D0214403

Political Protest and Prophecy
under Henry VIII

FOR YOU

"Who is it that says most? which can say more
Than this rich praise, that you alone are you?"

Political Protest and Prophecy
under Henry VIII

SHARON L. JANSEN

THE BOYDELL PRESS

© Sharon L. Jansen 1991

All Rights Reserved. Except as permitted under current legislation
no part of this work may be photocopied, stored in a retrieval system,
published, performed in public, adapted, broadcast,
transmitted, recorded or reproduced in any form or by any means,
without the prior permission of the copyright owner

First published 1991 by The Boydell Press, Woodbridge

The Boydell Press is an imprint of Boydell & Brewer Ltd
PO Box 9, Woodbridge, Suffolk IP12 3DF, UK
and of Boydell & Brewer Inc.
PO Box 41026, Rochester, NY 14604, USA

ISBN 0 85115 258 9

British Library Cataloguing-in-Publication Data
Jansen, Sharon L.
    Political protest and prophecy under Henry VIII.
    I. Title
    942.05
    ISBN 0–85115–258–9

Library of Congress Cataloging-in-Publication Data
Jansen, Sharon L., 1951–
    Political protest and prophecy under Henry VIII / Sharon L. Jansen.
        p.   cm.
    Includes bibliographical references and index.
    ISBN 0–85115–258–9 (alk. paper)
    1. English literature – Early modern, 1500–1700 – History and
criticism. 2. Politics and literature – Great Britain – History – 16th
century. 3. Protest literature, English – History and criticism.
4. Great Britain – Politics and government – 1509–1547. 5. Great
Britain – History – Prophecies. 6. Prophecies in literature.
I. Title.
PR418.P65J36   1991
820.9'358–dc20   91–26089

The paper used in this publication meets the minimum requirements
of American National Standard for Information Sciences –
Permanence of Paper for Printed Library Materials, ANSI Z39.48–1984

Printed in Great Britain by
St Edmundsbury Press Ltd, Bury St Edmunds, Suffolk

CONTENTS

PERMISSIONS

I wish to thank the Bodleian Library, British Library, Folger Shakespeare Library, and the Public Record Office (London) for permission to quote from their manuscripts.

I would also like to thank Medieval & Renaissance Texts & Studies (Binghamton, New York), for their cooperation here with my references to Humphrey Welles and the prophecies from his anthology (Bodl. Libr. MS Rawlinson C.813).

ACKNOWLEDGEMENTS

When the journey is complete, it is a pleasure to thank those who have helped along the way.

I owe a great deal to the staff members of the many British libraries where I have worked. Most of the time, these men and women remain nameless, but without their help, advice, effort, and tolerance, I would not have had access to the material I have used in this book. Closer to home, I could not have undertaken this project without the help of the reference staff at the Robert L. Mordtvedt Library here at Pacific Lutheran University, especially Laura Lewis, without whose inter-library-loan expertise and cheerful willingness to find even the most obscure books and articles I would have been unable to start my journey, much less finish it.

I have also received a great deal of advice and many suggestions from colleagues both near and far. I owe special debts of gratitude to Professors Kathryn Kerby-Fulton and Tony Edwards, University of Victoria, B.C., Canada; to Professor Valerie Lagorio, University of Iowa; to Professor Greg Walker, University of Queensland, Australia; to Professor Robert E. Lerner, Northwestern University; and to Professor Kathy Jordan, an itinerant friend and scholar now on her own scholarly journey here in the U.S. In their own individual ways, they have made my travels much easier and far less lonely.

Many colleagues at Pacific Lutheran University have helped me at various stages of my trip. Professor Philip Nordquist, Department of History, not only kept me from some embarrassing historical errors but, during his long tenure here, has built the Library's Tudor history holdings. I thank him every time I find a book I did not expect to find on our shelves. Professor Rochelle Snee, Department of Languages, has helped a great deal with the idiosyncratic Latin that threatened to overwhelm me at times. Professor Paul Menzel, Department of Philosophy, and Professors Tom Campbell and Chuck Bergman, Department of English, provided help in more ways than I can even begin to list. Thank you for keeping me company along the way, and for providing me shelter or distraction when I needed it. And a special thanks to Kay Whitcomb, our hardworking departmental miracle worker — my constant interference on her computer kept her from finishing many of her own travels on time.

My dear friend, Professor George Arbaugh, Department of Philosophy, has been a constant support and a source of inspiration through the many ups and downs of this journey. Thank you for always being there when I need you.

And finally, for the last twenty years, Professor David C. Fowler, University of Washington, has been a faithful companion on my many scholarly ventures, including those early, tentative efforts. Thank you for your unfailing wisdom, kindness, and generosity.

ABBREVIATIONS

BL	British Library, London
Bodl. Libr.	Bodleian Library, Oxford
CUL	Cambridge University Library, Cambridge
E 36	Exchequer, Treasury of Receipt, Miscellaneous
EETS ES	Early English Text Society, Extra Series
EETS OS	Early English Text Society, Original Series
Folger	Folger Shakespeare Library, Washington, D.C.
Index	Carleton F. Brown and Rossell H. Robbins, *The Index of Middle English Verse* (New York, 1953).
KB	King's Bench
LP	*Letters and Papers, Foreign and Domestic, of the Reign of Henry VIII, 1509–1547*, ed. J.S. Brewer, *et al.*, 21 vols. and *Addenda* (London, 1862–1932).
Lambeth	Lambeth Palace Library, London
Manual	*A Manual of the Writings in Middle English, 1050–1500*, ed. J. Burke Severs (New Haven, 1975).
OED	*Oxford English Dictionary*
PRO	Pubic Record Office, London
Short Title Catalogue	A.W. Pollard and G.R. Redgrave, *Short Title Catalogue of Books Printed in England, Scotland, and Ireland, 1475–1640* (London, 1926).
SP	State Papers, Henry VIII
SP Scot	State Papers, Scotland
Supplement	Rossell H. Robbins and John L. Cutler, *Supplement to the Index of Middle English Verse* (Lexington, Kentucky, 1965).
Taylor	Rupert Taylor, *The Political Prophecy in England* (NewYork, 1911).

A NOTE ON THE TRANSCRIPTIONS

I have used many kinds of sixteenth-century documents in this study: personal letters, trial records, public pronouncements, official memos and notes, "literary" collections, and printed books, among them. In both the extracts and the complete texts printed here, I have made an effort to preserve the flavor and texture of the original sources yet to make them readable and accessible for modern readers. I have retained the spelling and word division of the originals, silently expanding their many abbreviations. Capitalization has been modernized, however. Punctuation has been added sparingly in the prose, more fully in the poetry. Where the originals are damaged or unreadable, the texts have been cautiously emended. Every attempt has been made to give sixteenth-century place-names their modern spellings. Some locales remain unidentified, however, and their names, as recorded in the state papers or as identified in the *Letters and Papers of Henry VIII*, have remained.

INTRODUCTION

On the second day of December in 1537, John Dobson, the vicar of Muston, was accused of numerous "crymes and defaultes" by his Yorkshire parishioners. Among their charges:

> Item, he saieth and hath reaported diuers tymes syns midsomer laste paste to sundrie his parishenes that he that bereth the eagle . . . shall spread his winges ouer all this realme. . . .
>
> Item, he saith and sins midsomer hath diuers tymes reaported . . . that the dun cowe . . . is . . . castene in hir stall and she shall come into England gyngling with hir keies and sette the Churche againe in the right feith.
>
> Item, he hath diuers tymes reaported and sayd . . . that when the crumme is brought lowe thene shall we begine Cristis crosse rowe. . . .
>
> Item, he saith that the mone shall kindle againe and take light of the sone. . . .
>
> Item, he seith that the cocke of the north . . . shalbe billid in the nek and the hed and aftir that he shall buske hym and brushe his fethers and call his chekins togiddire and aftir that he shall doo greate aduentures.
>
> Item, he seith the skalop shelles shalbe brokene and goo to wreke.

This strange talk of eagles, cows, chickens, and sea shells seems now to be little more than nonsense, but it evidently was not regarded as such by Henry VIII's Council of the North, investigating the rebellions of the Pilgrimage of Grace. On 3 December 1537, the day after these accusations were reported, the Council examined the offending vicar. The surviving records of the case contain two petitions, drawn on the same day, to the King and his Council "by youre poore supplicante John Dobson, preste." The vicar admitted the charges made against him by his parishioners, adding even more of what still seem to be harmless predictions:

> . . . the ruff shuld bee rufullie rente and the clergye shuld stand in steare and fight as the seclers were and whenne the blake fleit of Norwaye was commed and gone aftir in Englond shuld there be warre neuer. Whan A. B. C. is brought downe lowe thene we will begin Cristis crosse rowe. Thene sone aftir of Sanneneforth of the south side shall there bee a bataile. A long man in red shall rise and goo

1

ouer at Darwyn staye. The raise of ceall shall shyne full bright of
Barwicke walles. . . .

But Dobson took no credit — or, rather, blame — for having been the
originator of these mysterious predictions. They were, he claimed, the
prophecies of Merlin, Bede, and Thomas of Erceldoune, authorities who had
foreseen that all these things should come to pass "aboute the yere of Oure
Lord God a thousand v hundreth and xxxvij." In his defense, Dobson
pleaded, "I knowe well I spake neuer of prophecye in no place but oon tyme
to an old man called Stephyn Rosse and oon Thomas Beforth and that was in
Lente . . . and a nother tyme a fourtnight before" to "oon or twoo" others, but
"of my conscience more prophecie I sawe neuer in all my lif."[1]

The Council pursued the elusive source of Dobson's prophecy at great
length but with little success. Dobson had told the Council that on 20
October of the previous year he had borrowed a roll containing the predictions from John Borobie, the prior of the White Friars in Scarborough. Duly
following the thread of their investigation, the Council took a deposition
from Borobie on the fifth of December. In explaining how he had come
across the prophecies, the prior said he had "chaunsed to mete with a certeine preste in the towne of Beuerley" who had showed him a prophecy that
began, "France and Flaundres shall arise." Borobie had then copied the piece,
fairly brief, onto "ij shetes of paper." That was in the spring of 1536, during
Rogation days, and Borobie never saw the priest "afore nor aftir." He admitted having met Dobson, in fact having invited him to "drinke a cope
within my chambre"; the vicar had there seen the prophecies, borrowed
them, and returned them to Borobie "within xiiij or xv daies."

Borobie then cast a wider net for the Council. He told his examiners about
a visit to a place he called "Werthrop." The vicar there had showed him a
small quire of prophecies beginning, "whenne the cok of the north hath
builded his neste." At that point Borobie did admit to a crime of sorts, but
hardly one of interest to the Council: "bicause I coud not tarie the reding of it
there I desyred hym to lette me haue it home and so he did and I neuer sente
it to him againe." From this "borrowed" quire Borobie had extracted two or

---

[1] For Dobson's testimony and the reports of the witnesses who follow, see SP
1/127, fols. 63–67. The transcription here has been silently emended. The documents
are abstracted in *LP* XII.2, 1212. Dobson's case was first mentioned by Madeleine
Hope Dodds and Ruth Dodds, *The Pilgrimage of Grace, 1536–1537, and the Exeter
Conspiracy, 1538* (1915; rpt. London, 1971), 1, 82–84, though there is some confu-
sion in the detail. Madeleine Dodds referred again to the case in her "Political
Prophecies in the Reign of Henry VIII," *Modern Language Review*, 11 (1916), 281.
Brief summaries appear also in Keith Thomas, *Religion and the Decline of Magic*
(London, 1971), p. 475 and in G.R. Elton, *Policy and Police: The Enforcement of the
Reformation in the Age of Thomas Cromwell* (Cambridge, 1972), p. 61.

three "clausis," copying them onto the same "ij shetes of paper afore rehersid." Borobie had accumulated his prophecies from a number of sources; a "litle tale of a cromme and the Cristis crosse rowe," also transcribed onto the sheets, had come from a gentleman in Scarborough named William Langdale.

While he was thus describing his own collection of prophecies, Borobie added that two years earlier one of his brothers had showed him a similar scroll. As far as he could "call to remembraunce," it spoke of "the blak flete of Norwaye" and "a child with a chaplet and many other thinges." When Borobie had inquired about the owner of this document, he had been told that it had come from a priest of Rudston named John Paikok. Borobie supposed the scroll he had seen had eventually been returned to Paikok, but, he said, "my broder did geue copie of the same scroll to the foresaid William Langdale."

Undaunted, the Council interviewed Langdale three days later, on 8 December 1537, still trying to untangle the threads of the case. Where had the prophecy originated? Langdale admitted that Borobie had told the truth; the Scarborough prior had seen a "litle roll of paper wherein was writtene a prophecye in ryme . . . which spoke of the lernyng of A. B. C. and K. L. M." As Borobie had claimed, Langdale had loaned him the roll. Borobie had returned it "within a few daies aftir that," but, "aboute the same tyme," had sent another roll of prophecies to Langdale. Langdale could not produce this second roll because he had left it "lyng in a windowe in his hous in Scardeburgh": "those prophesies and . . . other his goodes and bookis were stolene and spoiled by the commons" during the Pilgrimage of Grace. Langdale had, however, gotten the same prophetic verses from Thomas Bradley, a priest at Ayton, "who told this deponent that he had it of Sir Richard Stapulton, priest at Cokbourne, and ferther he cannot depose."

Still tracing the source of the prophecy, the Council found Bradley and interviewed him on 11 December. Bradley confirmed that he had gotten the prophecy from Richard Stapleton, who "red a writing in the butterey at Ayton in Pikringlight aboute Mighelmas was a twelfmoneth in the tyme of commocion." Bradley had made a copy of the prophecy "in the chapell." There was no doubt it was the same item; the priest recalled the prophecy had mentioned Merlin, Bede, the letters A, B, and C, and a crumb in a man's throat. Bradley had returned the original to Stapleton, and "a daie aftir or twoo came William Langdale to Aton and herd of it and he asked me it and I gaue hym it and neuer had it more aftir."

In a deposition of 14 December, the priest Richard Stapleton described his meeting with a parish clerk of Croft, William Langley. Langley had told Stapleton about "oon litle prophesie" that Stapleton wanted to see. Since Langley did not have the prophecy with him, he had agreed to send it to Stapleton. Langley had been as good as his word, forwarding the prophecy with a servant named John. According to Stapleton, "as I remembre there was certeine lettres in it and crummes." He also added a few stylistic notes: it was "not paste xij lynes and wente in meter." Later, while travelling on his master's business to Ayton, he had given a copy to Bradley, and while returning home had given the original, along with "billis of rekenynge," to a kitchener at Gisburn. Stapleton's deposition concluded, "wheddir he hath it or no I knowe not for he estemed it but litle and sins that tyme I neuer see it."

There the investigation stopped. The source of the prophecy repeated by Dobson was never found, but it is not clear whether the Council failed to trace William Langley or decided the tangle of evidence was not worth further sorting or simply ran out of energy. Whatever the case, the matter was reported to Henry VIII on 18 December, and the Council's summary of the charges made against Dobson show how his prophecies were understood by those who had heard them. What seems now to be utter nonsense was really a series of very specific and topical seditious appeals, a potent mixture of political and religious propaganda.

According to his accusers, Dobson had declared,

> certeyne prophecies againste Yowre Grace and your realme in thre pointes. Oon is that Yowre Highnes shulde bee drivene oute of yowre realme and aftir [return] to the same againe and bee content to take the thirde parte thereof. The seconde is that the egle, which by theire reaporte he saith is themperoure, shuld spred his wingis ouer all this realme. The thirde is that the dunne cowe, whiche by theire reaporte he said is the pope of Rome, shuld gingle hir keies and come into this realme and sette it in the right feithe againe.

The threat of Dobson's words was serious. The Council had jailed the unfortunate Dobson, and asked for further instructions.[2]

Shortly after, on 19 January 1538, Bishop Tunstall wrote to Cromwell about several troublesome cases, Dobson's among them. Tunstall reported that Council members had turned to the justices of the assize for their opinions about the spreading of such "rumours" — Tunstall was concerned that many more cases involving charges like these would arise.[3] The assize justices must have been advised to treat the case harshly, for the Council of the North reported to Henry VIII on 7 April that Dobson was one of four people found guilty of treason during the Lenten assizes at York. The vicar had been convicted of interpreting prophecies and executed.[4]

Dobson's case is a remarkable one, for the original accusations against him seem bizarre, not to mention trivial. They involve birds, beasts, heavenly

---

[2] SP 1/127, fol. 97 (*LP* XII.2, 1231)
[3] SP 1/128, fol. 124 (*LP* XIII.1, 107)
[4] SP 1/131, fol. 56 (*LP* XIII.1, 705)

bodies, letters of the alphabet, and mystifying references to a "black fleet" and a "long man in red." But no matter how ridiculous such prophecies may at first seem, the Council, Cromwell, and the King obviously regarded them as serious offenses. And Dobson's case, though remarkable, is not an isolated incident. The state papers of Henry's reign include a surprising number of stray copies of prophecies, of references to mysterious prophecies heard or read or reported, of trials and examinations of men and women who, like Dobson, were caught spreading prophecies, and even of prophecies duly collected by the King's government, reinterpreted, and then offered as support for Henry's political and religious reforms.

Something of the danger of Dobson's prophecies can be reckoned from the surviving documents. As the Council of the North reported, the eagle was a reference to the emperor, who would invade the realm. The dun cow was the pope, who would turn back Henry's religious change. The letters "A. B. C." were to be "brought low," and these letters referred to Anne Boleyn and Cromwell, while alphabetic predictions about "K. L. M." were offered as support for Katherine and Lady Mary. The "long man in red" is obviously a reference to Reginald Pole, who had been made a cardinal and sent by the pope to raise support for the northern rebels. The pun on "crumb" and Cromwell is fairly obvious, but many of the references that are now more obscure must have been clear to Dobson's contemporaries, who recognized them as heraldic charges and badges. The symbol of the eagle, for example, came from the Hapsburg eagle badge, and thus the obvious danger of any prediction that it would spread its wings "over all this realm." The "jingling keys" were a likely reference to the crossed keys of St. Peter displayed on the papal insignia. The moon was the badge of the Percies, and it was "to kindle again." The cock was the crest of the Lumleys, and it was "to do great adventures." The scallop shell was the device of the Dacres, and it would be broken and go "to wreck."

Part of Dobson's difficulty doubtless arose because he was so rash — or so foolish — as to have spread his prophecies after that collection of rebellions known as the Pilgrimage of Grace. In his summary of this series of disruptions in the North during late 1536 and early 1537, J.J. Scarisbrick emphasizes the seriousness of this outbreak of rebellion in Henry's realm: ". . . presumably because it fought for the wrong side and because it failed, the Pilgrimage has often been treated by historians as a minor, peripheral upset wrought by a few provincial conservatives, a somewhat pathetic rising which could never have succeeded against Henry's solid regime. But the truth is that, if it had wanted, it might have swamped him."[5]

The government's response to rebellion, so harshly illustrated in the fate of

---

[5] *Henry VIII* (Berkeley, 1968), p. 342. Scarisbrick's summary and analysis of

Dobson, was swift and severe. Earlier in his reign, Henry and his ministers seem to have tolerated prophecies and prophesiers. They were bothersome but not really dangerous. After the "commotion," however, things were different.

Prophecies like those made by Dobson had a long history in England. The number that survive show just how popular they were and, at various times during their five-hundred-year history, how very influential. But, as Dobson's case illustrates, they are now very confusing. Only one book on the subject has been attempted, *The Political Prophecy in England*, published by Rupert Taylor in 1911.[6] In the preface to his volume, Taylor realized he had opened "a new field for investigation by students of literary history," and thus admitted he made "no pretense of detailed study." He concluded, with more than mere scholarly modesty, "I do not pretend in any case to have written the final word."

Aside from the deliberate obscurity of the prophecies, our confusion comes from trying to figure out just where and how they fit into an understanding of the past. What follows here is an attempt to make them somewhat less confusing. Since, as Taylor discovered, the "whole field" is far too broad to cover, I have narrowed my effort not just to one century or even to one king's reign, but to one tumultuous decade, the 1530s. After a brief survey of the origins and development of the form of English political prophecy, I turn at once to the political records involving the prophecies, and then to the texts themselves, most of which have never been published. Until now, no one has attempted to connect the surviving historical documents and references to the texts of the prophecies themselves. A few literary critics have examined the poems but not their historical context and political implications; historians have on occasion recorded the place of prophecy in contemporary events, but have not examined the texts to discover what the prophecies

events (pp. 339–48) are exceptionally clear, but the most thorough is the work by Madeleine and Ruth Dodds, cited above.

For more recent work on the Pilgrimage, see C.L.S. Davies, "Popular Religion and the Pilgrimage of Grace" in *Order and Disorder in Early Modern England*, ed. Anthony Fletcher and J. Stevenson (Cambridge, 1985), pp. 58–91; G.R. Elton, *Reform and Reformation: England, 1509–1558* (Cambridge, Mass., 1977), Chapter 11, "The First Crisis of the Reformation"; and M.E. James, "Obedience and Dissent in Henrician England: The Lincolnshire Rebellion, 1536," *Past and Present*, 48 (1970), 3–78.

Other studies of the Pilgrimage that take into account political prophecy are A.G. Dickens, *Lollards and Protestants in the Diocese of York, 1509–1558* (Oxford, 1959) and "Secular and Religious Motivation in the Pilgrimage of Grace," *Studies in Church History*, 4 (1967), 39–64. See also D.M. Loades, *Politics and the Nation, 1450–1660* (London, 1974), pp. 179–86.

6 Rupert Taylor, *The Political Prophecy in England* (New York, 1911).

actually said. My aim here has been to combine these efforts: to determine as far as possible the role of prophecy in the events of the decade and to discover in as great a detail as possible just what it was that people like John Dobson were hearing, reading, copying, collecting, trading, and — on more than this one occasion — dying for. Beyond illustrating the texts of the political prophecies, I hope to suggest *how* and *why* such political poetry was so powerful as political protest.

Even though I have so narrowly defined my investigation, I still feel, like Taylor, overwhelmed by the material — by the wealth of detail in contemporary records, by the number of manuscript sources, by the deliberate obscurity of the texts. If I succeed only in conveying a sense of the enormous appeal these prophecies had and still have, even today, I will feel myself to have done them some measure of justice.

CHAPTER ONE

The Political Prophecy in England

The title of this chapter is borrowed from the only full-length study of the form, *The Political Prophecy in England*, published by Rupert Taylor in 1911. The very number and confusion of the prophecies seem to have overwhelmed Taylor as he worked. In his own rather exhausted words, ". . . a thorough study of the material is impossible at this time, for available material is too scanty and the whole field too large."[1]

The void noted by Taylor still exists. R.H. Robbins's section on political prophecy in the *Manual of Writings in Middle English* (1975) contains surprisingly few references not found in Taylor's bibliography of texts. Although several notable recent editions and critical analyses have appeared, relatively little has been done to continue the work begun by Taylor.[2]

Perhaps the greatest difficulty in studying the prophecies lies in their very

---

[1] Taylor, p. ix. As just a brief indication of the problems faced by anyone interested in studying political prophecy, there are nearly 200 Latin manuscripts of Geoffrey's *Historia* and another seventy containing his *Prophetia Merlini* as a separate text. These numbers don't include later manuscripts that have chronicles or prophecies incorporating passages of Geoffrey. (For these figures, see Eckhardt, cited below in full, n. 5.)

[2] Taylor, n. 1, pp. 1–2; Robbins, "Political Prophecies," in Vol. 5 of *A Manual of the Writings in Middle English*, ed. J. Burke Severs (New Haven, Conn., 1975), pp. 1714–25. More recent discussions of prophecy include Keith Thomas, *Religion and the Decline of Magic*, pp. 461–514; V.J. Scattergood, *Politics and Poetry in the Fifteenth Century* (New York, 1972); Erwin Herrmann, "Spätmittelalterliche englische Pseudoprophetien," *Archiv für Kulturgeschichte*, 57 (1975), pp. 87–116; Alison Allan, "Yorkist Propaganda: Pedigree, Prophecy, and the 'British history' in the Reign of Edward IV," in *Patronage, Pedigree and Power in Later Medieval England*, ed. Charles Ross (Totowa, New Jersey, 1979), pp. 171–92; Charles Ross, "Rumour, Propaganda and Popular Opinion During the Wars of the Roses," in *Patronage, the Crown and the Provinces in Later Medieval England*, ed. Ralph A. Griffiths (Atlantic Highlands, New Jersey, 1981), pp. 15–32; J.R.S. Phillips, "Edward II and the Prophets," in *England in the Fourteenth Century*, ed. W.M. Ormrod (Dover, New Hampshire, 1986), pp. 189–201; Alistair Fox, "Prophecies and Politics in the Reign of Henry VIII," in *Reassessing the Henrician Age: Humanism, Politics, and Reform*, ed. Alistair Fox and John Guy (Oxford, 1986), pp. 77–94; and John Taylor, *English Historical Literature in the*

nature. Deliberately obscure and willfully ambiguous when they were written, they have become more bewildering with the passage of time. Filled with veiled topical allusions, disguised historical figures, and vague prognostications about future triumphs and calamities, the prophecies were intended to be confused and confusing. But even what must have been fairly clear to contemporary eyes has now become almost incomprehensible. For modern readers, the simplest references are difficult to decipher.

Contributing to the problem is their adaptability. Political prophecies were popular in England from early in the twelfth century until quite late in the seventeenth. During this five-hundred year period, all that was required to "create" a new prophecy was to compile the predictions of an older piece — or older pieces — and then to give them a new interpretation in light of current events. Consequently, the same images and lines appear in many different prophecies. More remarkable, entire prophecies reappear again and again; minor alterations are made in an already existing prediction, and then the whole piece is recirculated with new application to contemporary events. Any single prophecy is apt to have been recycled so often that its original shape and meaning are almost impossible to trace. Still, what makes a prophecy so interesting is not only the date or place or even the occasion of its original composition but the specific use to which it was put in any of its many variations. For successive versions of any prophecy there were clearly new aims and new interpretations. Each version reflected the needs of the moment and the attitudes of its compiler; each might be read as an expression of uneasiness and of a desire for change.[3]

1. Origin and Development

The strange prophecies delivered by John Dobson in 1537 have their origin centuries earlier. The historian Nennius (fl. 796) related "The Omen of the Dragons," in which the terrible fight between two dragons, one white and one red, was interpreted as a prophecy of the conflict between Saxon and Briton. The eleventh-century "Vision of Edward the Confessor" sounds as if it could have come from the mouth of our sixteenth-century vicar: "If a green tree is cut in the middle and the part lopped off is moved . . . from the stem, when the part moved away shall of its own accord and without the aid of any

---

Fourteenth Century (Oxford, 1987), especially Chapter 12, "Political Poems and Ballads."

[3] For an illustration of the successive versions of one text, see Sharon L. Jansen [Jaech], " 'The Marvels of Merlin' and the Authority of Tradition," *Studies in Medieval and Renaissance History*, 8 (1986), 35–73.

human hand unite itself to the trunk and begin to flourish and bear fruit, then for the first time can a respite from such great evils be hoped for."[4]

But the real source of political prophecy in England was Geoffrey of Monmouth, who had the genius not only to recognize a great story but also to figure out the best way to tell it. Near the mid-point of his *Historia regum Brittaniae*, Geoffrey "recorded" a series of prophecies that Merlin delivered to King Vortigern, among them:

> The Boar of Cornwall shall bring relief from these invaders for it will trample their necks beneath its feet. . . .

> Six of the Boar's descendants shall hold the sceptre . . . and next . . . will rise up the German Worm. The Seawolf shall exalt this Worm. . . .

> The Red One will grieve for what has happened, but after an immense effort it will regain its strength.

> Calamity will next pursue the White One. . . .

> The Lion's cubs shall be transformed into salt-water fishes and the Eagle of Mount Aravia shall nest upon its summit. . . .

> Thereafter, from the first to the fourth, from the fourth to the third, from the third to the second shall the thumb be rolled in oil. . . .[5]

And so on. Geoffrey "compiled" an impressive array of prophecies that included a zoo full of animals, a land full of natural disasters, and a sky full of astronomical wonders. These *Prophetia Merlini*, as this section of Geoffrey's narrative came to be called, actually "predicted" a number of *historical* events, for example the British defeat by the Saxons and the coming of the Normans. It then launched into what may be regarded truly as *prophetic*, the future restoration of the British.

While it is easy enough to credit Geoffrey with the "invention" of English political prophecy, it is not so easy to account for what followed. Scores — perhaps hundreds, depending on how they are counted — of prophecies were

---

4 Quoted by Taylor, p. 8.

5 Geoffrey of Monmouth, *The History of the Kings of Britain*, trans. Lewis Thorpe (Penguin Classics, 1966), Book VII.3–4. On the question of Geoffrey's claim that he merely transcribed, rather than invented, the prophecies, see J.S.P. Tatlock, *The Legendary History of Britain* (Berkeley, 1950), pp. 403–21. For an excellent discussion of Geoffrey's prophecies and his contributions to the development of the political prophecy in England, see the introduction to Caroline D. Eckhardt, *The Prophetia*

adapted from Geoffrey and now survive. Attempts to explain the development of the form and to categorize these texts are almost as confusing as the prophecies themselves. Here, for instance, Taylor ran into trouble, at various times trying to classify the prophecies by the methods of disguise they employed, then by their sympathies — English, Welsh, Scottish, or Irish — and at last settling on what he called the "major monuments" of the late fourteenth and early fifteenth centuries: "The Prophecy of the Six Kings to Follow King John," *The Prophecy of John of Bridlington*, *The Prophecy of Thomas of Erceldoune*, and *The Prophecy of Thomas à Becket*.[6]

This is much the same system Robbins used, dividing the texts into four major groups as they had been "fathered on famous figures of British prophecy": Merlin (from Geoffrey's *Historia*), Thomas Becket, John of Bridlington, and Thomas of Erceldoune. Robbins made only too clear the difficulties of his system. For example, in the twenty or so manuscript sources of "The Cock of the North," which he identified with John of Bridlington, the prophecy is variously ascribed to Merlin, Bede, Bridlington (rightfully), Erceldoune, and, for good measure, "Banester," and "Herryson." Robbins wisely included a sizable fifth classification: "miscellaneous." His is a telling commentary on the problem of trying to show clearly how political prophecies developed as a form: "The confusion of texts, the transfer of lines from one prophecy to another, the continuation of medieval prophecies into manuscripts as late as mid-seventeenth century, all confound an already confounded situation."[7]

In his survey of the genre, Keith Thomas performed a remarkable job of making sense of the kinds of prophecies by taking one of the other tacks suggested by Taylor, the methods of disguise employed. The most common type of prophecy is, in these terms, the Galfridian (from Geoffrey of Monmouth), those prophecies that employ animal symbols — Geoffrey's Boar of Cornwall, for example. A second kind of prophecy is called Sibylline, from the so-called *Oracula Sibyllina*, and uses alphabetic references (usually the

---

Merlini of Geoffrey of Monmouth: A Fifteenth-Century English Commentary (Cambridge, Mass., 1982).

Eckhardt comments on the significance of Geoffrey's *Historia* and its prophecies: ". . . it was surely the most influential history book of the Middle Ages" (p. 3). The historian T.D. Kendrick also discusses the influences of the book:

> Within fifteen years of its publication not to have read it was a matter of reproach; it became a respected textbook of the Middle Ages; it was incorporated in chronicle after chronicle; it was turned into poetry; it swept away opposition with the ruthless force of a great epic; its precedents were quoted in Parliament; two kings of England cited it in support of their claim to dominion over Scotland; it was even used to justify the expenditures of the royal household . . . (*British Antiquity* [London, 1950], p. 7, as quoted by Eckhardt, p. 3).

6 Taylor, pp. 48–82.
7 Robbins, p. 1531.

initial of a name).[8] Thomas's third type of prophecy is the "painted prophecy" — an illuminated scroll or picture.[9] To Thomas's categories based on method should be added prophecies based on other miscellaneous phenomena, including prophecies by the use of numbers, dice, stars, and Dominical letters.

For our purpose here it is not necessary to rewrite the history of the political prophecy. It is enough to know that the form had its origins centuries earlier, and that after Geoffrey's twelfth-century *Historia* its popularity increased. By the end of the fourteenth century, four main groups of prophecies had developed, each deriving from a single work or around a central figure. Prophecies of Merlin have their origins in Geoffrey's *Prophetia*, the most popular example of which became, after the early fourteenth century, "The Prophecy of the Six Kings to Follow King John": the Lamb of Winchester (Henry III), the Dragon (Edward I), the Goat (Edward II), the Lion (Edward III), the Ass (Richard II), and the Mole (Henry IV). The prophecy retained its popularity, and in the typically adaptable way of political prophecy, was reinterpreted in the 1530s so that the Mole referred to Henry VIII.

The longest and most elaborate of all the political prophecies was the fourteenth-century *Prophecy of John of Bridlington*, a carefully planned Latin poem with commentary, dedicatory epistle, and three introductory essays. *Bridlington* was itself translated into English, but the two most popular and useful prophecies linked with John of Bridlington's name are "The Cock of the North" and "When Rome is Removed into England," both of which figured in the upsets of the 1530s. Thomas of Erceldoune, a late thirteenth-century poet who acquired a reputation for prophecy, was held in equally high esteem, and notable collections of prophecies attributed to "the rhymer" were made, but the one that will most concern us is "The Prophecies of Rymour, Bede, and Merlin," a sixteenth-century adaptation of material from *Thomas of Erceldoune*. The prophecies associated with Becket seem originally to have referred to the wars of Edward III in France, but by the sixteenth century numerous popular prophecies were attributed to him.

In the sixteenth century, as Taylor noted, the tendency was to combine the separate prophecies, collecting them into one larger piece. Still, it is possible to trace their separate origins as well. It is also possible, to see their relationship to other sources. The use of animal symbols, for instance, recalls the style of Biblical prophecy in the Book of Daniel, Revelation, and Esdras, while certain elements in their narratives reveal some similarity to the apocalyptic tradition of the Emperor of the Last Days. Despite these apparent

---

[8] For an introduction to the Tibutrine Sibyl and selected translations, see Bernard McGinn, *Visions of the End: Apocalyptic Tradition in the Middle Ages* (New York, 1979), pp. 41–49. For the most complete text and discussion, see Ernst Sackur, *Sibyllinische Texte und Forschungen* (1898; rpt. Turin, 1963).

[9] Thomas, pp. 461–63.

similarities, the methods and aims of the political prophecies were quite different, as their texts will show.[10]

2. Methods

Something of the devices and disguises used in political prophecy is in order here. Although the methods used vary from prophecy to prophecy, the more obvious techniques are all evident in the examinations of witnesses in the case of John Dobson.

Most striking is the use of animal symbols. These animals are neither the monstrous beasts of Biblical prophecy nor the abstract personifications of beast fable or allegory. They are simply symbols used to designate a specific man or family or country. Animal symbols seem at times to have been assigned arbitrarily, but they were particularly suitable for a society used to heraldic images, as we can see in the case of the prophecies of Dobson. There, for example, the eagle, from the Hapsburg eagle badge, was recognized as a symbol for the emperor, while the cock was clearly regarded as a reference to the crest of the Lumleys.

The use of alphabetic references, usually initial letters, is also popular. Such references figure in Dobson's case as well, when "A. B. C." referred to Anne Boleyn and Cromwell, and "K. L. M." to Queen Katherine and Lady Mary.

In one of the introductory essays to the Latin *Prophecy of John of Bridlington*, the commentator explained at some length the methods used in prophecy. In addition to the use of *arbitrary names*, explained as the adoption of animal symbols, the writer of the commentary identified nine other devices in a fairly complicated system of prophetic reference. Included are *accidental designation*, a name derived from a distinctive mannerism, surname, or heraldic device; *equivocation*, an ambiguous word like "cancer," which can refer to the crab, the zodiac, or, in animal symbolism, the king of Scotland; *metaphor*, when, for example, a ship is referred to as a "wooden horse"; *words made from Roman numerals*, such as "cuculi," from "CCLXI"; *etymologized translation*, when the parts of an English word are translated as, for example, "Mortimer" translated as "mare mortis"; various *enigmas*, such as "si quis taurum, caput

---

[10] For a clear and succinct examination of these differences, see the introduction to McGinn.

An extended study of one such religious prophecy is the subject of Robert E. Lerner's *The Powers of Prophecy: The Cedar of Lebanon Vision from the Mongol Onslaught to the Dawn of the Enlightenment* (Berkeley, 1983). Lerner addresses the differences between apocalyptic and political prophecies as he discusses BL MS Cotton Vespasian E.vii, pp. 101–03 and 111–13.

amputat, inde fit aurum" — "if anyone cuts off the head of a bull (taurum), gold is made thereby (aurum)"; and three other techniques, *division of words*, *ambiguous words*, and simple *abbreviation* — following Taylor, I will leave these alone as "confusion worse confounded."[11] While a technical classification of such devices does seem confusing, the use of the moon, from a heraldic badge, to refer to the Percy family, and the pun on "crumb" to refer to Cromwell, are clear enough, and we will see examples of these techniques at work in various items during the trials and examinations of the 1530s.

More important, from my point of view, is the way prophecies combined fact and fiction. The greater part of most political prophecy was really history disguised as prophecy: historical events were treated as if they had not yet occurred. It was a kind of "retrospective prophecy" — the prophecy was made to seem as if it antedated the historical events it narrated. By such a "prediction" of historical events, a political prophecy gained credibility. The obvious intention of disguising history as prophecy was that a reader or listener would be able to see for himself (or herself) that many predictions had already been fulfilled and would thus consider the rest of the prophecy equally inspired.

But perhaps the most important technique of political prophecies was their adaptability. Although new prophecies do appear, reworked versions of older predictions are far more common, and even "new" compositions include familiar symbols and long passages adapted from earlier pieces. A prophesier went to great lengths *not* to be original: what made the prophecies so appealing, in fact, was not originality at all but their familiarity. They were attributed to men and women of the past who had long been recognized as prophets and who had no personal interests in the difficulties of the present. The prophecies' familiar references and motifs were also ways to emphasize their reliability. These were not strange and unfamiliar predictions; they had a long and recognized history. They carried with them the authority of the past.[12]

History and tradition thus became powerful political tools. The use of prophecy as a way of influencing political events fits quite naturally into the

---

[11] Taylor, pp. 5–6, with a phrase later echoed by Robbins, see above p. 12 and n. 7. An interesting examination of the various *stylistic* features common in political prophecy is found in Margaret Mary O'Sullivan, "The Treatment of Political Themes in Late Medieval English Verse, with Special Reference to BM Cotton Roll ii.23," Diss. University of London 1972. In her fourth chapter, "Style and Language. . . ," O'Sullivan includes many common features, among them the use of didactic tags and phrases ("as I thee tell," "I dare well say"), alliterative words and phrases, deferential appeals to the judgment of readers ("ye may well trust"), affirmative phrases ("truly," "it shall be so"), appeals to authority, expressions that refer to the progress of the prophecy ("shortly to tell"), and expressions of time and place ("on a day" and "at the last"). I wish here to thank the librarians at the University of London who very helpfully provided access to O'Sullivan's work.

[12] On this subject, see Thomas, pp. 501–14.

more general medieval interest in prophecy. In the face of conflict and instability, how were events of the present to be understood? Prophecy was, in R.W. Southern's words, "the chief inspiration of all historical thinking"; it was ". . . at once a source of information and interpretation, of hope and fear, and of assured truths which needed to be distinguished from the grossest errors and frauds."[13] Like their religious counterparts, political prophets sought truth in the midst of confusion.

3. Influence

It may still be hard to believe that political prophecies played any real part in contemporary events. Like Shakespeare's Hotspur, complaining of Glendower, we may prefer to dismiss them:

> . . . sometimes he angers me
> With telling me of the mouldwarp and the ant,
> Of the dreamer Merlin and his prophecies,
> And of a dragon and a finless fish,
> A clip-winged griffin and a moulten raven,
> A couching lion and a ramping cat,
> And such a deal of skimble-skamble stuff
> As puts me from my faith (I Henry IV, III.i.142–49).[14]

However, another contemporary critic, Francis Bacon, found the prophecies worth his attention if not his praise. In "Of Prophecies," he wrote, "My Judgment is, that they ought all to be Despised, And ought to serve, but for Winter Talke, by the Fire side. Though when I say Despised, I meane it as for

---

[13] "Aspects of the European Tradition of Historical Writing: 3. History as Prophecy," *Transactions of the Royal Historical Society*, 5th ser., 22 (1972), 160. Among the many works on prophecy in the Middle Ages, besides the work of McGinn, already noted, see Norman Cohn, *The Pursuit of the Millenium: Revolutionary Millenarians and Mystical Anarchists in the Middle Ages* (1957; rev. ed. New York, 1970 [Cohn's work is controversial, but the reference here is valid]); Marjorie E. Reeves, *The Influence of Prophecy in the Later Middle Ages: A Study in Joachimism* (Oxford, 1969) and "History and Prophecy in Medieval Thought," *Medievalia et Humanistica*, NS, 5 (1974), 51–75; Richard K. Emmerson, *Antichrist in the Middle Ages: A Study of Medieval Apocalypticism, Art, and Literature* (Seattle, 1981); and Lerner, *The Powers of Prophecy*.

[14] On Shakespeare's familiarity with political prophecy, see Sharon L. Jansen [Jaech], "Political Prophecy and Macbeth's 'Sweet Bodements,'" *Shakespeare Quarterly*, 34 (1983), 290–97 and Marjorie Garber, "'What's Past is Prologue': Temporality and Prophecy in Shakespeare's History Plays" in *Renaissance Genres: Essays on Theory, History, and Interpretation*, ed. Barbara Kiefer Lewalski (Cambridge, Mass., 1986), pp. 301–31.

as Beleefe. For otherwise, the Spreading or Publishing of them, is in no sort to be Despised. For they have done much Mischiefe: And I see many severe Lawes made to suppresse them."[15]

Despite such scepticism, political prophecies were taken seriously by many.

On this subject, Taylor recalled that Geoffrey of Monmouth had written his *Prophetia Merlini* at the request of Alexander, Bishop of Lincoln, in Geoffrey's words, "a man of the greatest religion and wisdom."[16] Geoffrey himself became bishop of St. Asaph in 1152. R.W. Southern referred to several of the "keenest students of Merlin, . . . university men with intellectual aspirations." In the midst of the Becket controversy, as one example, John of Salisbury turned to the prophecies of Merlin, while John of Cornwall translated some "newly discovered" Merlin prophecies for the Bishop of Exeter, "himself a distinguished canonist and administrator." And Gerald of Wales, "one of the most ambitious and experimental historical writers of the late twelfth century," went further than anyone else in seeking unknown prophecies and trying to fit them into his contemporary histories, "writing what he called a *Historia Vaticinalis*."[17]

Richard the Lionheart consulted the prophet Joachim of Fiore; Robert Grosseteste received prophecies from one of his correspondents.[18] The historian Froissart wrote of being entertained by hearing prophecies of Merlin predicting the future of John of Gaunt's descendants, Richard II studied political prophecies, and Adam de Usk used Bridlington's prophecy in 1372 as an argument against taxation.[19] Henry IV visited the shrine of John of Bridlington, while his son Henry V maintained, in the words of his most recent biographer, "a fervent devotion" for Bridlington and regarded the Yorkshire prophet as "his special patron." Numerous collections of prophecies survive from the period of the Lancastrian-Yorkist civil wars; John

---

[15] Francis Bacon, "Of Prophecies," in *The Essayes or Counsels, Civill and Morall*, ed. Michael Kiernan (Cambridge, Mass., 1985), p. 114.

[16] *History*, Book VII.1.

[17] ". . . History as Prophecy," pp. 168–69.

[18] Taylor, p. 83.

[19] For Froissart's comments, see John Bourchier, Lord Berners, trans., *The Cronycle of Syr John Froissart*, ed. W.P. Ker (London, 1901), 6, pp. 340–41 and 399.

Froissart's interest in prophecy and the studies of Richard II are discussed in John Webb, "Translation of a French Metrical History of the Deposition of King Richard the Second . . . accompanied by Prefatory Observation, Notes, and an Appendix . . . ," *Archaeologia: Or Miscellaneous Tracts Relating to Antiquity*, 20 (1824), 260–64.

For the comments on Usk, as well as brief asides on Henry II and Edward I's interests in prophecy, see R.H. Robbins, ed., *Historical Poems of the XIVth and XVth Centuries* (New York, 1959), pp. xlv.

Paston mentions Hogan the prophet and "hys profesye" in several letters written from London to his son in 1473.[20]

But, beginning in the fifteenth century, it seems to me that the interest in prophecy starts to shirt, almost imperceptibly at first. In 1402, a law passed against Welsh prophecies, "the cause of the insurrection and rebellion," brought a friar to the gallows. Another law passed in 1406 was aimed at Lollards using prophecy to predict the overthrow of the king.[21] Prophecies also figured in various cases of fifteenth-century treason by word. According to J.G. Bellamy, "At the beginning of the reign of Edward IV Oliver Germaine of Tesbury, Wiltshire, was accused with others of conspiring to imagine the death and destruction of the king on 14 May 1461 at Wilton where '*in prophesiis ut falsi heretici*' they announced that Henry VI was still the king and should have his crown." Germaine was sentenced to a traitor's death.[22] Long consulted by the powerful and influential, prophecies seem to have gained a wider audience. And they have become more than a vision of the present as the fulfillment of the past and as a preparation for the future.

By the sixteenth century, I would argue, political prophecies are not simply a way of understanding the present. They have become a way of shaping the present. They have become weapons, wielded deliberately, if sometimes wildly, by a very different class of person than Geoffrey of Monmouth, Froissart, or powerful families fighting for the interests of Lancaster or York. By the

---

[20] On Henry IV's visit see James H. Wylie, *History of England Under Henry IV* (London, 1896), 3, p. 336.

On Henvy V's devotion to Bridlington, see Desmond Seward's *Henry V: The Scourge of God* (New York, 1988), pp. 40 and 62.

On the use of political prophecy during the York and Lancastrian conflicts, see Allan, "Yorkist Propaganda" and Ross, "Rumour, Propaganda and Public Opinion." Collections of prophecies made during this period include British Library MSS Cotton Vespasian E.vii and Cotton Roll ii.23; Lambeth Palace MS 306; Trinity College Dublin MSS 432 and 516; Bodleian Library MSS Ashmole Roll 26, Bodley 623, and Hatton 56; Caius College Cambridge MS 249; and National Library of Wales MS Peniarth 50. For a more complete list, see Robbins, "Political Prophecies," pp. 1714–25.

For John Paston's references to the prophet Hogan, see Norman Davis, ed., *Paston Letters and Papers of the Fifteenth Century* (Oxford, 1971), 1, Nos. 273, 274, 277, and 361.

[21] On the 1402 trial see *Eulogium Historiarum sive Temporis*, ed. Frank S. Haydon (Rolls Ser. 9–3; London, 1863), pp. 391–94; Isobel D. Thornley, "Treason by Words in the Fifteenth Century," *English Historical Review*, 32 (1917), 556–61; and Wylie, 3, 334.

On the 1406 law, see *Rotuli Parliamentorum* (London), 3, p. 508, cited by Taylor, p. 105; see also Thomas, p. 470 and Robbins, *Historical Poems*, p. xliv. Scattergood comments (p. 22), however, that there is no conclusive evidence that prophecies in particular or political poetry in general had any actual effect.

[22] John G. Bellamy, *The Law of Treason in England in the Later Middle Ages* (Cambridge, 1970), p. 119.

1530s, those who chose the weapon of prophecy were those who had few other weapons to hand. They were ordinary men and women farthest from all sources of political decision and control. And those who found an element of power in the authority of prophecy used it in a kind of desperate attack *against* authority — the authority of King and parliament. In this war against authority, prophecy appealed to a higher and older authority — the authority of tradition.

Interestingly, in a discussion of Cromwell's attempts to manipulate public opinion during the 1530s, D.M. Loades comments on the *government's* use of tradition, noting the "careful formulation" of Cromwell's allegations of the "usurpation by the papacy of power traditionally and properly belonging to the English crown": "precedent was of the greatest importance, and the best way to persuade [the common man] to accept a new situation was to represent it as the revival of an old one."[23] Cromwell's device was both subtle and effective. We may speculate about the extent to which it might have resulted from the minister's recognition of the power and persuasion of political prophecy, with which he was well familiar.

We shall examine at some length those who used political prophecy in the 1530s. But prophecies continued as powerful political propaganda well after Henry's death. The act of 1542 making the uttering of any such prophecies a felony without benefit of clergy was repealed in 1547 at the time of Edward VI's accession in an act repealing all the felonies of the previous reign, but a new act against "fond and fantastical prophecies," imposing various fines and penalties, was passed three years later. This act of 1550 was repealed on Mary's accession, then reimposed by Elizabeth in 1563.[24] Thomas refers also to what he calls "the routine machinery of Tudor government" — proclamations, orders by the Privy Council, instructions to justices, and inquiries by bishops — taking aim at prophecies and those who spread them. With more energy than most who have studied political prophecy, the indefatigable Thomas traces the influence of prophecy through the nineteenth century, although, as he says, "evidence suggests that after the seventeenth century such prophecies were not usually taken seriously by educated persons."[25]

But during the 1530s, political prophecy was regarded as very serious indeed, as we shall see.

[23] Loades, p. 165.

[24] 33 Henry VIII, C.XIV; 3 and 4 Edward VI, C.XV; 5 Elizabeth, C.XV (Thomas says this statute was first debated in 1559).

[25] Thomas, p. 493. As an exception, however, note Arno Mayer's discussion of Hitler's use of such prophecy in his eastern campaign: "Hitler appropriated a vital strand in Europe's collective memory. He commended himself as prophet and crusader for a millenarian cause . . . ," naming his operation against Soviet Russia "Operation Barbarossa." See *Why Did the Heavens Not Darken: The "Final Solution" in History* (New York, 1988), esp. pp. 216–22. For the reference I am indebted to a reader at Garland Press.

CHAPTER TWO

Trials and Examinations of the 1530s

Political prophecies had always been most popular during periods of crisis. Many surviving texts and manuscripts date from the Lancastrian-Yorkist civil wars, for example, while a number of prophecies circulated at the time of Henry VII's fight for the throne.[1] But Henry VIII's reign was untroubled by serious conflict — or by the powerful anti-government propaganda that political prophecy was to become — until some twenty years after he had ascended the throne.

1. Background

To detail the crises erupting in England during the tumultuous fourth decade of the sixteenth century is a formidable task. By the time the King's "Great Matter" had come to involve individual conscience with affairs of state, Henry's divorce was only one issue in a series of disputes: crucial events in England during the 1530s were an integral part of more widespread theological, ecclesiastical, social, and political controversies. For me to attempt here a comprehensive account of this European revolution would be at once presumptuous and unnecessary. A brief review of the background against which

---

[1] On this see W. Garmon Jones, "Welsh Nationalism and Henry Tudor," *Transactions of the Honourable Society of Cymmrodorion* (Session 1917–18), pp. 1–59; Glanmoor Williams, "Prophecy, Poetry, and Politics in Medieval and Tudor Wales," in *British Government and Administration: Studies Presented to S.B. Chrimes*, ed. H. Hearder and H.R. Loyn (Cardiff, 1974), pp. 104–16; and John Guy, *Tudor England* (Oxford, 1986), p. 9. On Welsh political prophecy, see Margaret E. Griffiths, *Early Vaticination in Welsh with English Parallels*, ed. T. Gwynn Jones (Cardiff, 1937).

Political prophecies may also have played a part in the rebellions against Henry VII led by Lambert Simnel, John de la Pole, and Perkin Warbeck; see Thomas and C.W. Previté Orton, "An Elizabethan Prophecy," *History*, 2 (January 1918), 207–18.

the political "prophets" and prophecies must be viewed is all that is required
— and attempted — here.[2]

Henry's struggle for a divorce began late in the 1520s. As it became increasingly clear that all Wolsey's efforts to achieve the desired end would fail, Henry began to search for a new way to accomplish his goal. The so-called Reformation Parliament met for the first time in November of 1529, the month after Wolsey died. During the next seven years, parliament sat in seven sessions and enacted 137 statutes; by 1536, Henry had not only secured his divorce, but the King and parliament together had effectively ended the influence of the pope in England.

The first acts of the November 1529 session were a warning to the Church; statutes that were passed addressed various clerical abuses, among them pluralism and non-residence. Parliament was adjourned in December of

---

[2] For this summary I have followed several historical narratives of events in England during the 1530s. As a basic account, I have relied on J.D. Mackie, *The Earlier Tudors, 1485–1559*, Vol. 7 in *The Oxford History of England* (Oxford, 1952), especially Chapter 10, "Royal Supremacy." I am especially indebted to G.R. Elton, *Reform and Reformation: England 1509–1558*, especially Chapters 6 through 8 ("The Battle for Control," "The Age of Reform," and "The Royal Supremacy"). Perhaps most impressive is J.J. Scarisbrick's account of events in *Henry VIII*, particularly "The Canon Law of the Divorce" and "The Struggle for the Divorce," "The Campaign against the Church," especially for its detailing of events surrounding the Submission of the Clergy, and "The Royal Supremacy."

For more recent revisionist analyses, I recommend John Guy, *Tudor England*, especially Chapter Five, "The Break wih Rome" and Chapter Six, "Henrician Government"; Alistair Fox and John Guy, *Reassessing the Henrician Age: Humanism, Politics and Reform* (Oxford, 1986); and C. Coleman and David R. Starkey, eds., *Revolution Reassessed: Revisions in the History of Tudor Government and Administration* (Oxford, 1986).

On the parliamentary actions of the decade, see S.E. Lehmberg, *The Reformation Parliament, 1529–1536* (Cambridge, 1970) and *The Later Parliaments of Henry VIII, 1536–1547* (Cambridge, 1977).

The more detailed and specialized work of Elton in *Policy and Police* and "The Law of Treason in the Early Reformation," *The Historical Journal*, 11 (1968), 211–36, and of John Bellamy in *The Tudor Law of Treason: An Introduction* (London, 1979) are also invaluable. On the difficult area of praemunire, see W.T. Waugh, "The Great Statute of Praemunire 1393," EHR, 37 (1922), 173–205 and more recently John Guy, "Henry VIII and the *praemunire* Manoeuvres of 1530–31," EHR, 97 (1982), 581–603. For a discussion on the statute in Restraint of Appeals, see Elton, "The Evolution of a Reformation Statute," EHR, 64 (1949), 174–79.

Political and religious changes of the decade are also detailed, from a different perspective, in A.G. Dickens, *The English Reformation* (New York, 1964), especially Chapter 6, "Statutes and Bibles: The Henrician Revolution," and Chapter 7, "The Great Transfer."

For the texts of many of the acts of the 1530s, see G.R. Elton, *The Tudor Constitution: Documents and Commentary* (Cambridge, 1960).

1529 and not called again for over a year, reassembling in January of 1531. In the mean time, however, Henry had taken further action on his own behalf. After unsuccessful attempts to enlist scholars from universities in England and throughout Europe on behalf of his divorce — unsuccessful not because such determinations failed to appear but because they failed to be very influential — and after equally unsuccessful jurisdictional skirmishes with the pope on the same subject, Henry struck back within his own kingdom.

Late in 1530, fifteen clerics, including eight bishops, were charged with various breaches of praemunire, a complex and complicated series of laws that had been passed in the fourteenth century to protect the king's rights against interference by foreign courts, particularly papal courts. By the end of the year an indictment for praemunire had been laid against the whole of the English clergy. In the face of this assault, the clergy sued for pardon, the convocations of Canterbury and York both paying heavy fines. Parliament, reassembling in January of 1531, ratified the pardon and enacted various minor statutes but was dismissed again at the end of March.

When parliament reconvened in January 1532, Henry was ready with a bill to halt payments of annates to Rome. In spite of strenuous opposition in both houses, the bill nevertheless was passed. The commons were also ready, presenting to Henry in March their Supplication against the Ordinaries. Their petition contained a long list of complaints about clerical abuses, particularly those of Church courts. The Supplication was forwarded by the King to Convocation on 12 April. The clergy prepared a reply, returned to parliament at the end of the month.

While the petition thus passed from commons to King to clergy and then back, Henry took matters into his own hands, laying before the Convocation on 10 May a number of demands that, in effect, set aside the Supplication. The "royal ultimatum" included three demands, in brief: "the clergy must make no new constitutions, canons, or ordinances without the royal license; the existing body of ecclesiastical law must be reviewed by a committee of thirty-two, half clerical, half lay, all chosen by the king; and the laws approved by the majority of the committee must receive the royal assent before they became valid."[3]

Parliament was prorogued on 14 May 1532. On 15 May, after "days of pummelling," a surrender of sorts was forced from the Convocation. A "battered minority, a 'Rump' Convocation," yielded, and finally passed the Submission of the Clergy. On the next day, 16 May, Thomas More resigned as chancellor.

Before parliament met again in 1533, Cranmer had become archbishop of Canterbury, Henry was married to Anne, and Cromwell had secured his place

---

[3] Mackie, p. 355. On the origins of the Supplication of the Ordinaries, see Mackie, p. 354 and Scarisbrick, pp. 297–98.

as Henry's chief advisor. The 1533 session of parliament passed the act in Restraint of Appeals, and there followed swiftly both a decision on Henry's first marriage in the King's favor in Convocation and a judgment on the validity of his second in Cranmer's court. In response, Clement VII prepared a sentence of excommunication against Henry (11 July), though, giving Henry time to mend his ways, he postponed its issue (until September).

The break of 1533 was completed by the acts of the next year. During its first session of 1534 (15 January to 30 March), parliament passed five major statutes: "the act of Dispensations, which provided that henceforth ecclesiastical dispensations, licenses, faculties and so on be supplied in England and not from Rome; the act of Succession which settled the dynasty's future and imposed an oath to be administered throughout the kingdom acknowledging the king's new marriage and its offspring; the act in Absolute Restraint of Annates, which finally halted all payments to Rome for benefices and provided for the appointment of bishops by the king alone; the act for the Submission of the Clergy, which consecrated in statutory form the Convocation's surrender of May 1532; and the Heresy act which declared that it was no longer heresy to deny the papal primacy."[4] Parliament reassembled for a second session in November, passing three other acts of importance. In addition to an act annexing to the King former clerical revenues, the act of Supremacy declared Henry head of the English church. Finally, and very important for our purposes, Parliament passed a new Treasons act that expanded the old treason of "compassing the king's death" to include attempts to "imperil the king's person" and activities "to the prejudice, slander, disturbance and derogation" of his marriage to Anne. More to the point, treason by word was as serious as by deed; treason could be committed by "writing or imprinting."

In 1535, for their opposition to the demands made by the act of Succession and the act of Supremacy, More and Fisher were arrested. Convicted of treason, Fisher was executed on 22 June, More on 6 July. Since Clement had died in September of 1534, his successor, Paul III, drew up a second sentence of excommunication, *Eius qui immobilis*, against Henry.[5]

In the Convocation of 1536, Henry and Cromwell produced the Ten Articles, a definition of the new church and a formulation of Henry's powers as supreme head. This was followed by Cromwell's own Injunctions for the remedy of church abuses and the means to improvement. Added to all of this, the dissolution of the monasteries began as well. Although Anne Boleyn was executed (and thus removed as a focus of controversy) in May, unrest burst into open rebellion in Henry's kingdom, first at Louth in Lincolnshire

4 Scarisbrick, p. 324.
5 Like the bull earlier drawn by Clement, the implementation of this second

(1 October), then in the East Riding of Yorkshire, followed by Durham and Northumberland. By the end of the month, rebellion had engulfed all the counties of the north. The reasons for rebellion were varied — religious, social, economic, and political — and the maneuvering by crown and rebel forces complicated. Discontent lasted into the next year, the King finally establishing the Council of the North which began to exercise royal authority late in the year. The imposition of law and order was Cromwell's real task throughout the rest of the decade. Consolidation of the realm meant not only continued efforts in Wales and Ireland but, more difficult, within the hearts and minds of individual subjects.

Foreign threats re-emerged as the decade drew to a close. In December 1538, Paul III finally issued his Bull of excommunication, drawn in 1535. There were fears of invasion from Scotland, from the Low Countries, from Spain, from France, or from all of them combined. The decade ended with numerous political executions including, in 1540, that of Cromwell himself.

2. Early Warnings and Strange Doings

The political and religious revolution of the 1530s was accompanied by what Scarisbrick has called "a new and long-lived disunity, inside a new sense of nationhood." We can see the growth of this disaffection in the increasing number of accusations, rumors, warnings, and predictions included in the state papers of the decade. Among the examinations of nuisance, sedition, and treason recorded there, political prophecies play a considerable part.

Prophecy of a sort had been involved in political events as early as 1521, playing a part in the fall of Edward Stafford, duke of Buckingham. At one point during Henry VII's reign, Buckingham had been discussed by "grett personages" as a suitable king. Thus he was one of Henry's most powerful and most dangerous subjects. Buckingham was summoned to London in May of 1521. Once there, he was charged with treason, convicted, and executed. Relevant documents in the case are few, and opinion varies as to whether the duke was actually guilty of anything more than his enmity for Wolsey.[6] But

excommunication was also delayed. Paul III ordered the execution of his Bull of excommunication on 17 December 1538.

[6] On Buckingham's mention during Henry VII's reign, see Helen Miller, *Henry VIII and the English Nobility* (New York, 1986). On Buckingham's "crimes" and guilt, compare Scarisbrick, pp. 121–22, Elton, *Reform and Reformation*, pp. 81–82, and Guy, *Tudor England*, pp. 96–97. Relevant documents include a letter from Henry advising Wolsey to keep a "good watch" on the duke (dated 1519 in *LP* III, 1 but which Scarisbrick says belongs to late 1520 or early 1521); *LP* III, 1233; and *LP* III,

the "evidence" in the case included Buckingham's alleged claims about his own destiny and about the King's future, thus "prophecies" of a sort. The charges against Buckingham were brought by a former servant, Charles Knyvet. Among other accusations, Knyvet revealed certain predictions that had been made to Buckingham in 1514 by Nicholas Hopkins, a monk from Henton, Somersetshire: that the King would have no male heir and that the duke should one day "have all." Buckingham himself may later have spread these predictions. Knyvet claimed the duke had made various threats against the King's life in 1520 and that he had said the death of Henry's son was divine vengeance. The accusations against him were enough to convict Buckingham of compassing and imagining the death of the King.

While these predictions were clearly regarded by Buckingham's contemporaries as dangerous "prophecies" of future events, it is important to distinguish between them and the riddling and ambiguous form of prophecy that is our concern here. Predictions like those made to and by Buckingham do look ahead to the future, but they are straightforward in their claims. What is to come may be strange or surprising, but it is clear enough: the death of male heirs was a divine judgment, Henry would be killed, Buckingham would become king. It is obvious why such predictions would be regarded as dangerous. It is much less obvious why the confused prophecies of John Dobson should be regarded as so dangerous.

Another case of straightforward prediction of the future is the celebrated case of Elizabeth Barton, the "Holy Maid of Kent." Like those supposedly made by Buckingham, the nun's claims could be understood by everyone, and they resulted in equally disastrous consequences for the young woman. Hers is a relatively well-known and documented case.[7] Briefly, the young woman

1283–84. For Buckingham's fall, see also Miller, pp. 45–50, F.J. Levy, "The Fall of Edward, duke of Buckingham" in *Tudor Men and Institutions*, ed. A.J. Slavin (Baton Rouge, La., 1972), pp. 32–48, and Barbara J. Harris, *Edward Stafford, Third Duke of Buckingham, 1478–1521* (Stanford, Calif., 1986), Chapter 8, "The Fall of the Duke of Buckingham."

[7] Elizabeth Barton's story appears in Mackie, pp. 361–62, Scarisbrick, pp. 321–22, Elton, *Reform and Reformation*, pp. 180–81, and Guy, *Tudor England*, pp. 138–39. Excellent analyses of the charges and legal decisions are in Bellamy, *Tudor Law*, pp. 23–30, and Elton, "The Law of Treason," pp. 220–21.

In this instance I have relied only on the abstracts of the documents found in *LP*, chief among them: IV.2, 4806; V, 1698; VI, 835, 869, 887 (Cromwell to Henry VIII, among other notes, telling the King he had made inquiries about the nun), 967, 1149, 1194, 1333, 1336, 1369, 1370, 1381, 1382, 1419 (Chapuys to Charles V), 1422, 1433, 1438, 1445 (Chapuys again, describing the charges and trial), 1460 (Chapuys on the execution), 1464, 1465, 1466, 1467, 1468 (a listing of those who had seen the nun's revelations and her confession), 1469, 1470, 1471, 1512, 1519 (Cranmer to Henry VIII, a kind of wrap-up of events), and 1546 (Cranmer to Archdeacon Hawkyns, an excellent summary of the case, with Cranmer's judgment suffered some sort of serious illness in 1525 while a servant in Aldington in Kent. She began to have visions, during which she uttered religious prophecies. After various examinations of her and an inquiry conducted by William Warham, archbishop of Canterbury, she entered a convent in Canterbury.

By 1527, her predictions had acquired a political tinge, and she began to prophesy against the King's divorce. Like today's rock stars and politicians, she seems to have had her "career" managed by a careful handler, in this case a monk of Canterbury named Edward Bocking. She was summoned by the King himself, whom she threatened directly, predicting his death if he divorced Katherine and married Anne. She sent warnings to the pope as well. Despite all this, she remained free to speak until July of 1533 when Henry finally ordered her arrest. After some legal maneuvering about the exact charges that could be made against her, she and several followers were condemned and executed in 1534.

Like Buckingham's, these were surely dangerous predictions, but they are very different than the ambiguous political prophecies that were also beginning to circulate. As early as 1512, Wolsey had supposedly been bothered by a prophecy of the kind that would become so troublesome in the 1530s. Included in a much later document are the details: "that one with a Red Cap [Wolsey, who was to become cardinal in 1515] brought up from low degree to high estate should rule all the land under the King, . . . and afterwards procure the King to take another wife, divorce his lawful wife, Queen Catherina and involve the land in misery" and that "after much misery the land by another Red Cap [Pole] be reconciled, or else brought to utter destruction." Cromwell took careful note of this prophecy, as the writer of the letter made clear: "Which prophecy the lord Cromwell knoweth and many and often times he and I have reasoned the matter. . . ."[8]

Wolsey may have been annoyed by this early prophecy, but by the 1530s both the times and the prophecies had become more dangerous. On 30

on the Maid's "feigned visions and godly threatenings"). Some of Barton's predictions may have been influenced by the techniques of political prophecy, however. Among the listing of thirty of her predictions sent to Cromwell in a letter on 25 November 1534 are two of interest in this regard: the twenty-seventh is the cryptic "Of 9. 9. 9. the reign of the King, how long he shall reign as saith a prophesy, which agrees with her saying" (the twenth-seventh year of Henry's reign would have been from 22 April 1535 until 21 April 1536), and the twenty-eighth, "Of three letters, A. F. G. by a prophesy in the hands of Holy Richard" (LP VI, 1466).

    [8] PRO 31/9 (LP XIV.1, 186). The document is found among the 1539 papers, but the prophecy was allegedly "showed and declared" when Henry's army was in Spain (1512). Cromwell often discussed this prophecy, recalling it particularly after Pole was created Cardinal in Rome in December 1536 and later legate to England. Quoted here from Roger Bigelow Merriman, *Life and Letters of Thomas Cromwell* (Oxford, 1902), 1, 204–05.

September 1530, one William Harlock was examined in the Tower before Sir Edmund Walsingham and Sir John Daunce about various prophecies he had been heard to pronounce. His case is an excellent example of the kind of person who came to be involved in political prophecy, and it provides a hint of the challenges that prophecies were to offer established authority.

Harlock seems hardly to be the kind of man to have posed much of a threat to Henry's position. In his deposition, he explained that he had lived with a "Doctor Austyn," a doctor "of phesyke and astronymer," who had died in Colchester nine years earlier, "of whome thys deponent had a kalendre of profysye wherin ther were pictures of kinges and lordes armes." These pictures were used as prophecy by Harlock and his associates. About a year before the time of his examination, Harlock explained that he had showed the calendar to one "Byrte of White Staunton in the countie of Somers[et-shire]" who "dyd interpreta[te], expounde, and declare parte of the contentes of sayd kalendre." According to Harlock, Byrte revealed "by the pyctures in the same kalender ther shuld be a grett bateille of prestes," but "what yere or tyme" the battle would be, he did not reveal. Further, Byrte said "that by thys kalender . . . ther shalbe iij yeres next followynge after the yere of Our Lorde God mille D and xxx moche truble and besynes."

His prophetic "calendar" had caused something of a stir in Somersetshire, for Harlock admitted that Sir Nicholas Wadham had threatened to punish him if he persisted in showing it around. He had promised to burn it; instead he had showed it to a goldsmith at Taunton, Richard Loweth. Harlock had his own ideas about how his prophetic pictures were to be interpreted. He told Loweth they were "off the dredfull dragon." But Loweth had his own book of prophecies: "the seyd Lowethe seyd that his boke showyd myche off the same and seyd farther that the seyd dragon sholde lande wythe the bare leggyd hennys." Then Loweth had taken a turn interpreting the prophecy: he believed the "dredfull dragon" was the Irish earl of Desmond, and the "lyon gentyll," also figuring somewhere in the prophecy, was "the kynge of Scottes."

A battle would take place, a "curtes knyght" would land, and "there shalle the blew bore mete the curtes knyght and geve batelle tylle they do swete and foome." Loweth showed Harlock many more prophecies "wreten in Walsh in a blakke booke," but Harlock could not remember any more of them. He *could* remember many others who had spoken prophecy, though, recalling an occasion about two years earlier when John Barbour of Norwich had read from a book of prophecy in the presence of Harlock, Roger Coper, a weaver named Robert, and Sir William, chaplain to a Mr. Hals. Harlock had been impressed by Barbour's book, but Sir William had told him that Hals had one even better, adding "by that boke, for my hedd, the Kinges Grace shuld not obteigne above thre yere." Sir William and Harlock had had some kind of falling out after their meeting, and Harlock had gone so far as to accuse Sir

27

William of prophesying before two sheriffs of Norwich, who evidently could not make much out of the matter, dismissing the mess with a memorable comment: "Thys ys but a tryffyllinge mater to come before the Kinge."

Finally, Harlock implicated still another prophesier he knew, Thomas Larke, who had met with Sir William Larke, a man named Richard Jones, and "one Lloid, of Appysham in Devonshyre." Thomas Larke's prophecy was that the "whytte lyon in the yere of Our Lorde God mille D xxx j shuld kylle a kinge in Englond." The prediction was interpreted by William Larke, who "supposyd" the white lion "to be the Kinge of Denmarke."[9]

Nothing seems to have resulted from Harlock's examination at the time, though it now demonstrates how complicated the links among prophecies and prophesiers could become. Harlock may, in fact, be the "old Horlock" referred to by a prisoner examined in the Ilchester jail (Somersetshire) two years later, in 1532; the prisoner, Thomas Cheeselade, reported that a fellow prisoner, John Richards, had repeated a number of prophecies he had had from "old Horlock" six years earlier, among them one that the King would be driven from the realm. If Harlock and "old Horlock" were the same man, Harlock would thus have been an active prophesier by at least 1526. And as if this were not confusing enough, Harlock, especially if he was, in fact, the "old Horlock" referred to, must also have been related to "one yonge Hurlok," who figured as a source of prophecies in the 1546 examination of William Laynam, who was himself active in spreading prophecies for some seventeen years, and whose name appears here and there in the state papers during the decade of the 1530s. In addition, the name of Richard Jones, perhaps the same Richard Jones mentioned here by Harlock, is associated with another noted case of magic and prophecy, that of William Neville.[10]

Harlock may also be linked indirectly to the most serious early case involving political prophecy, that of Sir Rhys ap Griffith. The young Griffith was executed on Tower Hill on 4 December 1531, and among the charges brought against him was the accusation that he had spread a seditious prophecy. According to the formal Indictment preferred against Griffith and his two servants, "et inter se colloquentes sepius repetendo et dicebant quod hec antiqua subsequens prophecia existit in Wallia videlicet that king Jamys

9 For all of this, SP 1/58, fols. 101–102 (*LP* IV.3, 6652).
10 For the 1532 examinations revealing the prophecies of "old Horlock," see E 36/120, fol. 76 (*LP* V, 759); SP 1/69, fols. 115 and 136 (*LP* V, 793 and 830); and especially SP 1/237, fols. 121–27 (*LP Addenda* I.1, 768). A 1534 catalogue of Cromwell's papers (E 36/139) includes a reference to "William Hurlock" indicating he is "a blind profeser" (*LP* VII, 923.).

On Laynam, see SP 1/92, fols. 34–47 (*LP* VIII, 565); BL MS Cotton Titus B.i, fol. 271 (*LP* XIV.1, 806); and SP 1/220, fols. 60–69 (*LP* XXI.1, 1027).

For Richard Jones's career, see below.

with the red hand and the ravens should conquere all England." The "red hand" was a reference to Owen Lawgoch, the last representative of the house of Gwynnedd. The "ravens" referred to Griffith himself, the head of the house of Dynevor, whose arms bore three ravens on a white field. (His grandfather, Rhys ap Thomas, had carried those same arms for Henry VII.) Ravens were also the arms of Owain ap Urien Rheged, a legendary Welsh hero — and thus a powerful symbol of challenge to any English king. In the words of this prophecy, then, James of Scotland would lead a great army that would conquer England for himself and Wales for Rhys ap Griffith. The threat that Scotland and Wales would unite to conquer England had a long history, and the hint of it here contributed to the conviction of the rash Griffith. Griffith certainly should have known the danger of prophecy, for on 30 January 1529 he himself had written to Wolsey about the capture "at great cost" of John Sant, who had spread a prophecy of the King's death.

The connection between the prophecies of Griffith and Harlock is indirect. "Old Horlock" had predicted that a peacemaker would march into England out of the west, and this prediction was recalled by the prisoners at the Ilchester jail after they had heard the news of Rhys ap Griffith's execution: "A little before Xmas last tidings came that one Griffith, a gentleman of Wales, should be beheaded and deponent showed the prisoners that 9 or 10 years ago one Horlock an old man showed him 'that the white hare should drive the fox to the castle of care and that the white greyhound should run under the root of an oak and that there should be such a gap in the west that all the thorns of England should have work enough to stop it."' The prisoners somehow linked the Welsh Griffith with the peacemaker predicted by "old Horlock" to come into England from out of the west.[11]

3. Dangerous Precedents

The prophecies revealed by the examination of Harlock and involved in the arrest and execution of Rhys ap Griffith are only a hint of what was to come. Two cases in 1533, though complicated and clearly troublesome, represent a kind of lull before the break of a storm of prophecy. The accused, William

---

[11] For the complete text of the Indictment and a discussion of the place of prophecy in Griffith's arrest and conviction, see W.L. Williams, "A Welsh Insurrection," Y Cymmrodor, 16 (1903), 33–41; see also Taylor, pp. 91 and 106, Glanmor Williams, "Prophecy, Poetry, and Politics," p. 112, and Glanmor Williams, Recovery, Reorientation, and Reformation Wales, c. 1415–1642 (Oxford, 1987), pp. 255–57.

For Griffith's letter to Wolsey, LP IV.3, 5190.

For the investigation of the Ilchester prisoners, see LP Addenda, I.1, 768.

Neville and Mistress Amadas, were to suffer no serious consequences for their predictions.

It is hard to decide whether those involved in the Neville case were fools or knaves. The records in the case are numerous, and the summary of the case offered by G.R. Elton is a delightful characterization of the "dramatis person- ae," "props," and unfolding scenes in a comedy of ambition.[12] The action could, of course, have wound up a tragedy for those involved but, in Elton's words, "in the end they proved more fortunate than their idiocy deserved." While there are many actors in this minor drama, the principal players were William Neville, who was one of the younger brothers of Lord Latimer, and Richard Jones, an Oxford scholar who involved Neville in this drama of magic and prophecy.[13]

There is a great deal beside prophecy in this case, including astrology, magical instruments like "styllatoryes, alembykes, and odre instruments of glasse," and even an attempt to make a cloak of invisibility. The sequence of events and the details of all the efforts of this conniving crew are well told by Elton. Our concern here is only with Neville's interest in prophecy. Among the evidence offered by Thomas Wood, an intimate of Neville's who was a part of all the action, is the accusation that "Nevyll shewed him that the Kinges Highness wold shortly ouer see and that he shuld neuer come agayne nor shuld . . . reigne the full of xxiiij[th] yere and that he knew wele bi dyuerse prophesies and said also that before this feast of Christmas the kinge of Scottes shulde make iij battells in England and shuld come in bi Worcester and optayne and that he wold be at oon of thies battelles him self."[14]

In his confession, Neville admitted to this knowledge, but said the prophecies had been made to him by Jones: "he told me þat none off Cadwa- ladres blode shulde reign longer than xxiiij[ti] yeres." The reference to the

---

[12] Elton, *Policy and Policy*, pp. 50–57. The documents are numerous: the original accusation of Neville (3 December 1532 — E 163/10/20; not found in *LP*); examin- ations of Thomas Wood, William Neville, George Neville, and Richard Jones (30 December — SP 1/72, fols. 196–207; *LP* V, 1679); a letter from Jones to Cromwell (SP 1/73, fols. 1–2; *LP* V, 1680); an arrest report for one of the minor actors in the case (12 January 1533 — SP 1/69, fols. 13–14; *LP* V, 712, misdated to 1532 there, according to Elton); another letter, in fragments, relative to the case (SP 1/73, fols. 3–4; *LP* V, 1681 — Elton says the letter is probably from Tyler to Jones); a report of additional information in the case (21 March — SP 1/75, fol. 38; *LP* VI, 257); and a few other appeals and petitions (SP 1/75, fol. 39, *LP* VI, 258; SP 1/238, fol. 119, *LP Addenda* I.1, 863). Several of these items are included in the catalogue of Cromwell's papers (E 36/139, fol. 48; *LP* VII, 923, item xxv).

[13] Richard Jones's name has already appeared in our narrative, in connection with William Harlock, above. It is not clear whether this is the same man, but it is an intriguing possibility.

[14] SP 1/72, fol. 196 (*LP* V, 1679)

"blood of Cadwalader" recalled the Welsh claims of the Tudor dynasty. Neville added more: "he told me þat Prynce Edwarde hadde issue a sonne which was conveyed ouer see and there hadde issue a sonne who is yet alive eythre in Saxonye or Almayne which I told him was not lykely seynce he was not herde off in all this tyme. Also þat eyther he or the kyng off Scottes shulde reigne next after the Kynges Grace þat now is."[15] Which "Prince Edward" Neville referred to is unclear — perhaps he meant Henry VI's son, Prince Edward, who had died in 1471, or he may have meant Edward IV's young son, Edward, Prince of Wales. In either case, such a reference to the sudden return of a long-lost young man with a legitimate claim to the throne who would become king of England was a powerful tool that was to become even more threatening later in the decade — as the records in the state papers and the texts of the prophecies will show. Neville's prediction about the "kynge of Scottes" is also very important since James V of Scotland, as the son of Henry VII's older daughter Margaret, also had a strong legitimate claim to the Tudor throne. Neville also admitted knowing that the duke of Buckingham and, more recently, "yong Ryse" had lost their lives for putting too much faith in such prophecies.

Nevertheless, Neville seemed to be a great deal of *his* trust in prophecies. According to Wood, Neville not only believed that he would succeed his brother, Lord Latimer, but that he would become earl of Warwick. Wood said Neville had explained how all this would happen. Latimer would first claim the Warwick title as a descendant of Richard Neville's uncle, and then *William* Neville would gain it by inheritance: "my broder shalbe slayn at oon of the said batteles and then shall I haue the warde of his sone and haue both his landes and therldome of Warwyk."[16]

Neville's ambitions might even have gone further: "a beyr whiche had ben long tyde to a stake shuld arise and make peace and vnytie . . . and the same William Nevyll named him self the bair. . . ." Both a bear and a ragged staff were part of the Warwick arms, and if Neville were to be the Warwick earl and to bring "peace and unity" to the realm after Henry's fall, he was perhaps patterning himself after the "kingmaking" earl of Warwick, Richard Neville. Thus the interest of the King's Council in all these matters was not misplaced. Neville might even intend to be king himself. Significantly, Neville was here quoting directly from a popular prophecy:

> Then shall a bere þat longe hath be tyed at a stake
> Causer of debate chefe as yt shalbe see
> A[t] many his cheine shall he shake
> And be chefe maker of pease and vnytie.[17]

15 SP 1/72, fol. 202 (*LP* V, 1679)
16 SP 1/72, fol. 196 (*LP* V, 1679)
17 For the accusation against Neville, SP 1/72, fol. 197 (*LP* V, 1679); the

Cromwell acted quickly in the affair, rounding up the principals and keeping them safe in the Tower. The first accusation against Neville and Jones, by Edward Legh, Neville's chaplain, was made on 3 December 1532. By 30 December, Neville, Wood, and Jones were all in custody and had been examined. The charges were certainly serious, encompassing talk of the death of the King. After the 1534 Treasons act, such talk would be punishable by death. However, those involved with Jones and Neville seem not to have actually plotted *taking* any action themselves. Jones and his fellow magicians were content to manipulate Neville, who in turn enjoyed the visions of all that would come to him as he sat back and waited for events to unfold. All survived their arrest. Neville went free, appealing to Cromwell in 1534 for financial help because of the losses he suffered in the affair.[18] By July of the same year he was once again part of the commission of peace in Worcestershire, and in 1537 his name appears as a trusted government servant during the investigations after events in the Pilgrimage of Grace.[19]

Richard Jones remained in the Tower for some time. From the Tower he wrote to Cromwell, promising to make him a philosopher's stone and to serve him "as one of your dogs." He claimed he had only intended to make a fool of Neville: "The most that I have offended was in laughing at his countenance."[20] In July of the same year, still in the Tower, he wrote to the mayor of Bristol, signing himself, "Your unacquainted orator." He offered comments about the clergy and the King's divorce, and said that if the mayor was unable to interpret his predictions, he should inquire "of Mr. Latimer's boy."[21] Jones's brother eventually obtained the scholar's release from the Tower.[22]

The same year, 1533, saw also the case of Mistress Amadas. She was not as prominent a person as Neville, nor is her case as complicated or as confused. In fact, there is only one document in the case, with no indication about how the woman made herself or her prophecies known. She may have been the wife of Robert Amadas, keeper of the King's jewels, in which case she would have had access to audience enough.[23] In any case, it is clear that she was quite a handful for anyone — husband or examiners — to manage. She had

prophecy appears in British Library MS Lansdowne 762, fols. 63v–65r, compiled during this decade. (See Appendix for a discussion of this manuscript.)

[18] *LP* VII, 1649

[19] See Elton, *Policy and Police*, p. 55 as well as *LP* VII, 1026 and XII.1, 234.

[20] SP 1/73, fols. 1–2 (*LP* V, 1680)

[21] For Jones's letter to the mayor, see *LP* VI, 873.

[22] For the letter of his brother, see SP 1/238, fol. 119 (*LP Addenda* I.1, 863).

[23] The examination of Mistress Amadas is found in BL MS Cotton Cleopatra E.iv, fols. 99–100 (*LP* VI, 923).

The next document in *LP* (VI, 924) is a record of accounts for Robert Amadas, ending "Information of certain words spoken by Mistress Amadas as within appeareth."

plenty to say on any number of subjects. Her examination is headed, "Hereafter folowyth some parte of suche vngracious rehersalles as Mistres Amadas at syndry tymes hath spoken befor dyuers persons." Included here are only the "ungracious rehearsals" that involve political prophecy:

> Furst, she said that she hath loked this twentye yere apon profecyes and this is the yere that her matteres shall come to passe.
>
> Item, she saith that the Kynges Grace is called in her boke of profecyes the moldwarpe and is cursed with Godis own mowth.
>
> Item, she saith His Grace shalbe bannysshid his realme as Calwalider was and or midsomer day the realm shold be counquered by the Scottes and her contre men and after that the clobbes of Essex shall dryve them forth again and a busshe in Essex shalbe worth a castell in Kent.
>
> Item, she saith that thar is a religius man alyve in an ilond and is called the ded man and he shall come and kepe a parlament at the Towr and it shalbe called the parlament of peace. . . .
>
> Item, she said . . . the dragon shall be kylled by mydsomer. . . .
>
> Item, she said the blasynge sterre was towerd that ilond frome whens the ded man shold come and said "nowe this geyre begenes to werke. . . ."
>
> Item, she said ther shalbe a battell of prelates and that the Kynge shalbe distroyed and ther shalbe neuer no kynges in Ynglond and the realme shalbe callid the land of conquest and be devyded in fower partes. . . .
>
> Item, she saith she hathe a rowyll wherin is payntyd and wryten all her profecyes.

Many of the other charges she made were directed specifically against the Boleyn family.[24] She claimed that Anne was a harlot, that Anne's father, the earl of Wiltshire, had been "bawde both to his wife and his two dowghters" (since Henry "hath kept both the mother" and the daughters), that the King had "many tymes" plied her, Mistress Amadas, "with tokens and large offerynge of gyftes to make her a hoore," but that she was one of only three "good weddid woman in Ynglond," the other two being Katherine and the duchess of Norfolk (rejected by her husband in favor of his mistress). Whether or not she was Robert Amadas's wife, she had marital problems of her own and strongly identified with Katherine: "because the Kynge hath forsaken his

[24] Mistress Amadas's attacks on Anne Boleyn were keenly political. For extensive analysis of and argument for the political influence and partisanship of Henry's second wife, see E.W. Ives, *Anne Boleyn* (Oxford, 1987). Note, however, the more qualified view of Anne's political influence in Retha Warnicke, *The Rise and Fall of Anne Boleyn: Family Politics at the Court of Henry VIII* (Cambridge, 1989).

wyfe he suffereth her husbond to doo the same bot the good emprowre shall delyuer all good wyfes when he commythe whiche shalbe shortly." Among her other enemies were the Lord Chancellor Audley, the Chief Justice Norwich ("that false Norwyge"), and Sir John Baker, the "false recorder of London," all of whom "shall surly be behedid."

Mistress Amadas may have been out of her mind, as one who heard her ravings concluded: "old Maister Whitnall thought after she had beyne madde or elles distraite." She may have been dismissed as a shrew, "with her continuall raylynge of bawdry and lecherye." Perhaps. But if she was mad, there was also method in her.

Mistress Amadas's "ungracious rehearsals" pulled together several of the threads of prophecy we have seen to this point, and she wove them into something of a coherent whole. Like Harlock some three years before, she foretold a battle of priests, a prophecy originating in Geoffrey's *Prophetia Merlini*. Harlock had said his calendar had predicted that battle occurring in three years' time, and there was Mistress Amadas, three years later, proclaiming the same thing. Her prophecy agreed with Harlock's in the invasion of the king of Scots as well, a prediction that Neville and his cohorts also made. In identifying Henry with the terrible "moldwarp," her prophecy again went back to Geoffrey, this time indirectly, through the very popular "Prophecy of the Six Kings to Follow King John." The sixth king was pictured as a terrible mole who would be driven from his kingdom, and although the sixth king had been originally identified as Henry IV, and the prophecies of the moldwarp used against him, Henry VIII came to be identified as the mole during the 1530s. Here also is a reference to the coming of a mysterious "dead man," whose arrival in England was to be so important. Like the equally mysterious "issue" of the "issue" of "Prince Edward" in Neville's prophecies, a deliverer would somehow arrive in England, in both cases from over the sea. Mistress Amadas foretold an arrival from an island, while Neville one from the continent. Or perhaps the emperor would be the conqueror — Mistress Amadas was clearly on dangerous ground here. Particularly noteworthy are her attacks on Anne Boleyn. As political tensions between England and Rome, and within England, between Church and state, grew, political stands were increasingly expressed in terms of support for Queen Katherine or for Anne Boleyn. But for all her political prophecies, Mistress Amadas had the authority of tradition behind her. Whatever her personal characteristics, her political characterizations were to the point.

Although Elizabeth Barton died later in the year for her predictions, Mistress Amadas did not. She suffered no serious consequences from the government for her prophecies, not even, apparently, arrest. But there is ample evidence that even though the woman herself was not taken seriously, political prophecies like hers were.

4. *The Gathering Storm*

As Henry's divorce from Katherine and Rome progressed, increasing numbers of strange claims and predictions were reported. In the fall of 1533, for example, Mary Baynton, a disturbed Yorkshire woman, wandered about spreading the tale that she was the King's daughter, forced to beg for her subsistence.[25] In June of the following year, well after Henry's marriage to Anne and after the first session of the 1534 parliament, the mayor of Hereford reported directly to Cromwell the "opprobrious words" of "Robert Stoper, alias Pewterer." Under examination, Stoper had confessed that he was, in reality, the king of England — that he was the eldest son and heir of the late earl of Wiltshire, by whom he meant Henry Stafford, who had recently died, brother to the duke of Buckingham whose execution for treason in 1521 has already been discusssed. Stopes also claimed that Queen Katherine's banner would once again be spread in England.[26]

Months later, Thomas Arundell, a curate in Chesterton, reported his parson, one Master Brown, to Cromwell. Arundell's charge was that Brown had in his possession a copy of a political prophecy. Brown had made his curate copy the prophecy for him. The self-righteous Arundell had done as he was told, but he had also made a second copy, retaining it "to show" to Cromwell. He must have intended to reveal the details of the prophecy in a personal meeting with Cromwell. He did, however, enclose assurances that he had refused to serve Brown any further. In late 1534, two priests were involved in a dispute over an incident that had occurred the previous year. Thomas Gebons accused his fellow priest, Ralph Wendon, of having quoted a prophecy that a queen would be burned in Smithfield. Gebons claimed that Wendon, who had called Queen Anne (redundantly) a whore and a harlot, interpreted the prophecy as a prediction about Anne Boleyn. But subsequent investigation revealed Gebons's own shady character and thwarted ambitions rather than Wendon's guilt. Still, the role of prophecy as a treasonable offense is noteworthy, as is the blame Anne took in the state of dissatisfaction and unrest.[27]

On New Year's Day of 1535, Eustace Chapuys, the Emperor Charles V's ambassador in England, set the tone for the year:

[25] *LP* VI, 1193

[26] For the mayor of Hereford's letter, see SP Scot. 4, fol. 172; for Stoper's confession, BL MS Cotton Titus B.i, fol. 171. Both are abstracted in *LP* VII, 802.

[27] On Arundell's charge, see SP 1/88, fol. 56 (*LP* VII, 1624). The document for Wendon's case is SP 6/7, numbers 6–10 (*LP* VI, 733). Though included among the 1533 state papers, the document belongs to 1534 (dated correctly by Elton, *Policy and Police*, p. 347).

Booksellers have been forbidden to sell or keep a prognostication lately made in Flanders, which threatens the King with war and misfortune this year; and some of the leading men of the Council have said that, matters being as they are, nothing is wanted to set the realm topsy turvy but to translate and publish the said prognostication in English.[28]

Adding to the political and religious turmoil, the weather was bad. In a letter to Lady Lisle, Anthony Waite reported from the Inner Temple the case of a man committed to the Tower for saying that the month, May, would be full of rain, the next full of death, and the third full of war. Waite said the man would be kept in the Tower until the truth of his prophecy were seen. Interestingly, the same letter mentioned a group of people from Flanders who were also examined for "strange" and "damnable" opinions — perhaps the prognostications Chapuys had reported to the Emperor earlier in the year.[29]

In August, two men "voluntarily declared" before a Worcestershire justice that Edmond Brocke, while going home from Worcester Market, had said to Margaret, wife of Thomas Higons, "It is long of the King that this weather is so troublous or unstable, and I wene we shall never have better weather whilst the King reigneth, and therefore it maketh no matter if he were knocked or patted on the head." Brocke was an old man, about eighty, and he pleaded his age, madness, and drunkenness as an excuse for his talk.[30] A letter from the bishop of Bath to Cromwell, in September, made weather a point as well — the bishop remarked on the constant rain for nine of the previous twelve months.[31]

The Treasons act passed by parliament in its November 1534 session went into effect on 1 February 1535, and Cromwell supervised the investigations that arose as a result of the new act. On 16 April instructions were sent to spiritual and temporal authorities to arrest any offenders. Those accused were to be examined and held, while all depositions were to be forwarded to the Council or to Cromwell directly. Almost no one and nothing seems too insignificant to have come to official attention.

Many of those reported to the government under the new act were clergy. The vicar of Halifax, for instance, was reported by a former servant for having repeated the rhyme "A-pon Herre all Yngland mey werre."[32] The abbot of Abingdon reported that his officers had taken into custody a priest who had a book of "conjurations" for finding hidden treasure and for consecrating a crystal so that a child could see "many things," presumably "things" in the

[28] *LP* VIII, 1 On Chapuys and his reporting, see Ives, pp. 72–75.
[29] SP 3/14, Lisle Papers (*LP* VIII, 771)
[30] *LP* IX, 74
[31] SP 1/96, fols. 183–84 (*LP* IX, 383)
[32] E 36/120, fol. 104 (*LP* IX, 404)

future. The abbot sent the book to Cromwell, noting that it included many ominous pictures, such as one of a sword crossed over a sceptre. The abbot asked Cromwell where he should send the offending priest.[33] Near the end of the year, a friar named Maydland was accused of necromancy. His magic contributed to his prediction of the King's "vyolent and shamefull" death and his wish that Anne, "that myschevous hore," would be burnt.[34]

All these show the increasing unrest in Henry's kingdom. More specific cases related to political prophecy need to be seen as a part of this general state of suspicion and tension. In a letter to Cromwell written in late May from Dorsetshire, Sir Thomas Arundel reported the predictions of Alexander Clavell. Clavell had commented first about the weather, but then he had gone on to make a now familiar prophecy about priests taking up arms: he lamented "the stormy wether and then the world sayinge hit was a hevy world and was lyke to be worse shortly, for he had herd say that the pristes wold ryse ageyne the Kyng." In his examination of Clavell, Arundel found that the predictions had come from an old man: "he herd hit off on off my faderes tennanttes . . . off the report off an old man callyd Payne dwellyng iij myles fro me." Since Payne was too old to make the trip to Arundel, Arundel made the trip to him. After questioning, Payne confessed that he had told "dyuerse men that the prystes schuld make a feld." Further, "the whit fawcon schuld come owte off the northe west and kyll allmost all the prystes."[35] The white falcon was Anne Boleyn's badge, and Payne's prophecy an another indication of the widespread resentment of her, and of the blame she received for events taking place in the country.

The investigations of Clavell and Payne ended after Arundel's examination. Perhaps, since Payne said the prophecies had come to him from a wise man dead for fifty years, it was felt the matter should be pursued no further. Much more serious was the investigation of the Carthusian monks undertaken at about the same time.[36] In interrogatories on the question of Supremacy, administered by Cromwell himself, John Leek, a clerk of Syon, revealed that he had been seen a "slanderous bill" about six months earlier, but at the time of his examination he could not remember which of his companions at the time had showed it to him. The question of who had had the document ultimately was not all that important. What became more important was tracking down the source of the prophecies.

Leek *said* that he had heard Thomas Skidmore *say* that John Hale, the vicar of Isleworth, *had said*, "the Kyng was molywarpe þat Merlyn prophecyed þat turnyd al vpe and þat the Kyng was accursed of Godes owne mowth."

33 SP 1/97, fols. 128–29 (*LP* IX, 551)
34 SP 1/99, fols. 67–68 (*LP* IX, 846)
35 SP 1/92, fol. 194 (*LP* VIII, 736)
36 For all this see SP 1/92, fols. 34–50 (*LP* VIII, 565–67).

When Skidmore was examined, he added that Hale had also claimed "þat the mariage betwene the Kinge and the Quene was vnlefull."

Hale's examination before the Council is pitiful. He began with a history of his recent problems — he had fallen and hurt his leg nearly a year before, he had been violently ill with a fever for some time, and during the trip he had made with Leek he had had several falls from his horse, from one of which, as he pleaded, he was "troubled in [his] wits as also by age and lack of memory." When he finally got down to repeating what he knew of the prophecies, he admitted having heard some of the predictions of Merlin from a prophesier named Laynam about two years earlier.[37] Once again an allusion to Rhys ap Griffith appeared, showing how closely his fate was identified with prophecy: Hale said Skidmore had talked about young Rhys, saying Welshman and priests were sorely disdained in those days.

The unfortunate vicar finally confessed that all the charges against him were true. But in his defense, he pleaded that his "wits" were "troubled by sickness" and that he was "aged and oblivious." He begged forgiveness from God, King Henry, and Queen Anne. Nevertheless, Hale was one of several executed in the persecution of the Carthusians. Among those found guilty along with him for their resistance to the Supremacy were three priors — John Houghton of London, Augustine Webster of Axholme, and Robert Laurence of Beauvale — as well as Richard Reynolds of Syon and three other monks. A month later Chapuys reported the popular reaction to the executions: "Already [the people] begin to murmur, because ever since these executions began it has rained continually, and they say it is the vengeance of God."[38]

One further case in the gathering storm of 1535 ended more happily, if not more justly. In November William Thwaytes, the parson of Londesborough (Yorkshire), was accused of various treasonous words. Thwaytes had made much of the news of the papal interdiction of England, and had openly claimed before "any convenient audience" that the King would be forced to flee from his realm. One of the witnesses against him said Thwaytes had spoken many prophecies of "fields," or "battles," that were to come. There were several witnesses against the parson, and he seems almost certainly to have been as guilty under the Treasons act as Hale had been.[39] At the York

---

[37] Laynam's name has appeared before; see above, p. 28 and n. 10.

[38] *LP* VIII, 949

[39] *LP* IX, 791 and VIII, 457 (Elton, *Policy and Police*, p. 58, says this is dated a year too early in *LP*). In addition to these documents, the notation "To move the King touching Thwayttes" appears in a list of "things to be moved on the King's behalf unto his attorney, to be afterwards . . . by the learned counsel against the next assembly of his Parliament." This document (*LP* VI, 1381) belongs to late 1533 and may refer to early rumors about the parson.

assizes, though, he was acquitted. About the case G.R. Elton concludes, "the depositions suggest rather that Thwaytes, guilty in fact, had the right sort of friends."[40]

5. The Storm Breaks

When the last session of the Reformation Parliament met in January 1536, it passed an act dissolving monastic houses worth less than £200 a year. Katherine of Aragon died on 7 January, and Anne Boleyn miscarried (a boy) by the end of the month. In April parliament was called into session again, but quickly found its business to include an investigation of Anne's "crimes."[41] By 30 May, Anne and those accused with her had been executed, and Henry had married for the third time. A new Successions act was passed in July, and Convocation was presented with Henry's Ten Articles. Cromwell issued the Injunctions for the remedy of abuses and the advancement of improvement in August.

During the early months of 1536, several cases involving political prophecy are worth attention. The first involved the abbot of Coggeshall, in Essex, who was examined on various articles, among them one that he had read a book of prophecy to his fellow monks. Depositions "of certain of the Convent against the Abbot" accused him of numerous financial and spiritual abuses and appealed to Thomas Legh, one of Cromwell's visitatorial commissioners, for a new abbot. But, in a letter directly to Cromwell, Henry Bourchier, earl of Essex, offered his support for the abbot, saying that he had been accused by a "simple person," one who had formerly been abbot himself and seemed therefore to have a personal motive for his attack. Nothing of the prophecies in the abbot's book is detailed.[42]

Much more of the kind of prophecies circulating in the country is seen in the information collected in Leicestershire against the abbot of Garendon, Thomas Syson. According to the documents containing the charges, the abbot claimed "thatt in þe yere of Our Lord a thousand and D and xxxv^ty þe church by my boke shall haue a grett fall" — so far, he was right — "and by xxxix^ti hit shall ryse agayne and be as hye as euer hit was." The abbot further prophesied "þe egle shall ryse with such a nombre þat þe Kyng shall go forth of þe realme." The King would later return and be killed. Like Mistress

---

40 Elton, *Policy and Police*, p. 58.

41 On Anne's miscarriage and its date, see Warnicke, pp. 191–205. On the parliamentary maneuvers of April 1536, see Ives, pp. 358–70 and Lehmberg, *Later Parliaments*, pp. 25–28.

42 SP 1/101, fols. 88–89, 153–61 and SP 1/103, fols. 215–16 (*LP* X, 94, 164, 774).

Amadas, the abbot identified Henry with the mole of "The Six Kings" prophecy: "þe molle is curst of Goddes one mouth, for he rotyth uppe þe churches as þe molle rotyth uppe þe molle hilles, and biffore þe xxxix[th] yere be come you by my boke shall here many thynges which I tell you nott of yett." Syson's house was dissolved that year, and he received a dispensation from his vows, but in October of the next year John Beaumont wrote to Cromwell, saying that Syson's prophecies of the previous year were still encouraging "divers persons" to rebellion.[43]

On 2 April a letter was sent to Cromwell about the parson of Wednesbury, Staffordshire, accused of treason. The letter-writer, John Whalley, said the abbot was a Scot, one who would also, "if well handled," declare "a great multitude of Papists in this country." Whalley added that the accused "had a book of prophecies."[44] One of the charges made against John Hill of Eynsham, Oxfordshire, in June was that "he trustyd to see the king of Scottes were the flower of Englond."[45] On the same day Sir William Goryng reported to Cromwell regarding charges made against the prior of Tortington. He informed Cromwell, "I have sent vnto yow the vere boke or the coppy of the sayd boke that the prior dyd rede as a profysy."[46] In a letter to the Emperor, Chapuys reported on the death of Anne Boleyn, including in them references to popular prophecies that had predicted her death. According to another account of Anne's death, now preserved in the Vienna Archives, "Thus, he who wrote this billet says that, according to old writings, he has seen the prophecy of Marlin fulfilled."[47]

Later in the year, as the North became increasing restive, the old prophecy of priests taking up arms seemed to have been fulfilled as well. In late September, the commissioners for the dissolution of the monasteries in Northumberland who were to investigate the canons of Hexham reported that the convent had armed itself with guns and artillery. As the commissioners approached the town, they heard the bells of both the town and the monastery. The house's gates were shut, and the prior appeared to the commissioners "in harness" — in armor. He told the commissioners that the monks were prepared to die rather than to surrender. After the commissioners retreated, according to reports of the townsmen, the monks "marched" out of their house "in harness," found the investigators out of sight, and "so they returned."[48] A few days later, the earl of Northumberland forwarded to

---

43 SP 1/125, fols. 90–91 (*LP* XII.2, 800).
    For Beaumont's letter, see SP 1/81, fol. 175 (*LP* VI, App. 10; misdated to 1533 according to Elton, *Policy and Police*, p. 71, using evidence of *LP* XII.2, 800).
44 *LP* X, 614
45 SP 1/104(B), fol. 225 (*LP* X, 1205)
46 SP 1/104(B), fol. 227 (*LP* X, 1207)
47 *LP* X, 911. For letters from Chapuys, see items 909 and 1069.
48 SP 1/106, fols. 222–24 (*LP* XI, 504)

Cromwell a report sent to him "of the obstinate and traitorous demeanour of the canons of Hexham."[49] Northumberland's letter reached the King himself by 5 October. Henry ordered the immediate apprehension, at any cost, of the "arrant traitors."[50]

All the incidents reported to the government were not so tense. Some are now quite sad, such as the letter from Richard Branborowe to Cromwell from late in October. The writer complained that Lord Hungerford had "wrongfully imprisoned" him in Bath "on a charge of speaking unseemly words." Branborowe didn't deny having spoken them; he wrote only saying "he never knew what [the] prophesy did mean," and that he was an old man with a wife and children. He begged Cromwell to write to the mayor of Bath "to accept sureties" on his behalf.[51] There is no record of what action Cromwell took.

Within a few days of the resistance of the canons of Hexham, the series of riots and rebellions known collectively as the Pilgrimage of Grace began. On 1 October 1536 there was a riot at Louth in Lincolnshire. Open resistance to the government spread quickly throughout the North, peace returning only in March of the following year. We have already noted the seriousness of this rebellion. Elton summarizes well the "King's vengeance." In Carlisle, seventy-four were hanged by the duke of Norfolk. Executions of the leaders of the rebellions followed, in London and Yorkshire, including the deaths of Sir Thomas Percy, the lords Darcy and Hussey, and George Lumley. As Elton concludes, ". . . since the pilgrims themselves seem to have caused the death of nobody, these are sad enough figures; yet a total of well below 200 people executed for raising a vast rebellion covering seven shires and threatening the safety of the whole realm — 200 out of perhaps 40,000 involved — is really astonishingly low, especially when it is remembered that over seventy of them were the victims of Norfolk's one act of savagery at Carlisle."[52] During the rebellion and its aftermath, political prophecies played an important part.

Early in February, in fact, Norfolk forwarded to Cromwell a copy of a prophecy collected during his investigations:

> A little boke was made in dede
> By the cownsaill of Marlin and Bede —
> Who so it doth rede writen shalbe
> That a litle cuntrey called Braytin
> Shalbe brought in such caas certayne

---

[49] LP XI, 535
[50] SP 1/106, fols. 257–58 (LP XI, 544) For a full account of the resistance at Hexham, see Dodds and Dodds, *The Pilgrimage of Grace*, 1, 75, 192–97.
[51] LP X, 809
[52] Elton, *Reform and Reformation*, p. 262.

And be compelled to begyn agayne,
At A. B. C. thait saide not Christes crosse
Therfore I like it the woorse;
Then toke Marlyn his horse and rode his way,
Bede bade still and made good chere,
And said, as ye shall after here
Howebeit I harde hym not swere,
"More ill cumethe of a smal note
As Crumwell set in a mans throte";
That shal put many other to payne, God wote,
But when Crumwell is brought in lawe,
And we rede owte the Christ crosse rowe,
To K. L. and M. then shall we knowe nowes;
The bere is bownd he was so wild,
Therefore he lost his ragged staff,
The care now he is fyled —
It was for cownsaill that he gave;
The white lyarde shalbe put owte of mynd
By cause he will not to the cownsaill assent,
They shall call hym vnkynde,
So shall they do Hamshire and Kent;
The fayre cressaunt shall loose his light,
Therefore England may make greate mene
With not the helpe of God alone;
The whit lyon shalbe layde to slepe
For envye of the axes clodge;
He shalbe bownd your deo sheld kepe,
The Talbot, your good dogge.[53]

Here are the now-familiar references to "A. B. C." (Anne Boleyn and Cromwell), to "K. L. and M." (Katherine and Lady Mary) and the pun on Cromwell's name. There are also allusions to those who participated in the rebellions, the crescent moon of the Percys, for example, and George Talbot, the earl of Shrewsbury acting for the King in York. In heraldry, a "talbot" is a hunting dog, used in the crest of the Talbots.

The prophecy Norfolk sent to Cromwell as he began his investigation of the rebellions is probably a good indication of the kind of prophecies Cromwell had received in the midst of the Pilgrimage from Lord Hungerford. Though the prophecies referred to have not survived, Cromwell's response has. In a letter to Lord Hungerford from Windsor, Cromwell wrote, ". . . I ha[ve] resceyved your lettres with the deposicions and confessions of certayne persons and a boke, wherin was writen amonges other thynges certain prophecies accordyng to your lettres. . . . And wher ye have commetted

[53] SP 1/115, fols. 175–77 (LP XII.1, 318)

Richard Sole and Richard Spicer to prison ye have done very well therin requyryng you they may remayne ther in saff and sure custodie and kepyng untill suche tyme as he shalbe further advertised of the Kynges pleasure in that behalfe."[54]

The prior of Malton, William Todd, was implicated for his part in Sir Francis Bigod's rebellion. His "part" seems mainly to have been inciting the rebels with prophecies. In his first examination, the prior described those prophecies: "vpon a xiiij or xvj yere ago [around 1523 or 1525?] . . . he sawe . . . a rolle in parchement of half a yarde in length and half a quarter of a yarde brode or thereaboutes wherin was a moone paynted growyng with a nombre of yeris growing as the moone did and where the mone was at full ther was a cardinall paynted and beneth hym the moone waned and twoo monkes paynted a-rowe, one vnder another hedlesse, and in the myddes of that roll was a stacke made as an overthwart partition and vnder that lyne in the nether parte of the rolle a childe paynted with axes and butchers knyves and instrumentes aboute hym."[55] Todd seems to have owned as well as to have seen this roll. He confessed, "which thing ofte tymes syns he shewed that he had seen as well to Bygod as to diuers others." He also admitted owning a book of prophecy "called 'Metodius.'" That book "lyeth vpen in his chambre for euery man to loke on."

In his defense, the prior claimed that, although he had a book of prophecies, he "never toke hym to intrepretate any parte of the said bookes," nor did he say anything at all "concernyng the Kynges Highnes or his affaires." Todd suffered the fate of the other rebels; he was sent to London and questioned again in late April, before the King's examiners, about his role in "this commotion."[56] His deposition is included with those of Sir John Bulmer, Sir Francis Bigod, Sir Thomas Percy, George Lumley, Lord Darcy, the prior of Bridlington, the abbots of Jervaulx and Fountains Abbey, Lord Hussey, and Robert Aske, among others, all of whom lost their lives. This final examination is now badly mutilated but does contain a few new details: that the king would be forced to flee his realm and would return to be content with one third of it, and that the church would suffer for three years but then flourish again.[57]

Also investigated at this time were the monks of Furness, who seem to

[54] Longford Castle MS as quoted by Merriman, *Letters of Cromwell*, 2, 35. Hungerford had earlier imprisoned Richard Branborowe for similar reasons; see above, p. 41.

[55] SP 1/116, fol. 165 (*LP* XII.1, 534) Interestingly, William Thwaytes, the parson of Londesborough investigated for his prophecies in 1535 (see above, p. 38), had apparently heard some of his "treasonable words" at Malton (SP 1/99, fol. 20; *LP* IX, 791).

[56] E 36/119, fol. 130 (*LP* XII.1, 1023)

[57] The entire collection of depositions is SP 1/119, fols. 73–87 (*LP* XII.1, 1087).

have given active support to the rebels. The most interesting accusations to emerge were those made against John Broughton. According to one witness, Broughton had prophesied, "in England shalbe slaine the decorat rose in his mothers bely," by which he meant, "Your Grace shall die by the handes of preestes for their churche is your mother and the church shall sley Your Grace." The abbot of Furness added further details: ". . . John Broughton dyd shew me one prophecie in the garden and I did ask hym how he dyd vnderstand it, and he shed me that A. B. C. and iij ttt shuld be all in one state and . . . the red rose shulde die in his mothers wombe."[58] As the abbot said, "this is a mervelous and a daungerous word," but no further details of the investigation appear in the state papers. Broughton's prophecy about the murder of the rose in his mother's belly obviously drew from the heraldic device of the rose and from prophecies popularly attributed to Thomas Becket, whose murder was supposed to have been predicted by the following: "the son shall slay the father in the womb of the mother." Or, Becket, a father of the Church, would be slain by Henry II, a son of the Church, in front of the altar, the Mother Church. Broughton provided his own interpretation of the lines in contemporary terms: the "red rose," Henry, would be killed in "his mother's belly," the Church.

Various other, less serious, charges were made as the Council of the North proceeded in its investigations. In Kent, a priest named James Fredewell was reported by a schoolmaster named Adam Lewes, if the charge can be believed, of predicting an invasion in the mysterious words, ". . . ther is another byrde a-bredyng that cam not forthe yett which wyll cum forthe before mydsomer þat the Kyng had neuer suche syns he was Kyng of Ynglond."[59] Also in Kent, Elizabeth Wood of Aylesham was taken to the Norwich jail after speaking "traitorous words" against the King, probably quoting a bit of prophecy when she said "with clubs and clouted shone shall the deed be done, for we had never good world since this King reigned."[60]

Richard Bishop of Bungay in Suffolk was also examined for speaking "certeyn wordes agaynst the Kynges Highnes." Bishop was investigated by the duke of Suffolk, Charles Brandon, who found him very difficult. Several accusations were lodged against him, and among them, not surprisingly, was a prophecy. Suffolk wrote directly to Cromwell about the case on 16 May, forwarding to him the examinations of Bishop and his accuser, Roger Seyman, and in Suffolk's words, "the copyes of the prophysye." He evidently found the prophecy a serious part of the case since he took time to track down its origins and progress: "I haue sent for the origynall of the same and

58 SP 1/118, fols. 1–8 (LP XII.1, 841)
59 SP 1/118, fols. 231–34 (LP XII.1, 990) On this report, see also Elton, Policy and Police, p. 66.
60 LP XII.1, 1301

hym that hathe yt and to knowe who hath hade copyes out of the saide boke. And further to knowe in what companyes the said copyes hath ben rede as nere as I can and further I haue sent for them that was at the redyng of the said copies with this Richarde Bysshope and to see what can be gotten of them."

Bishop's was a version of the "Six Kings" prophecy. According to his accuser, Robert Seyman, the lines he heard had alluded to the King as a mole. The mole was to be "subduyde and put downe." The prophecy also predicted the landing of "the prowdest prynce in all Cristendome," who would "mete with other ij kinges and shale fyght and shalbe put a-down and the whyte lyon should optayne." It is not clear from all this *who* would emerge as king. Seyman's summary of the prediction is garbled. But Bishop's own confession is more clear on the subject of the prophecy. In his confession, sent by Suffolk to Cromwell, Bishop "knewe where was a certan prophecye wich if the said Robert wold come to Bungay he shuld here hyt redde and that on man hadde taken payn to wache in the nyght to write the copye of the same. And if so be as the prophecye saith ther shalbe a rysyng of the people this yere or neuer. And that þe prophecye saith that the Kynges Grace was signified by a mowle and that ye mowle shuld be subduyt and put down. . . . Also he said that the prophecy saithe that thre kynges shall mete . . . and the prowdest prince in Crystendome shuld be ther subduyt and that the whyte lyon shuld stey all that besynes at length and shuld obteyne."

Suffolk was unhappy about the results of his investigations. At first recalcitrant, Bishop eventually confessed to some of the charges made against him, those above, for example. But the prophecy cited was only one of his "wordes agaynst the Kynges Highnes." More serious, he had also been charged with inciting rebellion, bringing into the south the dangerous spirit of the northern rebellions so recently subdued. Bishop had admitted a great deal, Suffolk wrote, "savynge he wold not conffesse in noo wyse that he spake that if three hundrethe good fellowes werre to gyther that they shuld haue company inoughe to subdue the gentillmen but I thynke surely he spake theym." Bishop must have been tortured by Suffolk, who added, "for nother by fayre meanes nor be fowlle I can make hym conffesse that ever he hard any such wordes of any body or that he spake any suche like wordes to any other person."[61]

The records do not show what happened to Bishop. Margaret and Ruth Dodds claim that both Bishop and his accuser Seyman were executed, citing a second letter from Suffolk to Cromwell ten days later.[62] There Suffolk wrote that he had not yet received the book of prophecy but that he would not "fail to accomplish" the King's pleasure "as to Seyman and Busshope and any

[61] SP 1/120, fols. 100–104 (LP XII.1, 1212)
[62] *Pilgrimage of Grace*, 2, 176–77.

other offenders."[63] Whatever happened to Bishop, Suffolk was still pursuing the source of the prophecies.

Only a few days later, on 11 June, the confession of a young man named Robert Dalyvell was sent to Cromwell:

> Furst, the saide Robert Dalyvell saythe that our sayde Soueraynge Lorde the Kyng shall not lyve nor be on lyve a month after the Feast of the Natiuite of Saynte John Baptiste which shalbe in the yere of Our Lorde God a thowsande fyve hundreth xxxviij[th] except he do amende his condicons.

> And further the said Robert Dalyvell sayth that after the saide tyme an horse of [10 shillings] price shalbe abli to beare all the noble blode of Englande.[64]

Cromwell was interested in Dalyvell's case; memoranda for the examination of Dalyvell in Cromwell's hand survive and reveal more of Dalyvell's whereabouts and the reasons for Cromwell's concern:

> Fyrst, to aske hym when he was last in Scotlande and what was the chance he went thether.

> Item, how longe he dwellyd ther and with whom.

> Item, what he herde ther of the Kynge and the realme and of whom he harde yt.

> Item, with whom he spake as he went into Scotlande in the northe or he went into Scotlande and in what place or places.

> Item, whether he hathe herde of any proffesyes of any persons in the northe in Scotlande or elles where within this realme.

> Item, yf he be acquayntyd with any relygyous person within this realme that hath telle hym any proffesyes or not.

> Item, to how manye he hathe tolde the matyers contaynyd in the two artycles. . . .

> Item, what he sayde to the Scottyshe man that told hym of the effectes of the matyer conteynyd in the twoo artycles and what answer he made hym.

> Item, how long it is agoo that the angell apperyd to hym and how often hit haste apperyd to hym.[65]

By the time Dalyvell answered Cromwell's questions, he had been transferred to the Tower. His responses there are dated 12 June. He had been in Scotland "a monyth before Lammas was twelffemonyth" (about April a year

[63] LP XII.1, 1284

[64] BL MS Cotton Cleopatra E.iv, fol. 159 (LP XII.2, 74)

[65] SP 1/121, fol. 93 (LP XII.2, 74)

earlier), having gone to Edinburgh to learn the craft of a saddler. He had stayed about eight weeks. On the prophecies he had heard: "he saythe he harde dyuers Skottyshe men, some of reputacyon and the more parte lyght parsons, saying as they redde vppon bokys of prophecye that their kyng shulde be Kyng of Englond and crownyd yn London byfore mydsomer day or wythyn one monythe after shalbe thre yerys." According to one of these Scots, "one Aleyn," "theyr kyng was best worthy to be Kyng of Englond for bycause he was next of blodde." (After the death in 1534 of Henry Brandon, earl of Lincoln, and before the birth of Henry's son Edward in 1537, James V of Scotland was, in fact, the King's closest legitimate male heir.) Further, "As to the fyfte artycle, he [Dalyvell] saythe ther was neuer Englyshe man þat euer red to hym any prophecyes nor tell hym any by mowthe butt he saythe when he was yn Skottlande the foreseyd Skottes þat raylyd byfore rede the prophecyes off Marlyn yn hys herynge sayeng yn euery poynt as ys expressyd yn the two artycles."[66]

Dalyvell thus refused to indict any Englishmen and, though pressed on the point, further refused to accuse any religious of having spoken prophecies to him. His examiner, Edmund Walsingham, the lieutenant of the Tower, added an ominous note to his report of Dalyvell's examination: "And accordyng to Your Lordshypyys commaundmente the Thursday at after noone I browght hym to the racke and ther streynyd hym vsynge suche cyrcumstance as my pore wytt wolde extende to butt more can nott I gett off hym then thys. Yester nyght I provye hym at hys fyrst commynge and abowtes viij of the clocke agayn and in the mornyng after ageyne by fayre menys and also by thretynynges." Dalyvell escaped with his life but not unscathed. He was sent back to Royston, Hertfordshire, and punished by having his ears cut off.[67]

The state papers contain many other references to those who were accused of spreading prophecies during the next few months. In late July Sir Henry Saville reminded Cromwell that John Lacy and his brother had spread a mocking rhyme in Halifax against the King during the time of the northern risings. The Lacy brothers, he warned, were still causing trouble.[68] At the end of August, Sir Roger Townsend sent Cromwell a book of prophecies.[69] John Beaumont wrote to Cromwell on 1 October reminding him of Thomas Syson's prophecies — the abbot had been investigated in early 1536 and his predictions were still causing problems.[70] In November Sir William Parr sent Henry Cowpar, a priest from Ockley, to Cromwell for his predictions about

---

66 BL MS Cotton Caligula B.i, fol. 130 (*LP* XII.2, 80)
67 SP 1/140, fols. 125–26 (*LP* XIII.2, 1090)
68 SP 1/123, fols. 91–92 (*LP* XII.2, 339)
69 SP 1/124, fol. 132 (*LP* XII.2, 602)
70 See above, pp. 39–40.

"L. M. and N."[71] The state papers also include a small sheet of paper, about 4½ inches by 8½ inches, containing the following verse:

> vj is com, v is goon wyth thris ten beware al men,
> vij wyth vij shall mete wyth viij[th] and viij many
> a thousande shall wepe *ad perabulum hanc*;
> if I shulde seye what it is I shuld haue no thanke,
> for he that ne rekketh where that he steppeth
> he may lightly wade to depe.

There is no indication of the source of the rhyme, or why, or how it found its way into the state papers.[72]

The year ended with the investigation and execution of John Dobson, the vicar of Muston, whose story has already been told in some detail.[73] Included here is his full confession about the prophecies he had heard and spread:

> To the Kinges Highnes and his mooste honorable Counsaill in the North Parties.
>
> Pleaseth it Youre Highnes that where youre poore supplicante John Dobson, preste, vicar of Mustone within the countie of Yor[k] had a rolle of prophecies of the prior [of] Whight Freres of your towne of Sca[rborough], the which prophecie to his knowlege [Merlin] and Thomas Ayslaydone did make [and such] thinges as is comprehendid therin [appear] hereaftir. Firste the said Thomas and Mer[lin] did reherce in theire aforesaid roll h[ow] the ruff shuld bee rufullie rente and the clergye shuld stand in steare and fight as the seclers were. And whene [the] blake fleit of Norwaye was commed and gon[e], aftir in Englond shuld there bee warre neuer. Whan A. B. C. is brought downe lowe, thene we will begin Cristis crosse rowe. Thene sone aftir of Sanneneforth of the south side shall there bee a bataill. A long man in red shall rise and goo ouer at Darwyn staye. The raise of ceall shall shyne full bright of Barwike walles. The Kyng of England shall haue all the keies of Christendome to governe soo long as God woll. The egle shall spred his winges and doo moch thinges. The cok of the north shalbe plucked and pulled and cursse the tyme that euer he was lord. The mone shall lose hir light and aftir shall take light of the sone againe. Thomas demaundeth of Merlion and Bede, saying, "when shall all thies thinges bee?" "Aboute the yere of Oure Lord God a thousand v hundreth and xxxvij." And of my conscience more prophecie I sawe neuer in all my life. . . .[74]

In this confession, Dobson tried to mitigate his guilt by shifting the meaning

71 SP 1/126, fols. 177–78 (*LP* XII.2, 1102)
72 SP 1/121, fol. 238 (*LP* XII.2, 184)
73 See Introduction.
74 SP 1/127, fol. 64

of his prophecies just a bit. Instead of the dun cow, or pope, coming into England with "her" keys to restore the supremacy of the Church, Dobson claimed he had said the King would have the keys to Christendom and the support of God to rule it. Similarly, the cock of the north, George Lumley, wouldn't only rise in the north and do great adventures but would fall, cursing "the tyme that euer he was lord." And Thomas Percy, the moon, instead of "kindling again" would lose his light. In spite of this subtle alteration, Dobson was found guilty of treason.

6. Threats from the Continent

Although he effectively quashed internal rebellion, Henry began to face mounting threats from outside his kingdom. As accusations of treason and sedition were vigorously tracked by the Council of the North and the indefatigable Cromwell, hints of invasion came to figure more frequently in their investigations.

Late in October 1537, Jane Seymour died, and Henry was quickly persuaded to look abroad for his fourth wife. His haste was perhaps due in part to what appeared to be the ending of hostilities between France and the Empire. Peace on the continent might mean that Catholic Europe would turn a united force against England.[75] In fact, while Henry's search for a suitable match dragged on, the Emperor Charles V did sign a ten-year truce with France, and the spectre of a Catholic crusade against Henry was then raised. On 17 December, Paul III prepared to formalize the Bull of excommunication and interdiction drawn up in 1535. Reginald Pole left Rome to raise the Catholic powers against Henry, including James V of Scotland.

During the early months of 1539 it appeared as if the Catholic invasion of England were imminent — from Scotland, from the Low Countries, from Spain, and from France. Though events soon began to turn in England's favor, the country was, as Scarisbrick has written, "seized with war-panic." War preparations and defenses were hurriedly begun.

In such volatile times, a new charge was issued to local courts of criminal jurisdiction:

Ye shall also enquire of tale-tellers and counterfeiters of news that import any hurt or damage to the King's person, or to any of his

---

[75] On Henry's negotiations for a fourth bride, see Scarisbrick, pp. 356–61. Scarisbrick's chapter "England and Europe, 1537–1540" (pp. 355–83) provides an excellent summary of events.

nobles and councillors, or to move disorder between his grace and his nobles or nobility, or whereby any nobleman or any his grace's councillors may incur the infamy and slander of the common people. These kind of people be to be abhorred and hated of any honest man. They go about utterly to extirp love, concord and quiet whereby any commonwealth flourishes, and to sow in their place sedition, disorder, variance and trouble — as the prophet witnesseth, fearing whose tongues be full of lying and slandering; their feet be swift to do mischief, kill, and slay. It is no way to reform evil if any were meant, but rather to kindle and increase it, and many times it procureth him that is gentle, loving and kind to be ungentle and cruel, and to do that that was never intended or thought. Yet it is no means to tame a lion with beating or pricking. In any wise note ye well such devilish persons and suffer them not to live among you. Such people God hateth and hath banished them his most glorious sight for ever and will reward them at length with eternal damnation, as the apostle testifieth. Be not yet, for the love of God, light of credence of such things. News, if they be naught, such as import him to any man, come they never so late come too soon. If there be or hath been any among you that hath reported or told any such news, by the oath that ye have made ye shall present his name, to whom, when and where he spake it.[76]

Many of the scares brought to Cromwell's attention after this charge involved crimes other than prophecies. In early January, for example, Fulk Vaughan was examined about a discovery that had been made in a London churchyard. The parish clerk had dug up a wax figure of a child with two pins stuck in it. Vaughan had taken the image to a scrivener named Pole to interpret its meaning. The investigation of the incident must have been a serious undertaking, since Vaughan was examined by Cromwell's secretary, Thomas Wriothesley, and a great deal of attention seems to have been paid to Vaughan and to Pole, who was something of an experienced conjuror.[77] It is hard to make anything out of this initial report. But a later document shows that the case of the wax child had been pursued for an entire year, and from that later evidence, in December, the ominous meaning attached to such an image becomes clear. This confession again shows the involved string of who told what to whom:

I, Rychard Guercey, do confesse that beyng in the kytchen in Korpus Krysty Collyge [Oxford] dyd say to Syr Martyall that I wolde tell hym suche noys as was schowed me and then I tellyd hym that ther was

---

[76] BL MS Additional 48047, fols. 63–64, as quoted by Elton, *Policy and Police*, p. 46.

[77] E 36/120, fol. 71 (*LP* XIII.1, 41) Elton neatly summarizes this incident in *Policy and Police*, p. 49.

one of Peckwaters Ynde [Inn] calyd Osmond whyche tellyd me that ther was a image of wax funde in London way the whyche had a knyfe stykynge thoure hys hede or hys harte representynge the princes parson and as that dyd consuyme so lykwyse schould the prynce.. . .[78]

The Council of the North was also called upon to investigate another stranger-than-usual case early in the year. A thirty-two-year-old widow with two children, Mabel Brigge, was executed in York in April for fasting. Her three-day fast was somehow "directed" against the lives of the King and Norfolk. Brigge had claimed she was *hired* to fast by Isabel Bucke. Brigge was convicted of encompassing the King's death, and the Council's investigations ultimately involved half a dozen people, several of whom were convicted with her, though of lesser crimes.[79] In August of the same year, some time was even taken to track down rumors about dreams. The mayor of Salisbury eventually took depositions from four local citizens who had either heard or spread the rumor that the image of Queen Jane had appeared to Henry in a dream and urged him to go on a pilgrimage to Mont-Saint-Michel.

As the year came to an end, a young tailor, Richard Oversole, was investigated for "talk" about the northern rebellion. While travelling from Northallerton, through London, to Canterbury, he lodged with Robert Knowe, a palemaker, who promptly reported that the youth (only seventeen, and on his way to his aunt, faithfully and carefully identified in the deposition as Isabel Forust, sister to his mother Joan) had said that only one Percy survived, that the King and Cromwell would flee the land, and this surviving Percy would make England shine as bright as St. George. Oversole admitted only to having said that if anything happened to the King, Percy would succeed him.[80]

Aside from these oddities, several cases involving prophecy came to light in 1538. The earliest of these is mentioned in a letter written from Dublin to Cromwell by Robert Cowley. Cowley reported several false tales he had heard, among them, "that Your Lordship hath sent a Walshe man hither to Saint Patrikes purgatory to enserche and inquire of a prophesy that a pellican shuld come out of Ireland and shuld doo many straunge, mervelous thinges in England." In July, Sir James Layburn reported to Cromwell that he was

---

[78] SP 1/141, fol. 67 (*LP*, XIII.2, 1200)
[79] SP 1/130, fols. 22–31 (*LP* XIII.1, 487) and SP 1/131, fol. 56 (*LP* XIII.1, 705) Elton discusses Brigge's case in *Policy and Police*, pp. 57–58.
[80] For the rumors in Salisbury, see SP 1/135, fol. 53–56 (*LP* XIII.2, 62). For Oversole's examination, see *LP* XIII.2, 996. There, Oversole's home is recorded as "Northalderton," but given Oversole's northern interests, this is likely an error for Northallerton in the North Riding of Yorkshire.

holding two men: the first, Alexander Stotson, a roving minstrel, the second, Isaac Dikson. According to Stotson's deposition, Dickson had attacked him while they were drinking together because the minstrel would not sing a "song" called "Crummock," a version of the "crumb well" prophecy we have seen before. Layburn had sent a copy of his reports to the Council of the North, but asked Cromwell directly to tell him what to do with both of the men he had in his custody. In Cornwall, a friar named Robert Elys said he believed the time for the fulfillment of old prophecies of the King's punishment had arrived.[81]

Late in 1538, as part of Henry's destruction of Cardinal Pole's family and supporters, and all remnants of the Plantagenet line, Sir Edward Neville was arrested and, along with Henry Pole (Lord Montague), Henry Courtney (the marquess of Exeter), and a dozen others, executed. Part of the evidence against Neville included prophecies. The marchioness of Exeter, examined on 6 November, said that she had heard Neville say, and even sing, "divers times," that the world would soon amend and honest men rule again. She reported a conversation with him at the time of the Pilgrimage of Grace when she had expressed fear for her husband's safety. Neville, she said, had replied, "Madame, be no afeared of this, nor of the second, but beware of the third." She had responded, "Mr. Nevell, you will never leave your Welsh prophecies, but one day this will turn you to displeasure."[82]

In the same month, Richard Swann, a young servant, was accused in Kent of having spread a prophecy. The report is especially valuable because it includes so many details of the predictions in question. According to the priest who was a witness against Swann, the servant had prophesied "that he should bee killed that neuer was borne and thys deponent demaunded who that was and the said Richard Swanne said hit was the prince and this deponent asked hym howe he knew that and he answered 'by a profecye' and saied further that the Quene beying in trauell a lady went to the Kinges Grace and saied that off two one must dye and that the Kinges Grace bad 'save the childe' and so the childe was cut out off the mothers womb." Another witness against Swann gave much the same evidence. The servant had told him, "a childe should bee killed that neuer was borne."

When Swann himself was examined, he admitted "that he founde a prophecie in London that 'the bore and the bere should play at the base and sette all Ynglond in a chace.' Also he saieth that he founde in the said

---

[81] For Cowley's letter, see SP 60/6, fols. 47–48 (*LP* XIII.1, 470); for Layburn's reports, see SP 1/134, fol. 131 (*LP* XIII.1, 1346) and SP 1/134, fol. 134 (*LP* XIII.1, 1370); for Robert Elys's story, see SP 1/242, fol. 103 (*LP Addenda*, 1370).

[82] Trial records for Montague and Exeter are in KB 8/11/2, the trial itself described in Miller, pp. 65–68. The testimony regarding Neville is abstracted in *LP* XIII.2, 765. Many other documents on the accused are included in *LP* XIII.2, through 830.

prophecye that 'a stoute knyght in a stowre hys bugle did blowe hys raches to reche to sle hym that neuer was borne' but he denyeth that he named it to bee the prince and further he saieth that he hard in Sussex raport that a lady went to the King and saied that 'off two one must dye or bothe' and so the King bad 'save the childe' but he [Swann] can not telle hys name that told hym for he was a straunger."[83] Once again we see the fate of the King's son figuring in prophecy.[84] About Swann's prophecy, G.R. Elton writes, "what it meant he no doubt could no more tell than we."[85] But Swann most likely knew exactly what he meant, for the very text he quoted to his examiners appears frequently in contemporary collections, as we shall see in the next chapter. As an interesting note, the reference to Prince Edward's unnatural birth ultimately has its source, like many other prophetic elements we have seen, in Geoffrey's prophecies of Merlin: "The bellies of mothers shall be cut open and babies will be born prematurely."[86]

The same themes — fear of invasion and the strange birth of Edward — kept reappearing in reports of prophecies in 1539. In January, Sir William Eure, the captain of Berwick, wrote to James V on Cromwell's orders: ". . .of late sundry bokes of balettes and diffamatory reallinges have been by some of your subjectes of evill disposition, yea and of a cancred malice, lewdly conceyved against your uncle, my Souerain Lorde and Maister." Eure sent sample copies of the prophecies, which he called "a folish flattering grounded upon fayned prophecies forged as it semeth purposely to impresse a grudge bitwen your said uncle and you." Eure asked James to "take suche ordre that the said balettes and diffamations maye be stayed and abolished."[87]

The state papers contain two responses from James. In a letter to the Bishop of Llandaff, James wrote that he had ordered a search for the authors of the "dispitfull and slandarus ballattes" and "fantastik prophetyis." He had, however, been unable to find anyone in his realm who had ever heard them — their source, he concluded must have been one of his dearest uncle's subjects. He himself never paid such attention to "sic trumparys."[88] Nevertheless, he did issue a proclamation forbidding his subjects to publish or read such ballads and prophecies, sending a copy of his proclamation in a second document now also found among the state papers. Sir William Eure wrote to send a copy of James's response directly to Cromwell.[89]

[83] E 36/120, fol. 58 (not in *LP*)

[84] The figure of Prince Edward, later Edward VI, assumes a remarkable role as a resurrected savior in later political prophecy. See Thomas, pp. 498–501 and Sharon L. Jansen [Jaech], "British Library MS Sloane 2578 and Popular Unrest in England, 1554–1556," *Manuscripta*, 29 (1985), 30–41.

[85] Elton, *Policy and Police*, p. 59.

[86] Book VII.3.

[87] SP 1/142, fols 187–88 (*LP* XIV.1, 178)

[88] BL MS Cotton Caligula B.i, fol. 309 (*LP* XIV.1, 232)

[89] SP 1/143, fols. 69–70 (*LP* XIV.1, 275)

Various other reports about dangerous prophecies made their way to Cromwell in the next few months.[90] The most interesting case is referred to in a letter from Cromwell to Henry VIII, dated mid-April. In it, Cromwell referred to a number of on-going investigations, including one of the prophet named William Laynam: "The examynation of Leynham sheweth that of a long season he hath ben a madd prophet. Assuredly as far as any man may iuge the man is but a pyvysh foule and no part of the spirit of true prophet can be found in hym. Many such foules have ben in tymes and as I think the feld of the world woll never be without such noyefull weddes amongest the good corn but hervest shal I trust make an end of them."[91] Laynam was lodged in the Tower at the time, his name having been associated with prophecy before — in 1535, John Hale had said that he had heard his prophecies two years earlier from Laynam.[92] Though Hale had lost his life for his prophecies, Laynam must have been released, because he continued his career. In 1546, in fact, he was once again in trouble, the state papers including not only a report of him but an examination of the man himself, who was still claiming that Henry VIII was the mole, the last of the six kings predicted by Merlin, that the Scots would "wynne the felde," that a "dead man" would rise, and that Henry would be forced to give up three-fourths of his realm "to kepe the fourethe." He admitted to having been active in spreading prophecies for at least seventeen years.[93] Interestingly, in this 1546 statement Layman referred to another prophet he knew, young "Hurlok," presumably a relative of the "old Horlock" examined at some length for his prophecies in 1530.[94]

Maybe by this time prophecies had again become more of a nuisance than a threat. Laynam clearly must have been released by Cromwell in spite of his continued prophesying. A second case in late 1539 seems to have ended similarly. In August depositions were taken from a tinker named John Wessel about a June conversation in the Bell at Tower Hill between a mariner named Roger Dycons and John Ryan, the keeper of the inn. Wessel had heard Ryan say "that the prophise shold saye indead that the prince shold reign and be kyng after the Kyng his fader, but . . . that the prophesy shewith that he shold be as grete a murderer as the Kyng his fader is and that he must be a murderer be kynde for he morthred his moder in his birth."[95] When Ryan was questioned, he admitted having made the prophecy: "he had hard an old prophesy of Marlyn as it had bene told hym by a man that had diuerse bokes of prophesye as he said to hym that Edward should succed Henry and

- 90 See *LP* XIV.1, 794 and 1027, for example.
- 91 BL MS Cotton Titus B.i, fol. 271 (*LP* XIV.1, 806)
- 92 See above, pp. 37–38.
- 93 SP 1/220, fol. 60–69 (*LP* XX.1, 1027)
- 94 See above, pp. 27–29.
- 95 SP 1/153, fols. 5–6 (*LP* XIV.2, 11)

were the crown of Englond and that ther sholde be more murder and traytours in his tyme then were in all the tyme of Kyng Henry his fader and . . . the same propheseyer said to hym, 'O thou child that merdred thy moder in hir wombe, thou shall haue so moche treson wrought in thy tyme more then euer thy fader had and yett shall thou prosper and goo forth.' "[96] He said he had heard the prophecy from a servant of the King called Robert. The case dragged on a little while longer. Another examination of witnesses was made, but the supposed prophecier in the King's service never was turned up. No further reference to Ryan or the witnesses appears, so apparently the matter was dropped.[97]

One serious case of prophecy did conclude in Exeter during August as this decade drew to a close.[98] There, on 10 August, an attorney named John Bonnefant was hanged and quartered after a conviction for treason. Bonnefant's "treason" took place during an evening's conversation with John Northbrook and Adam Wilcocks. After dinner they began talking of contemporary prophecies, specifically two separate predictions. One was of the cursed mole, which they took as referring to Henry, the second a Welsh prophecy of a dun cow and a bull, which they regarded as a prediction of the King's downfall. They must all have known such prophecies were dangerous because they burned the copies they had consulted.

After leaving Bonnefant, Northbrook and Wilcocks grew uneasy, since, as they agreed, lawyers like Bonnefant were so crafty. Fearful that the attorney might reveal their crime, they decided to act first, disclosing what they knew to the mayor. Bonnefant was arrested, a commission of inquiry was formed, the lawyer charged with the crime "that he should say the King was a molde warpe" and that Henry would cause the destruction of the realm.

While Bonnefant was executed, his associates fared little better. Northbrook lived thereafter in great infamy, his descendants having "bad success." Wilcocks "fell accursed and was distracted of his wits." He died "most miserably."

It may well be that, about this time, the intense interest in political prophecies was parodied in the anonymous and fragmentary Tudor interlude *Albion, Knight*.[99] Although much of the drama's plot isn't clear, the piece itself is both political and satirical in intent. Still, from the six surviving leaves it is clear that England, personified in the interlude as Albion, is torn

[96] SP 1/153, fols. 50–51 (*LP* XIV.2, 73)
[97] SP 1/153, fol. 74 (*LP* XIV.2, 102). On this see Elton, *Policy and Police*, p. 62.
[98] For all the details of this case, see Frederick J. Furnivall, *Ballads from Manuscripts* (London, 1868–72), 1, 476–77. The case is not included in the state papers but in local guildhall records.
[99] Printed in John S. Farmer, ed., *Six Anonymous Plays*, 2nd ser. (London, 1906), pp. 117–32.

apart by dissension "between the commons and Principality [royal power]" and "between lords spiritual and lords of the temporality." Among the causes of discord are Principality's efforts to acquire "more to his lucre in every deal," his failure to "apply for [the] defence" of the common weal, and his tolerance of the "maintenance and bribery" suffered by "the poor commons." Justice, who has come to Albion's aid in this period of "great abusion," is opposed by Injustice, supported by his swaggering, armed "fellow," Division. At his first appearance, Division spouts a cryptic rhyme that begins,

> Have in a rusk
> Out of the busk
>   A lusty captain.
> A boar with a tusk
> A sturdy lusk
>   Any battle to derain.
> A stallion stout
> To bear it out
>   In everywhere.
> And never to lout
> For a knave's clout
>   Though my head it bear.

Although the date of the interlude is uncertain, the discord within Albion corresponds to the turmoil of the late 1530s. And Madeleine Dodds has argued that Division's verse, quoted in part here, represents a parody of Robert Aske and the rebels' verses in the Pilgrimage of Grace.[100] The "lusty captain" may well refer to Aske, and the "boar with a tusk" and the "stallion stout" do seem to recall prophetic devices, the image of a boar and his tusks coming from the well-known prophecy of Thomas Becket. If this interlude does belong to this period, it is a further indication of the widespread familiarity with political prophecy.

---

[100] Dodds, "Political Prophecies," p. 283. On the relationship between early Tudor drama and its role as propaganda in support of governmental policies and the English Reformation, see James C. Bryant, *Tudor Drama and Religious Controversy* (Macon, Georgia, 1984).

Aside from Dodds's assumption that *Albion, Knight* was written soon after the Pilgrimage of Grace, see Farmer's discussion of the problems of dating in his notes, pp. 327–29. Farmer indicates the play may have been printed in 1565–66, but rejects dates of composition in the 50s or 60s because the political situation doesn't correspond to the turmoil essential to the play. Farmer concludes a date during Henry's reign is much more likely. In his bibliography of anonymous Tudor plays, F.P. Wilson [*The English Drama, 1485–1585*, Vol. 4, p. 230 of *The Oxford History of English Literature* (New York, 1969, p. 230] accepts a range of dates from 1537 to 1565.

Shakespeare's later dramatic allusions to political prophecy have already been mentioned; see Chapter One, n. 15.

7. The Government's Counter-Offensive

It should be clear from all of this that Henry's government took a serious view of the prophecies and prophesiers. The government's primary response to the challenge to authority they offered was in the prompt and thorough investigations supervised directly by Cromwell. There were, however, a few efforts at "counter-prophecy" undertaken on Henry's behalf. An earnest effort to counter the effects of prophecy was made in Yorkshire shortly after the Pilgrimage of Grace. There, in 1537, a fairly obscure provincial poet named Wilfrid Holme wrote *The fall and evill success of rebellion*.[101] Holmes's work was not a factual history but, in A.G. Dickens's words, "anti-treason propaganda." Holme's work began as a dream vision. The poet-dreamer encounters Anglia, a princess who asks him to recount the events of the "late commotion." In addition to his discussion of the rumors that preceded the risings, of the rebellion itself, of the rebels' articles and the King's replies, and of the Royal Supremacy, Holme added a final section entitled "Of the Mouldwarp" to his narrative. There he treated the political prophecies that had been a part of the events. Holme did not dismiss the prophecies as nonsense. Instead, he argued rationally in his poem that Henry could not be the mole, the last of the "six kings" that followed King John. Since Henry III had always been counted as the Lamb of Winchester, the first of the six kings, Henry VIII was obviously the *twelfth*, "except ye skippe at pleasure / To take heere one and there one your purpose to defende?" And aside from the pure mathematics of the thing, according to Holme, Henry certainly did not have any of the characteristics of the dreaded "mouldwarp":

> The prophesie of the Mouldwarpe, declareth he shal be
> A Caitife, a Cowarde, with a helderly skin:
> But is he a Caitife, when playnely we may see
> His portrature and vigor a very Herculine?
> And is he a cowarde the truthe to define,
> When in Fraunce and in Scotlande his noble chiualrie,
> And in many places mo so gloriously doth shine,
> That he is accounted a Gemme in actiuitie?

---

[101] See A.G. Dickens, "Wilfrid Holme of Huntington: Yorkshire's First Protestant Poet," *The Yorkshire Archaeological Journal*, 39 (1956), 119–35. This appears, in slightly altered form, in Chapter Four of his *Lollards and Protestants in the Diocese of York*, pp. 114–31. See also Dodds, "Political Prophecies," p. 281 and *Pilgrimage*, 1, 84–85.

For the text of the poem, see Pollard and Redgrave, *Short Title Catalogue* (London, 1956), Nos. 13602–3. I am indebted to the Folger Shakespeare Library, Washington, D.C. for making available to me a facsimile of Holme's work.

In fact, Holme argued, Henry had fulfilled Merlin's prophecies of the final return of the Britons to rule, since Henry VII "Cadwalladers bloud renued," and Henry VIII "maketh Britons by the number plural." Henry not only fulfilled Merlin's prophecies, but all those Holme could gather together:

> This is the Britishe Lion by Sibilla prophesied
> This is the Egle surmounting, which Festome hathe notified,
> This is the king anoynted, which S. Thomas specified,
> This is the three folde Bul which Siluester magnified,
> This is the king which S. Edward in words glorified,
> Which shuld win Jerusalem with all the holy land,
> And many realmes mo with the crosse [of] Christ crucified,
> By his abundant fortitude without dint of hand.
>
> Is not his grace a Lion and accompt his audacitie,
> And a prodigious Egle high volant in things divine,
> And anointed with faith by the spirite of veritie,
> And of faith, hope and charitie, a fierce Bul in trine:
> He hath obtained Christes crosse as they did vaticine,
> With the heavenly Jerusalem aboue Ezechias,
> Repairing the true temple in vertuous wayes to shine,
> Maumetrie destroying as the vertuous Josias.
>
> Ye this is he which hath made al the Romain bels to ring
> Without pul of hand, their false tongs papistical,
> Hauing oile in his lampe he is a maiden king,
> Though they take it otherwise by their senses carnal,
> And in the true vale of Josaphat the scripture canonical,
> There no doubt but his grace is sepelite.
> For doubtlesse all the English prophesies autentical,
> Concerning these matters by the king is whole condite.[102]

Whatever his interest on Henry's behalf, Holme's influence cannot have been great, for he died within a year of *The fall*'s composition, and his work was not published until 1572. Much more eager to work on the government's behalf was Thomas Gibson, a printer and pamphleteer. Gibson was evidently known to Hugh Latimer, who had become bishop of Worcester in 1535 and who gave Gibson a recommendation to Cromwell in 1537. Sometime shortly therafter, Gibson wrote directly to Cromwell, offering him a very curious work. Gibson sent Cromwell a collection of "dyvers prophecies that shewyth of a king which shall wyn the holy crosse and also dyuers realmes." These "darke prophecies" had been made to "avawnce the fame and glorye of Charles," the emperor, Gibson said, but he had reinterpreted them to show that it was Henry, not Charles, who was to be the victorious king.[103] Gibson's

---

[102] *The fall and evill success*, I.i verso and I.iii recto-verso.
[103] BL MS Cotton Cleopatra E.vi, fols. 401–06 (*LP* XIII.2, 1242). For a brief

work seems to have been sent to Cromwell so that Cromwell might avail himself of the prophecies — and, of course, their collector — in the government's propaganda effort. Gibson's work was not a unique compilation; in the traditional of political prophecy he had merely accumulated and reassembled popular prophetic works. His real contribution to the "Sayings of the Prophets" he had collected was his reinterpretation, or gloss. Since the originals of Gibson's prophecies were among the anti-government prophecies circulating in the realm, we will examine his text in detail in the next chapter.

Cromwell seems to have made no use of Gibson as a propagandist or as a printer. But among the men he did employ in his full-scale propaganda campaign was Richard Morison.[104] In 1539, Morison introduced a counter-prophecy in Henry's favor in *An exhortation to styrre all Englyshemen to the Defense of theyr countreye*.[105] He took the authority of the prophetic tradition a step backwards. His prophecy was not merely one "lately commen out of wales," but was "founde in scripture," in the book of Esdras.

The prophecy is of a terrible eagle, defeated ultimately by a lion:

> There is mention made of a proude Egle, that so moche toke vpon her, that al princes, all kyngdomes were troden vnder her fete. What and whom this Egle figureth, we can not doubte, if we wol beleue goddes owne exposycion. It sygnyfieth . . . the kyngdome of Antichriste, the reigne vndoubtedly of the byshoppe of Rome. . . . Nowe by the Lyon, who is ment, the texte sayth nothynge. What if I contende, the noble HENRY the VIII to be this Lyon?[106]

discussion of Gibson, see Elton, *Reform and Renewal: Thomas Cromwell and the Common Weal* (Cambridge, 1973), pp. 20–21. Gibson is also mentioned by Thomas, p. 477, and by Alistair Fox, "Prophecies and Politics," pp. 92–93. Fox's is a curious work, primarily a summary and recapitulation of Taylor, Dodds, and Elton. Fox indicates that Gibson's work is based on the text in BL MS Lansdowne 762, but such is simply not the case. See the text of the "Sayings of the Prophets" in the next chapter.

[104] On the government's anti-papal propaganda, see W. Gordon Zeeveld, *Foundations of Tudor Policy* (Cambridge, Mass., 1948), especially Chapters 6, 7, and 8, and, most impressively, Elton, *Policy and Police*, Chapter 4, "Propaganda," and *Reform and Renewal*, Chapter 4, "Cromwell and His Men."

[105] See Zeeveld, pp. 232–33, noted also by Dickens, *Lollards and Protestants*, p. 130. On Morison's work for Cromwell, see Elton, *Reform and Renewal*, pp. 55–61, and *Policy and Police*, pp. 185–86, 190–93, 199–207.

For the text of the work, see Pollard and Redgrave, *Short Title Catalogue*, No. 18110. Again, I wish to thank the Folger Shakespeare Library for making available their copy of a facsimile of the work.

[106] *An exhortation to styrre all Englyshemen*, D.iv verso–vi.

In his conclusion, Morison interprets his prophecy, giving to it the "correct" meaning:

> Se ye not, to what honour god calleth our nation? may not we reioyce, that god hath chosen our kyng, to worke so noble a feate? God sayth, a Lion shall teare this tirantes auctorite in peces. . . . Let this yelling Egle approche towarde vs, let her come with all her byrdes about her, let a traytour cary her standard: doth not god say, her wynges shall be cut, her kyngedome waxe feble, the Lyon waxe stronge, and saue the residue of goddes people, filling them full of ioye and comfort, even while the worlde endureth.[107]

Still, such propaganda was evidently not enough to handle the threat of political prophecy. In a final effort, the government passed in 1542 an act "Touchyng Prophecies uppon Declaracion of Names, Armes, Badges, and etc.":

> Where dyvers and sondry persones, making theyre foundacion by prophecies, have taken uppon theyme knowledge as it were what shall become of theyme whiche beare in theyre armes, cognysaunce, or badge feldes, beastes, fowles, or any other thing or thinges whiche hathe ben used or accustomed to be put in any of the same, or in any uppon the lettres of theyre names, have dyvised, descanted, and practised to make folke thinke that by theyre untrew gessys it might by knowne what good or evyull thinges shulde coome, happen, or be done, by or to suche persones as have and had suche armes, badges, or cognisaunces or had such lettres in theyre names, to the greate perill and destruccion of suche noble personages of whome suche false prophecies hathe or shulde herafter be set fourthe, wherby in tymes paste many noble men have suffered, and (if theyr Prince wolde gyve any eare therto) might happe to do herafter; for remedye whereof be it enacted by the Kinges Highnes with thassent of the lords spiritual and temporall and the comons of this present parliament, that if any persone or persones prynte or wryte, or elles speake, sing, or declare to any other persone of the King or of any other persone, after the firste daye of Julie next coomyng, and suche false prophecies uppon occasion of any armes, feldes, beastes, fowles, or other suche lyke thinges accustomed in armes, cognisaunces, badges, or signetes, or by reason of lettres of the name of the King or of any other persone to thintent to set further suche prophecies, that thenne everye suche offence shalbe deamed felonye, and thoffendres therin and theyre counsellers and abettoures and everye of theyme, being therof convicte by thordre of the commen lawe afore suche as have or shall have power and auctoryte to here and determyne

---

[107] *An exhortation to styrre all Englyshemen*, D.vii verso–viii.

felonyes, shall suffre suche paynes of deathe, forfaictures or landes, goodes, and catalls as in cases of felonye at the comen lawe is determyned and appointed, without priveledge of clergie or sanctuarie to be allowed to theime or any of theime.[108]

[108] 33 Henry VIII, CXIV (LP XVII, 28).

CHAPTER THREE

The Texts of the Prophecies of the 1530s

Very little of the government's reaction to the political prophecies of the 1530s makes sense if all we consider are the fragmentary references now surviving in the state papers. Cromwell's correspondents, for example, often referred only to "a prophecy" in their reports, while the examinations such as those conducted by the Council of the North usually recorded only a few details of the prophecies under investigation. Clearly, all those concerned at the time — uneasy authorities, determined investigators, troubled witnesses, accused prophesiers — were so familiar with the prophecies that there was little need to add more than the fact that the subject of their inquiry was "a prophecy of Merlin" or a prophecy of "the dreadful dragon."

Only by examining in some detail the texts of the prophecies so popular and troublesome during the 1530s will we be able to understand why the government reacted so strongly during this decade of crisis. A few of the texts were included among the state papers themselves, but many more are found in the manuscript collections of the period. What follows is a collection of the prophecies circulating when men like John Dobson and John Hale lost their lives.[1]

---

[1] For full details of the manuscript sources of the prophecies, textual notes and comments, and other pertinent bibliographic information, see Appendix.

1. "The Prophecies of Rhymer, Bede, and Merlin"

COMMENTARY

Perhaps the most popular prophecy of the decade was "The Prophecies of Rhymer, Bede, and Merlin." The piece is fairly long, certainly the longest of the prophecies that now survive. In outline, "The Prophecies" consists of three visions. The poem begins much like a *chanson d'aventure*: an unidentified narrator, while travelling "over a lande besides a lee," has a strange encounter. He meets a "little man" who promises to reveal some strange "tidings."

The first scene he presents is of a "crouned quene" and two armed knights, who represent Saint George, patron saint of England, and Saint Andrew, patron saint of Scotland (ll. 17–88). The queen steps between the two knights to stop their "striffe" and "follye." The three figures vanish, to be succeeded by a second vision, actually a series of disguised historical events (ll. 89–295). This second section of the narrative begins with a spotty history of the Lancastrian and Yorkist wars. The strange little man describing the wonders "foresees" a period of great strife, a coming time of "grett battelles," falsehood, envy, and dissension:

> This shall reigne vnto the space
> Off xxx yeres and three,
> In Ingelande shalbe lakke of grace
> Soo muche trayson shalbe (ll. 113–16).

The thirty-three year reign of treason he thus "foretells" corresponds to the period between the Duke of York's rebellion in 1452 and the battle of Bosworth in 1485.

The "little man" then "predicts" Henry of Richmond's landing in England: "Ther shall entre at Milffort Haven / Vppon a horse off tree / A banneshed buron" (ll. 139–41). He also "foretells" the death of a white boar (the heraldic device of Richard III) at Bosworth and the crowning of Henry Tudor. The remainder of this second section of the poem's narrative skips rapidly over Henry VII's reign and death, concentrates for some time on the battle of Flodden (ll. 177–279), and winds up with an allusion to Henry VIII's exploits in France in 1513 (ll. 280–83).

The third scene, which unfolds in the remainder of the poem (ll. 288–615), contains the material that is of special interest to us here, the actual political propaganda. This section of the poem begins with the arrival of a mysterious young man:

> A childe withe a chaplett shall raye hym right
> With many a hardye man off hande,
> And many a helmett that gliderethe bright,
> And he shall come ouer Salwey Sandes (ll. 296–99).

The prophecy is quick to point out that the mysterious young man "askethe noo thing butt his right" (l. 302). After this initial glimpse of the Childe, the action shifts to the terrible destruction of the battle of Sandiford, a battle the young man's arrival seems somehow to precipitate. When the carnage is over, the narrative returns to the "childe," whose career occupies the rest of the prophecy. Something more of his background is revealed at this point. According to the vision, the Childe is foreseen as performing "a dede / That is doughtye and deere" (ll. 442–43). The prophecy adds, "In handes he shalbe taken att nede / And brought vnto his blode full neere" (ll. 444–45). He is saved "from drede" and then is reconciled to a "barne" or "baron" of his own blood. When peace returns to England after his victory in battle, the Childe travels to London and calls a parliament (ll. 456–71).

Once peace is established in England, the Childe appoints as protector the "baron" to whom he had earlier been reconciled and who is described as a "cosyn off his [the Childe's] kynne" (l. 481). Leaving behind his chosen protector, the Childe undertakes a conquest of the continent. He marches triumphantly to Paris, where he is given the key to the city (ll. 488–93). He proceeds to Rome, where he is honored by the pope. After leaving Rome, the Childe marches to Jerusalem, fights against the Turks, and visits the shrine of St. Catherine (ll. 494–527). His earthly career is capped by his recovery of the Holy Cross, which he sends to Rome (ll. 528–44). But the young conqueror dies before he can return to Rome himself. Following a series of miracles, the Holy Father carries the Childe's body to Cologne, where it is placed next to the bodies of the kings of legend (ll. 560–83).

After the Childe's burial the prophecy's narrative returns to England and the protector:

> Then he þat was protectour Engelonde wythin
> Hathe wrought soo worthelye
> In London they shall crowne hym kynge
> With grett solempnite;
> Then soo noble shalbe thys realme
> In that tyme when thys shalbe,
> Fyve and fyftye yeres Engelonde within
> Soo longe his reigne shalbe (ll. 584–91).

The prophecy insists on the worthiness of the protector in the Childe's absence and on the blessings in store for England because of his true service:

falsehood will vanish, truth "shall redye be," and men will live in charity (ll. 592–95).

While this third section of the prophecy is a rather straightforward narration of the Childe's career, there is one fairly long digression. In the passage recounting the fearful battle of Sandiford (ll. 336–439), attention shifts for a time from the Childe to a whole series of images that appear and then disappear in rapid succession. One of these images is of a "derffe dragon" who enters the fray (ll. 356–67). This dragon is introduced, briefly described, and then disappears from the scene until several stanzas later, where it is summarily destroyed by a bear (ll.416–17).

Another intriguing vignette is of an eagle (ll. 372–75, 384–99, 408–15, 432–35), whose actions are interwoven with those of the dragon and bear. This eagle is an active participant in the great battle, killing a king, resting for a time on an island, then returning to the battle after being summoned by a "faire ladye." Aided by a "rampyng lyon mekell off pride," the eagle achieves a victory at Sandiford; the prophecy then turns again to the Childe and his career.

This summary of the prophecy's narrative can do no more than suggest the poem's general structure. What narrative there is consists in the overall frame: a strange "little man" delivers a series of prophecies to an unnamed listener. The word "narrative" may, in fact, be misleading because it may imply a unity and coherence that really do not exist in the poem. There are three separate visions in the piece, and the only coherence is supplied by the continuing presence of the "little man" as narrator. The first vision, of the two armed knights and the crowned queen, is quite short and very easy to interpret. The second vision is history disguised as prophecy; but this second section of the poem is still important because, as we have seen, it is by such a "prediction" of historical events that a political prophecy gained its credibility. The obvious intention of disguising history as prophecy was that any reader would be able to see for himself that these "predictions" had already been fulfilled and, realizing that, would consider the rest of the prophecy equally inspired.

What is most difficult to understand is how the third vision, the prophecy of the coming of the "childe withe a chaplett," was used as propaganda. Who is this curious young conqueror supposed to be? Why was this text so inflammatory and dangerous? Earlier in Henry's reign, the prophecy could, of course, have been interpreted in the King's favor — it would have been a very flattering picture of Henry's future. But once Henry had broken with the pope, the Childe who was honored in Rome *by* the pope certainly could not be Henry.

In his discussion of this prophecy, J.A.H. Murray suggested that the landing of the Childe might at one time have referred to the arrival of John

Stuart, duke of Albany, in Scotland.[2] This is an intriguing possibility. Albany had lived all his life in France, but in 1515, at the invitation of the Scots lords, he had come to Scotland to act as co-regent with Margaret Tudor and to strengthen French influence there. Albany and the lords eventually gained possession of the boy-king, James V, but Albany left for France shortly afterward. However, he did return to Scotland twice more, once in 1522 and again in 1523, each time landing with arms and men.[3] If we follow Murray's suggestion, then, the glorious Childe might have once been interpreted as Stuart, and the "bairn" or "baron," to whom the Childe was reconciled and for whom, after the death of the Childe, a long and peaceful reign was predicted, would have been James V of Scotland.

By the 1530s, references to Albany would have been out of date. However, the trials and examinations of the period are remarkably consistent in suggesting who this victorious Childe might be. As early as 1532, William Neville had said Henry would not complete the twenty-fourth year of his reign. In the prophecies that led to his arrest, Neville had referred to the mysterious son of the son of a "Prince Edward," saying that "eyther he or the kyng off Scottes shulde reigne next after the Kynges Grace þat now is." Mistress Amadas, too, had said "the realm shold be counquered by the Scottes." John Hill "trustyd to see the king of Scottes were the flower of Englond" while Roberty Dalyvell, the saddler who lost his ears, "harde dyuers Skottyshe men . . . saying as they redde vppon bokys of prophecye that their kyng shulde be Kyng of Englond."

Given the uneasy state of Henry's realm in the 1530s, any piece that predicted the arrival of a young conqueror who would once again unite all England was bound to have been quite popular among the various disaffected and rebellious parties. The figure of the Childe clearly represented a new king, probably a Scots king, and the prophecy thus was an inflammatory piece of anti-government propaganda. Since James V was indeed the King's closest legitimate male heir after the death in 1534 of Henry, earl of Lincoln, and before the birth in late 1537 of Henry's son, any predictions about the succession of a Scots king would clearly have been understood as a reference to James V.

It is also possible to begin to unravel the meaning of other allusions in the prophecy, the fight between the dragon and the bear, for example. During the terrible battle of Sandiford, the "derffe dragon," who is "thinking to wynne" (l. 365) is destroyed by a bear, who leads a "ryall route" (l. 323) and who holds the dragon's head up in victory (ll. 416–17). Among the many accusa-

---

[2] *The Romance and Prophecies of Thomas of Erceldoune*, EETS, OS 61 (London, 1875), p. lxxxiv.

[3] Mackie, pp. 305–12. For a full account of Albany's career, see R.G. Eaves, *Henry VIII's Scottish Diplomacy, 1513–24* (New York, 1971).

tions made against William Neville is one that is of special interest here, for Neville had claimed that "a beyr whiche had ben long tyde to a stake shuld arise and make peace and vnytie"; he had then "named himself the bair and erle of Warwik." The bear in the prophecy might thus be similarly interpreted as a victorious rebel, especially considering the bear was one of the heraldic devices of the "kingmaking" Warwick earls. It seems clear that the dragon, its opponent in battle, was regarded as Henry, from the Tudor heraldic dragon. Mistress Amadas, for example, identified the King as a dragon when she claimed, "the dragon shall be kylled by mydsomer."

The eagle who takes such an active part in the great battle precipitated by the Childe's landing must surely have been regarded by those who read and disseminated the "Prophecies of Rhymer" as the Emperor Charles V, Katherine of Aragon's nephew. (The eagle was a Hapsburg badge.) Mistress Amadas had prophesied that the Queen would be delivered by the emperor, and the abbot of Garendon later prophesied that "þe egle shall ryse with such a nombre þat þe Kyng shall go forth of þe realme." One of the charges brought against John Dobson in 1537 was that he had claimed the eagle, "which is thempoure," would spread "his winges ouer all this realme," and would "rule it all" and "aftir that shall neuer bee king in [England], but all shalbe holden of thempoure." In the prophecy here, the eagle, weary of fighting, is recalled to battle by a "faire ladye" who speaks with a "voyce clene" (ll. 388–89). The eagle is renewed by the "counsell off that faire ladye" and is eventually victorious in the fight. If the eagle was understood as Charles V, the "fair lady" must undoubtedly have been seen as the discarded Queen Katherine and, after Katherine's death in 1536, as her daughter Mary.

After examining such evidence, we can begin to feel the spirit of the "Prophecies of Rhymer, Bede, and Merlin." The prophecy worked by using methods that had been valid for centuries and by relying on the authority of men traditionally regarded as prophets — Thomas of Erceldoune (the "rhymer"), Bede, and Merlin. In spite of its many difficulties — the obscurity demanded by the form and the confusion that has grown with the passing of centuries — we can see the piece as a deliberate and dangerous piece of propaganda, aimed at unseating Henry and turning back the flood of his reforms. The prophecy foresees the coming of a new king who will, in his grace and strength and wisdom, return England to the blessings of Rome. In aid of this young conqueror, the prophecy predicts revolution from within as well as intervention from without.

If we return for a moment to the documents of the 1530s, we can see not only how the prophecy was interpreted but also how widely it circulated. Specific details from "The Prophecies" appear frequently in the examinations preserved in the state papers. In one of the first cases investigated during the decade, William Harlock described his calendar of prophecies, which he said referred to "a grett bateille of prestes." This prediction appears at the beginning of the prophetic section of the poem discussed here:

> Holye Churche shall harnes hente
> And three yeres stande on stere,
> Mete and fyght vppon a bente
> Even as they seculers were (ll. 304–07).

This is also a part of the prophecies of Alexander Clavell and John Payne, interviewed by Sir Thomas Arundel in 1535, and of William Thwaytes, acquitted of the charge of treason at the end of the same year.

"The Prophecies" was obviously one of the texts John Dobson had copied. In his final confession he recalled, "First, the said Thomas and Merlin did reherce in theire aforesaid roll how the ruff shuld bee rufullie rente and the clergye shuld stand in steare and fight as the seclers were. And whene the blake fleit of Norwaye was commed and gone, aftir in Englond shuld there bee warre neuer." Immediately after the lines predicting priests would take up arms, quoted above, "The Prophecies" continues, "The roffe off it shall ruffully be rent / And stande in grett dangere" (ll. 308–09). Further, "A king shall come out off Norwey, / The blake flete, with mayne and might / Ther enemyes boldelye for to assaye" (ll. 317–19). Dobson had said his prophecies came from John Borobie. Among other identifiable texts, Borobie confirmed the popularity of "The Prophecies"; he admitted having read a scroll containing a piece about "a child with a chaplet" and "the blak flete of Norwaye."

Other details from the poem are referred to in the state papers, but less specifically. Several examinations refer to the invasion of a force from Denmark, to bears, and to "dreadful" dragons, all of which appear here. And it is easy to see how a line like "Then shall the northe rise ageynst the southe" (l. 328) would have made this piece especially popular during and after the northern rebellions of the Pilgrimage of Grace. In fact, when Wilfrid Holme, the Yorkshire poet, wrote in defense of Henry, "Ye this is he which hath made al the Romain bels to ring / Without pul of hand," he seems to have been responding directly to "The Prophecies": "All the belles off Rome att ones . . . / They shall ringe wythin this wones / Without helpe of mannys hande" (ll. 552–55).

TEXT

Well on my waye as I forthe went
Over a lande besides a lee,
I mette a buron on a bent —
Me thought hym semely for to see;
I prayed hym wyth good intent   5
To abyde a while here with me,
Some vncothe tithinges in vereament,
To tell me what hereaftur shulde be:

"When shall all these warres be don
Or trewe men lyffe in leithe and lee,   10
Or when shall falshede be founde from home
And trouth shall blowe his horne on hye?"
He saith, "Man, sett thy foote on myne
And ouer my shulder loke thow nye;
The fairest sight I shall showe the fyne   15
That euer see man of thy countree."

Over a lovely lande as I was lente
A semely sight me thought I see:
A crouned quene, in verament,
With a cumpanye off angeles free;   20
Hur steed was grett and daupull greye,
Hur paterns was of silke off Inde
With perle and perrye sett full gaye,
Hur steede was off a ferlye kynde.

Soo ryall she was in hur arraye,   25
I stode and musyd in my mynde
All the clerkes on lyve this daye
Soo faire a ladye can not fynde;
An angell knelled on his knee
And other many vppon that lande   30

---

2 *lee* a protected or sheltered spot
3 *buron* berne; a warrior or knight, sometimes simply a man
7 *vncothe tithinges* unknown tidings
10 *leithe and lee* peace and harmony
15 *fyne* is used as an intensifier: "I shall show you the very sight" or "the fairest sight."
22 *paterns* pattens; foot-gear
23 *perrye* perrie; precious stones or gems
24 *ferlye* (adj.) ferly; wonderful, marvelous

Went to that fairest off felicite
And gaffe hur a holiwater sp[r]ingeles in hur hande.

Hur crowne was graven in graynes three;
She halowed the gronde with hur hande —
Both frith and feld and forest free —   35
And I behelde and styll dyd stande,
She halowed itt bothe farre and nere,
The angeles aftur hur dyd hye;
She said, "Iesu that bought vs dere
Here must many a ded course lye.   40

"Here must burons be brought on bere
And 'well awaye' shall they crye,
Iesu that bought mankinde soo dere
Vppon ther solles haue marcye";
Then I loked ouer a louely launde   45
That was a selcouth thing in syght,
I see ouer a bent a buron rydaunte,
He semed in felde as he wolde fight.

With shilde bright and shafte in hande
He shoke his speire ferselye with tene   50
Right cruell and kene as he might stande;
He bare a shelde of siluer shene,
A crosse off gooles therin I dyd see;
He carped wordes cruell and keene
And shoke a shafte off somer tree   55
And past forwarde vppon the grene.

An other armed knight I see,
In his criste he bare, I weene,
A redde lyon that did ramping be;
He spake wordes cruell and kene   60
To that other buron that was hym bye;
The crowned quene rode them betwene

32 *sp[r]ingeles* springels; sprinkler for holy water
33 *graynes* grains; colors
35 *frith* land grown sparsely with trees
40 *course* corpse
46 *selcouth* rare, strange
50 *tene* teen; anger, wrath
53 *gooles* gules; the color red in heraldry
59 The verb construction *did ramping be* (l. 59) is quite unusual. A similar construction also appears in l. 525.

Right as faste as she might hye,
She sayes, "Man, what doo you meane?

"Stynt your striffe and your follye,   65
Remembre that ther ben sayntes in heyven
And from my dere son commyn am I
To take this felde you twoo betwene
Where ever itt fall in burghe or bye";
She said, "Seynt George, thou arte my dere knight,   70
Ofte wronge heires hath don the teene;
Saynt Andrewe, yet thou art in right.

"Here shalbe Gladesmore þat shall glade vs all,
That shalbe glading of our glee,
Þer shalbe Gladesmore where euer itt falle   75
Butt not Gladesmore by the see;
On Cachemore a coke shall crowe
Ofter then tymes three,
In the thride yere a ferle shall falle —
Att Yernes Broke a king shall dye."   80

This crouned quene vanishede awaye
With hur cumpanye of angeles bright,
Soo did bothe these knightes that daye,
Noo more I see them in my sight;
To that little man I toke the waye   85
And prayed hym with mayn and might
More of this matter he wolde me saye,
He answered me with reason and right.

"I wolde tell the with trewe intent,
Butt I haue noo space to bide with the   90

71 The *wronge heires* probably are Henry IV, Edward IV, Richard III, and Henry VII.
73–76 The riddle-like reference here is to the legendary battle of Gladsmoor.
Gladsmoor is the first of the three great battles of prophetic predictions, and all three
(Gladsmoor, Seton and the Sea, and Sandiford) are mentioned in this prophecy; for a
discussion of these three legendary confrontations, see Murray, pp. lxxviii–lxxix. As
an interesting note, the battle of Gladsmoor became traditionally identified with the
battle of Barnet. Murray suggests (p. lxxix) that this identification was made because
of its horror and its effect on the struggle between Lancaster and York. See also the
chronicle of Holinshed and Drayton's *Polyolbion*.
    The passage puns on the moor of the gledes (the birds of prey and the carnage that
draws them), the word "glade" (an opening in the wood, which the *OED* says may
have the connotation of a "sunny space"), and "gladdening" (*glading* in the
prophecy).
79 *ferle* (n) ferly; a wonder or marvel

To tell the the trouthe, in verament,
Whatt shall falle or Gladesmore be;
Distincion amonges lordes shalbe lent
Off them that is of blode full nye,
Where many a man shall their be shent   95
And doughtillye in battell dye.

"Charite shalbe laid awaye
That riffe in land hathe bene,
Come shall teene and traye,
This man can mell and meane,   100
These that loves well to dye
Belife shalbe traied by teene,
In battell buryns shall them araye,
Right dulfully by deene.

"Grett battelles in Engeland men shall see,   105
Be itt wronge or right,
The son ageynst the father shalbe
Right fercelye for to fight;
Then shall trouthe be baneshed ouer the see
And faile bothe meane and might,   110

93–94 Murray regards these lines as references to the disputes between the Nevilles and the Woodvilles.

The word *distincion* should probably be understood as "dissension," though no such spelling is recorded.

99 *teene and traye* teen and tray; anger and affliction

100 *mell and meane* mele and mean; speak and mean or say

102 *belife* quickly

104 *by deene* indeed

107–08 Murray sees this as a specific reference to Clarence and his father-in-law Warwick. As Warwick was preparing to meet Edward at Barnet, Clarence treacherously deserted his father-in-law to return once more to the Yorkist cause and to aid Edward IV in his campaign to regain the throne. See E.F. Jacob, *The Fifteenth Century, 1399–1485*, Vol. 6 of *The Oxford History of England* (Oxford, 1961), p. 567; for more specific detail, see M.A. Hicks, *False, Fleeting, Perjur'd Clarence* (Glocester, 1980).

Murray's identification is interesting, but the reference here may in fact be to the battle of Towton. Some 50,000 men participated in that battle, including about three-fourths of the surviving adult nobles. Peter Saccio comments, "For centuries after, it was believed that Towton exemplified the most horrible results of internecine warfare: men were thought to have slain unknowingly their own fathers or sons" (*Shakespeare's English Kings*, New York, 1977, p. 141). The tradition of fathers killing sons at the battle of Towton led to Shakespeare's depiction of the battle in *III Henry VI*, and the same tradition may be reflected in this prophecy.

109–16 The thirty-three year reign of falsehood and envy corresponds to the period between the Duke of York's rebellion in 1452 and the battle of Bosworth in

Then shall falshede and envye
Blowe ther hornes on height.

"This shall reigne vnto the space
Off xxx yeres and three,
In Ingelande shalbe lakke of grace   115
Soo muche trayson shalbe;
A king shall reigne without rightwisnes
And putt downe blode full hye,
Anoder shalbe lost for lake of grace
To here shall be grett pettye.   120

"Yet shall dethe haue a dynt
In turnament off fight,
He that hathe Engelond hent
Shall make hym lowe to light;
Then men weneth that warre shall stynt   125
Butt itt rises newe on heght,
Then shall twoo prynces harnes hent —
With treason ther dedes ben dight.

"Wronge warkes loketh aftur wrake
With dedes vnwisely wrought;   130
Seynt Bede on boke did make
When the prophecye was sought,
That God, He will vs to grace take
When all Engelond is on lofte;
A duke shall suffre for ther sake   135
Whiche he to dethe hathe brought.

"When euery man wenes þat warre is gone
And rest and peace shalbe,
Ther shall entre at Milffort Haven
Vppon a horse off tree   140

1485. On the events of 1452, see Ralph A. Griffiths, *The Reign of Henry VI* (London, 1981), pp. 666–710.

Lines 109–12 are based on the abuses of the age formula; see Robbins, *Historical Poems*, No. 49, for example.

117–18 The king reigning *without rightwisness* is identified by Murray as Edward IV.

119–36 This passage is packed with allusions difficult to decipher. Mentioned here are a second king *lost for lake of grace*, one who has seized England, two princes who perform treasonous deeds, and a duke who suffers *for ther sake / Whiche he to dethe hathe brought*. Murray identifies Warwick in ll. 123–24. It is possible that the duke of ll. 135–36 is Richard, duke of Gloucester, later Richard III. The other figures, the second king and the two princes, are not easily identified. The king *lost for lake of grace* might be Henry VI, restored to the throne from 1 October 1470 to 11 April

A banneshed buron that is boren
Off Brutes blode shalbe;
Throughe the helpe of an egle anon
He shall broke Bretten to the see.

"Besides Boseworthe a feld shalbe pight,   145
Ther mete shall boores twoo
Off diuerse collours shalbe right
The on shall the other sloo;
A hartes hede with tynes bright
Shall worke his enemyes woo,   150
The whit bore to dethe shalbe dight:
The prophesye saith soo.

"Aftur, lordes shall to London ryde
That mekell is off prise,
A parlement shalbe sett ther in þat tyde   155
And shall choce a king att ther devise;

1471 before his murder in the tower in 1471. The prophecy expresses sorrow at this
king's loss (l. 120). The two princes might conceivably be George, duke of Clarence,
and Richard, duke of Gloucester, who as Edward IV's brothers might be regarded as
princes. They certainly seized their armor and executed "treasonous" deeds (at least
according to a Lancastrian viewpoint).

123 *hent* seized
127 *harnes hent* put on armor (*harnes* for "harness," or armor)
129 *warkes* works, deeds; *wrake* hostility
131–34 Within this long passage is the first reference to Bede as a source of
prophetic visions. Bede's reputation as a prophet is based in part on his *Explanatio
Apocalypsis*, a commentary on the Apocalypse and a discussion of the Antichrist.
139–44 Here is a passage with easily identifiable references: Henry Richmond
(later Henry VII) is the *banneshed buron* who enters the kingdom at Milford Haven.
The reference in l. 142 (*Brutes blode*) is to the traditional belief that the British are
descended from Brutus, and the *egle* (l. 143) presumably stands for the Stanley crest,
specifically here Lord Stanley. An interesting metaphor is used to describe Richmond's ship in l. 140.
145 *Boseworthe* A ballad called "The Rose of England" celebrates the battle of
Bosworth, at the same time employing an allegory of England as a garden. The
participants in the battle are designated by their heraldic charges and badges. For the
text, see Michael Bennett, *The Battle of Bosworth* (New York, 1985), pp. 169–70
(Appendix 5). *pight* pitched
146 The reference to heraldic charges is often used in political prophecy. In this
case the two boars are heraldic designations; Richard's badge was the white boar,
while the badge of John de Vere, earl of Oxford and the commander of Henry Tudor's
vanguard, is the blue boar.
149 *hartes hede* A heraldic reference to Sir William Stanley.
151 *dight* sent
154 *mekell* much

Euery man wenes large and wyde,
Thinke they be sett att prise,
Yet he shalbe called in that tyde
The kinge off covetyse.   160

"When Sondey goys by B and C
And prime by iij and twoo,
Then selcolthes men shall see
That semes not to be soo;
Burons in battell shall beyton be   165
And barons off blode full bloo,
The iiij[th] leeff off the tree shall dye
That lost hathe bowes moo.

"A fether from heght shall fall in haste,
His name shall turne to tree,   170
Dulffull dedes shall warnes waste,
Make folkes to felles to flye;
Traytours shall towres taste
And doutles be don to dye,
All London shall tremble in haste   175
A dede king when they see.

159–60 The reference here is to Henry VII, whose reputation for avarice was widely accepted and has become the stuff of tradition. In his biography of Henry VII, S.B. Chrimes (*Henry VII*, Berkeley, 1972, pp. 309–13) examines the evidence for and against the king's rapacity. See also John Guy, *Tudor England*, p. 66.

161–68 These lines are taken from a separate prophecy called by Robbins in the *Manual* "A Prophecy by the Dominical Letters."

161–62 The method of dating employed here is by the use of Dominical letters. The year referred to as B may be 1484, 1491, or 1502, and C may be 1490, 1501, or 1507. The reference to prime is to the hour of sunrise, here to occur at five a.m. These designations are intended to help the identification of the events that occur in the passage that follows. The formula is a popular one in prophecies.

161–76 The prophecy here sketches out a number of *selcolthes* (for "selcouthes," or "wonders") that will occur in the years designated by the Dominical letters B and C. Of course, there will be battles. Murray believes ll. 167–68 allude to the extinction of almost all of Edward III's descendants. The feather that falls "in haste" from height in ll. 169–70 may be a reference to the badge of the Prince of Wales, three ostrich feathers; Prince Arthur died in April 1502. The word *warnes* (l. 171) may be for "warrens," a cluster of buildings; *felles* (l. 172) for fells, downs, or moorlands. The allusion to traitors in l. 173 may refer to the plots organized around Lambert Simnel and Perkin Warbeck. The reference to a *dede king* in l. 176 is presumably to Henry VII, who died in 1509.

"A prince shall bowne hym over a flode,
Over the stremes staye;
Those þat were neuer off concyons good
Shall breke trewse on a dey —   180
Mekell bale burons bruen
When they cast ther truth awey —
Then in Ingelonde men shall here newes
And a king slaine on a dey.

"Betwen a treytise off truse   185
Withe a false assente
A castell sone shall loste be
Vppon a revere, in verament,
Betwen Seyton and the see,
Then shalbe warre, in verament   190
And many a towne brent shalbe
And warre shall waken in violent.

"That many a wiffe shall wydoo ben
Then shall wacon woo and orthe
And burons in battell shalbe bowne;   195
Ther shall come ouer the water off Forthe,
Well arayed in golde, a redde lyon
With many a lorde out off the northe
For to beyte ther enemyes downe —
Mikell blode with hym is brothe.   200

"Out off the southe shall entre right
A whit lyon vppon a deye
Ageynst the redde lion for to fight
Butt ther shall begyn a dolfull fraye;
Ther shall dye many a doughty knight   205
And ladyes shall crye, 'weale awaye,'

177–279 This rather long passage chronicles the battle of Flodden (1513) and the subsequent death of James IV. The prophecy identifies the battle of Flodden with the legendary battle of Seton and the Sea (ll. 185–92).

177 This may refer to Henry VIII's departure for battle in France in 1513. *bowne* boun (intrans.); set out

184 Evidently this line foreshadows the death of James IV.

194 *orthe* wrath

195 *bowne* boun (trans.); prepared (himself)

196–97 This is the traditional designation for the king of Scotland.

202 *a whit lyon* is the chief English fighter in the prophecy. Henry VIII's forces had been left in the hands of the seventy-year-old earl of Surrey, Thomas Howard. In consequence of his victory, Henry VIII restored the dukedom of Norfolk to the Howard family. The lion here may refer to Howard.

Men off churche fercelye fight
With shafte and shelde them selffe to assaye.

"Est and west, northe and southe,
Shall semble rially in ther arraye,   210
Att Milnffelde they shall spley banners couthe
Ageynst the redde lyon that daye;
Ther shall begyn at Yernes mouthe
Many a doughtye knight, in faye,
And many thatt daye be putt to dethe,   215
Att Floden Felde begyns the affraye.

"At Branston Hill shall semble a yarde
And bright bannars the[y] shall displaye
And many frekes shalbe a ferde
And fewe to beire ther lyffe awaye;   220
Those that is brede off vnkethe yarde
Shall doutles lose ther lyffe thatt dey;
The redde lion was neuer a ferde,
He shalbe doutles dede that dey.

"A beme full borle ther shall blowe   225
Vnder a mountayne vppon a lee,
A faire egle that men doo knowe
Shall make a hundred standertes to swe;
Ther shall freikes full frely falle
And off them he shall wyn the mountayn hye,   230
Doughtye knightes shall clepe and calle
And many a man that dey shall dye.

"A bull and a basterde to geder shall mete,
Shall fight in felde ful manffullye,
The rede blode shall ren as reigne in strete   235

207–08 An archbishop, two bishops, and two abbots fought and died for the
Scots at Flodden.
211 *couthe* known or recognized
217 On 9 September the Scots marched from Flodden Edge to meet Surrey in
the open field by Branxton Brook. *yarde* for "rod," clan
219 *frekes* men
220 *vnkethe yarde* unknown stock
225 *beme* trumpet; *borle* burly, goodly, excellent
227 *a faire egle* Sir Edward Stanley, commanding the English archers, took a
notable part in the battle. Afterwards he was created a baron, the King himself
choosing the title Monteagle, "in consideracion that his awncestors bare in their
crest an eagle" (see Miller, *The English Nobility*, pp. 16–17). The eagle here and in l.
254 may well refer to Stanley and his command of the left wing at Flodden.

And many a doughtye that dey shall dye;
The rede lyon shalbe made meke
And come downe from the mountayne hye,
Belive be fallen downe vnder feete
And in Yernes broke slayne shalbe.   240

"A whit lion shall kepe a stale,
An admirall shall come from the see
And doo his enemyes mekell bale,
Shall dryve them to the mountayn haye;
Ther shall begyn a doleffull swale   245
When the Almanakes blode begynneth to flye,
Ther fairest floure ther lost shalbe.

"The mule and the mairemedeon shalbe awaye
And don dolfullye too dye,
The gold anker shalbe slayn that daye,   250
Soo shall the bason with bers three;
A whit lyon in harnes gaye
Shall feght that daye full manfullye
To helpe the egle in all he maye,
And make his enemyes fayne to flye.   255

"The daye shall fade, bothe leyme and light,
The night shall entre vppon them soo,
Their enemyes ther shalbe put to flight
Withe blodye wondes and hartes woo;
Then shall they call and crye on hight   260
On feithffull frendes that is agoo,

239 *belive* belife; quickly, immediately
241 *stale* position in battle
242 *admirall* refers to Thomas Howard, appointed admiral of England in 1513 after the death of Sir Edward Howard.
246 *the Almanakes blode* The word "Almanakes" is probably a corruption of Albannaich, a term used to designate Scottish Celts (the term derives from Albanactus, son of Brutus).
248 The mule and the mermaid remain unidentified, as do many of the other figures taking part in the battle (the bull, and bastard, for example). In the actual battle, Lord Dacre, leading a mounted contingent, took notable part in the fighting, and he may be disguised here.
250 *the gold anker* is likely to be another heraldic device; the reference, then, is probably to a warrior with the crest of a ship with an anchor of gold.
251 Once again a heraldic device. The term *bason* here is most likely a variation of "basin" or "basinet," a helmet. The helmet bears the crest of three bears.
256 *leyme* leam; gleam of light

Ther shall they misse many a ryall knight
That full gladely to the felde did goo.

"On the morowe the daye shalbe full bright,
The peopple shall semble faire in feere,   265
Some with heuy hartes and some with light —
Whoo fyndes his frendes shall make good chere;
But the rede lyon vnto dethe is dight
By the voyce off a woman clere;
Ther shall they fynd hym full right   270
Or elles they wiste nott whoo he were.

"Then leyve euery lorde shall take
And bowne them whome in ther cuntrey,
Some wythe wyke and some with wrake
Whoo hathe loste their frendes free;   275
Butt the rede lyon, well I wotte,
To London town brought shall he be,
The white lyon shall graythe his gate
And to London shall carye thatt free.

"Then shall happon suche a chaunce   280
That prince that is beyonde the floode
ij townes shall take that longe to France
With little sheding of Cristen blode;
Boldely his peopple he shall aduance
And nother spare for golde ne good: 285
Bridlynton to this prophecye grantes
And soo did Bede that well vnderstoode.

"When euery man said itt shuld be warre,
Arsaldowne, then prophesyed hee,
And said, 'In Engelonde itt shulde not deire,   290
when vij yeres commyn and gon shuld be';
In haste ther is a messengere

264–79 The remaining two stanzas of this passage chronicle the death of
James IV. The word *wyke* (l. 274) is for ill, and *wrake* for enmity or distress. The
phrase *graythe his gate* (l. 278) should be understood as "prepare the way."
280–83 This is apparently the last historical event mentioned in the prophecy: the
taking of Therouanne and Tournai by Henry VIII in France in 1513. At this point,
the real "prophetic" material begins. For the partisan interpretation of these "predictions," see the "Commentary."
286–89 Since the real predictions are now underway, it is obvious that an attribution to well-respected prophets will help to reinforce the accuracy of the claims.

In Almanake from over the see,
That many a man shall suffre dere
Throughe his falshede and subtiltye.   295

"A childe withe a chaplett shall raye hym right
With many a hardye man off hande,
And many a helmett that gliderethe bright,
And he shall come ouer Salwey Sandes;
On Sanesmore begynnethe the fight,   300
Wher lordes shall light vpon that lande,
And askethe noo thing butt his right
Yett shall his enemyes hym withstande.

"Holye Churche shall harnes hente
And three yeres stande on stere,   305
Mete and fyght vppon a bente
Even as they seculers were;
The roffe off itt shall ruffully be rent
And stande in grett dangere
Tyll the syn off symonye be shent   310
That they haue vsed here.

293 *Almanake* See above note, l. 249
296 ff. The remainder of the prophecy concerns itself with the career of this young conqueror.
299 *Salwey Sandes* may refer to some point of landing from Solway Firth, on the west coast at the border between England and Scotland.
300–03 Murray suggests that these lines may allude to the landing of the duke of Albany, an intriguing possibility. For a discussion of Albany's adventures in Scotland, 1522–24, see Mackie, pp. 305–12.
304–11 Madeleine Hope Dodds refers to these lines. Here, she believes the image of priests taking up arms and fighting as *seculers* comes originally from Geoffrey of Monmouth's *Vita Merlini*; in Geoffrey's day, most bishops found themselves fighting either for Stephen or for Matilda as the two contested the crown of England. Dodds believes that during the first stages of the Reformation under Henry VIII, priests were once again plunged into a life-or-death struggle — and thus the reappearance of the reference to priests bearing arms. See "Political Prophecies in the Reign of Henry VIII," pp. 276–84.

Wolsey had begun closing monasteries as early as 1518 after obtaining a Bull authorizing him to reform the monasteries. Wolsey's actions were a precedent for Cromwell, and in 1531 the idea of a general confiscation was being discussed. In 1535 Cromwell was commissioned to begin a general "visitation" of the monasteries, and by 1536 began to close them (Mackie, pp. 375–79). During the 1536 Pilgrimage of Grace, rebellion, the canons of Hexham actually did take up arms in defence of their institution. See Madeleine Hope Dodds and Ruth Dodds, *The Pilgrimage of Grace*, 1, 75, 192–97, and Chapter Two, pp. 40–41.

In l. 308, *itt* seems to refer to *Holye Church*.

"A duke out off Denmarke shall hym dight
Into Engelonde vppon a deye,
Þat shall make many a lorde full lowe to light
And many a ladye to saye 'wealeawey';   315
Then freikes in felde fercelye shall fight,
A king shall come out off Norwey,
The blake flete, with mayne and might
Ther enemyes boldelye for to assaye.

"In Bretten lande shalbe a knight   320
That shall make on them a fellon fraye,
A bitter beire with mayne and might
Shall bringe a ryall route that daye —
Ther dye shall many a stalworthe knight —
And dryve them to the floodes graye,   325
They shall loose bothe saile and fight;
A crowned king shalbe slayne that daye.

"Then shall the northe rise ageynst the southe
And the eest ageynst the west,
Care in cuntrey shalbe couthe   330
Vntyll covetous be downe caste;
Out of a den shall draw an wulffe

317–19 Dodds again asserts that this comes originally from Geoffrey, whose Merlin foretells the invasions of the Saxons, Danes, and Normans. The original meaning may have been forgotten, but the predictions of hostile invasion were still the stuff of prophecies.

321 *fellon* felon; cruel, terrible

323 On the significance of the bear who destroys the dragon (ll. 416–17), see the "Commentary."

328 The reference to the rising of the North against the South would have taken on new meaning after the Pilgrimage of Grace. This geographic opposition may also recall the conflicts between north and south during Richard III's reign, specifically the rebellion of 1483 ("the duke of Buckingham's rebellion") in which the southern and western counties rose in opposition, as well as the final battle of Bosworth, where Richard derived his support from the north.

Furnivall (1, 301–09) prints a 1536 poem "An Exhortacyon to the Nobylles and Commons of the Northe," an address to "the northorne pepull," who are the "faithfull pepull" in contrast to "thes Sothourne herytykes." The poem claims that "the englysch commontie" will support a northern rising — which would oppose "this curseide cromwell," "cursyde heresie," the destruction of "chrystes lawe," and the "wtter confusion" of the state. Furnivall believes the poem to have been written just before the Lincolnshire risings by "a Northerner to Northerners." (The piece does end with a reference to Henry's "vndowdtyd wiff, qwen lady Jhane," a plea for pardon if "we do offende," and a pious "God Save oure Kynge.")

Right radely in the reste
And shall come in att the south syde
And beyte downe off the beste.   335

"On the southe side Sondiforde shall sorowe be sene
Vppon a Mundey in the morning gaye,
Wher gromes shall grone vppon a grene
Besides the grayves graye;
Ther standeth a castell in a mountayne clene,   340
This Arsalladonne dyd saye,
Whiche shall doo their enemyes tene
And save Ingelonde that daye.

"To geders ther shall mete with banners bright
Crowned kinges three,   345
And hewe on other with mayn and might
Vntill on off them slayne shalbe;
The blakke flete of Norwaye shall take þer flight
And be full fayne to flee,
They shalbe dryven over rocke and cliffe   350
And many on drowned shalbe.

"They shall flete in the salte stronnde,
Ferre forthe on the foome,
xx^ty thousande without dynt off hande
Shall lose ther lyves euerychon;   355
A derffe dragon, I vnderstande,
Shall come ouer the foome
And with hym shall bring a ryall bannde
And ther lyves yett shalbe forlorne.

"This derffe dragon, I vnderstande,   360
That comethe over the floodes browne,
When his tayle is in Irelande
His hede shalbe in Stafforde towne;

333 *radely* radly; quickly
336 The great battle of Sandiford proper begins. It is interesting to note that in a circular letter sent out by Henry VII shortly after the battle of Bosworth, Henry claimed that Richard was killed at a place called "Sandeford": "Richard duke of Gloucester, lately called King Richard, was lately slain at a place called Sandeford, within the shire of Leicester." For the full text of the letter, see Chrimes, *Henry VII*, p. 51.
338 *gromes* grooms; men
356 The *derffe dragon* is clearly intended as Henry, from the Welsh dragon device. *derffe* derf; wicked, fierce, dreadful

He shall soo boldelye bring his bande
Thinking to wynne and inioye —   365
Besides a well ther ys a forde,
Ther he shalbe beyton downe.

"On Snapes More ther shall begynne,
Thes doughtye men and dere,
With sterne stedes to geders thring   370
And hewe on helmetes clere;
An egle shall mounte wythout letting
And freshely feght on feere
And in a forde shall kille a king:
This Merlyn said in prophesye.   375

"Knightes shall counter in riche araye
And hewe on helmettes clere,
A gerfacon shall mounte that daye
And iij marleons in fere;
On Gladesmore, I dare well saye,   380
Dye shall mony a knighte,
Whoo shall beire the gree awaye
Noo segge can rekyn aright.

"The egle shall soo weree be
For feghting, as I wene,   385
He wyll take an ilande in the see
Where herbes is faire and alsoo grene;
Ther shall mete hym a faire ladye
And speke shall with voyce clene,
'Helpe thy men right egerlye —   390
Loke where they in battell bene.'

"Then shall the egle buske with pride
Through the counsell off that faire ladye,
Entre shall in on the southe side
And shall make xx^{ty} standertes to flee;   395
A ramping lyon mekell off pride

365 *inioye* for "enjoy"
370 *thring* gather, push forward
372 On the interpretation of the victorious *egle* which kills a king, see the "Commentary."
378–79 *gerfacon* and *marleons* are heraldic charges
380–83 The reference again here to Gladsmoor is quite inexplicable.
392 *buske* prepare (himself)
396–97 This seems to be a reference to a heraldic device.

In siluer sett with hermen free
Shall helpe the egle in that tyde
Where shall manye a doughtye dye.

"In a forest standes okes three,   400
In a frithe all by ther on,
Besides a hedeles crosse off tree
A well shall rynne off blode alone;
Merlyon said in prophesye
That in the forde ther standes a stoune,   405
A crowned king shall heded bee
And ther to lose his lyffe alone.

"The egle shall ferselye feght that daye —
To hym shall drawe his frendes neere,
A ravand hounde all a ronnande without deley   410
Shall ring the shawes bothe ferre and nere;
Burons shall on helmettes laye
Doleffull dinttes on sydes seere,
Twisse forsworne, I dare well saye,
Ther songe shalbe on sorowe here.   415

"The derffe dragon shall dye in feght,
The beyre shall holde his hede on hye,
A wilde wulffe lowe shall light,
The brideled stede shall manffullye
In felde ageynst his enymyes fight,   420
The double flowre mayntene shall he,
A swanne shall swyme with mayn and might:
This Bede sayeth in prophesye.

"The bull of Westmerlande shall bell and beire
The boldest best, in verament,   425
He shall afterwardes withouten warre
Be made iustice from Tyne to Trent;
A basterde shall doo dedes deere —

400–03 Murray compares this reference to three oaks beside a wooden cross to
Thomas of Erceldoune, ll. 569–78 and 629–30.
410 The *ravand hounde* is likely a heraldic reference. *ravand* raving
411 *shawes* shaws; thicket or small wood
418–23 The *wilde wulffe*, *brideled stede*, *double flower*, and *swanne* are presumably
heraldic references.
424 Ralph Neville is the earl of Westmorland. His father, also Ralph Neville, had
supported Richard at Bosworth, but was pardoned by Henry VIII. *bell and beire* bellow
and bear (off "the boldest best")

The foxe he shall in handes hente,
The fullemarte shalbe disfigured in feere   430
What side that euer he be on lent.

"Then shall the egle call on heght
And saye, 'This felde is owres to deye,'
Then shall aliens take ther flight,
Ther songe shalbe 'weale awey';   435
The doble roose shall laughe full right
And beire the gree for euer and aye
When false men shall take ther flight,
As Arsaldonne hym selffe dyd saye.

"Then spake that hollye man þat men call Bede,   440
In prophecye saithe he in feere,
A childe with a chappelett shall doo a dede
That is doughtye and deere;
In handes he shalbe taken att nede
And brought vnto his blode full neere,   445
He shalbe saved that dey from drede
With a prince that hathe noo pere.

"Off that baron he shall haue petye
That to hym is leeffe and dere
And afterwardes in prophesye,   450
As clerkes saye in feere,
He shall reigne in welthe and ryaltee
Fyve and fyftee yere;
Then shall lordes off counsell be
That doughtye is and dere.   455

"When all this is comprehendyd to an ende
Then may men byde and blyne,
To London these lordes shall wende
With that noble kynge;
Then all warres is brought to an ende   460
That hathe be Ingelonde wyth in
And suche grace God shall send
That exiled shalbe all syn.

430 The *foxe* and *fullemarte* are probably heraldic references. *fullemarte* foumart; polecat
436 *the doble roose* Again, most likely a heraldic device, perhaps the Tudor double rose.
457 *blyne* blinnen; cease, stop

"Then a parlement he shall make,
That king off highe degree,
Truse in Engelonde shalbe take
With his blode full nye,
Then shall goo woo and wiked wrake
That longe in Engelond hathe be,
Then shall all sorowe in Englond slake:
This saithe the prophesye.

"When the blake flete of Norwey is commyn and gon
And drenched in the fome soo free,
Mekell warre hathe ben beforne
Butt aftur that shall non be;
Then shall trowthe blowe his horne
Trulye loude and hye;
He shall reigne bothe even and morne
And falsehede shall banisshed be.

"Then shall the king a protectour make,
His cosyn off his kynne,
Then the faire flode shall he take,
Vncouthe landes with inne,
For to feght for Iesu sake
That dyed for all our synne,
And he shall worke bothe woo and wrake
Or ever he byde or blynne.

"Att Harefleete he shall doo battelles three,
Thys prince off mekell might,
And to Parys wend shall he
Wythe many a doughtye knyght;
Ther they shall yolde hym vppe the kaye
Off all that cytye wight
And then to Rome wend shall he
Wythe many a doughtye knyght.

"The pope off Rome wythe processyon
Shall mete hym that same dey,
And all the cardinalles shalbe bowne

465

470

475

480

485

490

495

464–71 After the horrors of years of turmoil, and after the fulfillment of the three predicted battles (Gladsmoor, Seton and the Sea, and Sandiford), peace and prosperity will be established again in England under the rule of the *childe*.
472–75 See the note on ll. 317–19, above. Dodds indicates that these lines in particular were later developed into an Armada prophecy.

In ther best arraye;
Ther shall knele three kynges with crowne 500
And homage make that dey
And many off the spirituall off Rome
shall bring hym on thee waye.

"To the rodes then shall he ryde,
Thys comelye kyng wythe crowne 505
And wynne his enemyes on euery side
And boldely beate them downe;
Ther shall advaile noo erthelye pride
In castell, towre, nee towne,
Butt gyffe them wyrking woundes wyde 510
That ageynst hym in battell is bowne.

"Then to Ierusalem this prince shall fare
As a conqueror off myght,
Seven mortall battelles shall he wynne ther
And the Turkes to dethe he shall dight; 515
Then to the sepulcre shall he fare
To see that gracious sight
Where Cryst for vs suffred sore
When he to dethe was dight.

"All the cyte off Ierusalem 520
Shall raye them in ryalte,
And for to fight shalbe full fayne
Vppon the heythen menye;
To Synaye that prince shall hym bowne,
Wher Seynt Kateren dothe buryed be 525
Seven heythen kinges ther shalbe slayne
That sight or ever hee see.

"Two and thritte battelles this crouned king

510 *wyrking* working; aching
512–35 The idea of a crusade died hard. Lord Darcy attempted something of a crusade in 1511 (Scarisbrick, p. 28), and as late as 1513 a crusade against the Turks was being considered in England (Mackie, p. 308). A crusading intention is clear in the 1518 Treaty of London (Scarisbrick, pp. 68–73) and in a letter to Pope Leo X in 1519, Henry VIII offered to go on crusade after the birth of an heir (Warnicke, p. 49).
524–25 The young king here visits Justinian's monastery of St. Catherine on Mt. Sinai. See Chapter 1 of David C. Fowler's *The Bible in Early English Literature* (Seattle, 1976).
Note also the curious verb construction used earlier in l. 59.

Shall wyn, I vnderstande,
And then the Holly Crosse shall he wynne   530
And bring itt into Crysten lande;
In haste ther shall be sworne to hym,
That darre nott hym wythstande,
Twoo and thrittye heythen kynges
He shall crysten wythe his hande.   535

"He shall send this riche relike to Rome,
To that worthye wones,
All the belles ther, I tell you sone,
They shall ringe all att ones;
The pope offe Rome shall mete itt with procession,   540
With all the cardinales for the nones
And all the senatours off Rome
Shall knele on knees att ones.

"Then to Ierusalem thys kinge shall hye
With many a Cristen wight,   545
In the vale of Iosaphat shall he dye
Wythout battell or fight;
Foure and thrittye kinges that cristened be
Shall take this worthye wight
And bringe hym to Rome right hastelye   550
Before the popes sight.

"All the belles off Rome att ones,
Yow shall well vnderstand,
They shall ringe wythin this wones
Without helpe off mannys hande;   555
The pope shall bowne hym to burye his bones
In Seynt Peters mynstre wher itt dothe stande,
Butt all the clerkes of Rome this ones
Shall nott sturre that beere wyth hande.

"Then the pope wythe many a hande   560
And cardinalles grett plentye
Shall bringe hym to the cyte off Collande
Where ther lyes kinges three
That offred to Iesu a riche relike
That might be borne and be   565

562–67 The body of the young king is taken to Cologne. According to tradition, the Emperor Barbarossa had discovered the bones of the Wise Men of the East (Gaspar, Melchior, and Balthazar) and had deposited the bones of the magi in the cathedral at Cologne.

In Betheleme that riall borough wythin
Off a mayden free.

"Then Balthaser shall speike on heght
And saye to Melcheser in feere,
'Make a rome, curteys knight,   570
Our fourthe brother is here';
A grate off golde hathe resyd in sight
Apon a good manere,
And ther they shall burye that worthye wight
Betwene these kinges dere.   575

"The pope shall laye in grave wyth his hande,
Trulye, that hollye kinge,
And all the lordes off faire Inglonde
He shall giffe them his blessing;
They shall bowne them ouer the stronnde,   580
Faire Engelonde wythin,
Manye shall waile and wring ther hande
When they here that tithing.

"Then he þat was protectour Engelonde wythin
Hathe wrought soo worthelye   585
In London they shall crowne hym kynge
With grett solempnite;
Then soo noble shalbe thys realme
In that tyme when thys shalbe,
Fyve and fyftye yeres Engelonde within   590
Soo longe his reigne shalbe.

"Then shall falsehede be banisshed for aye
And truthe shall redye be,
Trewe men bothe night and daye
Shall liffe in charyte;   595
Daylly me thinke we ought to praye
To God in Trinyte
To exile all wykednes for aye
Praye we vnto Our Ladye."

I prayed this little man in feere   600
That he wolde trulye vnto me saye

584–91 This stanza recounts the protector's becoming king and his fifty-five year reign of peace, predicted in ll. 448–53, above.
600–03 The focus here shifts back to the unidentified narrator who began the poem.

89

When shall this ende withouten werre
Or when shall come that dey;
He said, "A long tyme thou holdest me here,
Butt yet I wyll the saye,   605
Off that I shall nott faile on yere
And thou take good hede what I saye.

"In the yere off Our Lorde, I vnderstande,
Fyffetene hundreth in fere
And on and thrittye followande   610
All thys shall apere;
The Hollye Crosse in to Cristen menys hande
That is worthye and dere
Itt shalbe brought, I vnderstande,
To Rome wythouten werre."   615

608–15 In this last stanza, the little man who has delivered the prophecies predicts that all shall be accomplished by the year 1531. This date becomes *a terminus ad quem* for this version of the prophecy.

2. "The Marvels of Merlin"

> Off all the merveles of Merlion, howe he makys his mone
> Take tende to his talking in talys wher he tellys
> Howe a lyon shalbe baneshed and to Berwyke gone,
> By the roose and the ragged staffe, by frith and by fellys.

So begins "The Marvels of Merlin," a cryptic bit of political prophecy that was, like "The Prophecies of Rhymer, Bede, and Merlin," very popular during the 1530s. The prophecy seems to have originated during the Lancastrian-Yorkist civil wars, however, and before examining its meaning in the sixteenth century, we will first see how it was used in the fifteenth.

According to C.L. Kingsford, the opening lines of the prophecy originally alluded to the northern campaign of Edward IV and the earl of Warwick in 1462 and 1463.[4] Although Kingsford doesn't explain his identifications, they are surely based on the symbols of the lion, rose, and ragged staff, allusions to heraldic charges. The rose is Edward's Yorkist device, the "ragged staffe" the badge of the earls of Warwick.[5] The banished lion is likely intended to be a reference to Henry VI (after a gold lion used as a supporter for his arms), who in 1462 had ceded Berwick to Scotland in return for armed assistance against the Yorkists, and who had fled to Scotland for refuge after Edward was declared king.[6]

The next lines introduce a king who raises his hounds to "slee hym that neuer was borne," a black crow, a white lion, a bull, a bastard, and a bear (ll. 5–12). Some of these references remain obscure. The white lion is especially difficult, since a white lion rampant was a traditional designation for the Yorkist dukes of Norfolk, but Edward IV, too, used a white lion, as a supporter for his arms. The bull may be another reference to Edward, who also used this animal as a supporter.

More hypothetical would be the identification of Henry Beaufort, duke of Somerset, as the bastard, the Beauforts having descended from John of Gaunt

---

[4] *English Historical Literature in the Fifteenth Century* (Oxford, 1913), p. 237. Rossell H. Robbins seems to accept Kingsford's interpretations; see his *Historical Poems*.

[5] Information about heraldry and heraldic devices has come from *Fairbairn's Book of Crests of the Families of Great Britain and Ireland*, 2 vols. in 1 (London, 1905; rpt. Baltimore, 1968); from A.C. Fox-Davis, *A Complete Guide to Heraldry*, rev. J.P. Brooke-Little (London, 1969); and from C.W. Scott-Giles, *Looking at Heraldry* (New York, 1962).

[6] E.F. Jacob, *The Fifteenth Century, 1399–1485*, pp. 526–27.

and Catherine Swynford. In 1463, Somerset had pledged himself to the Yorkist cause after his capture by Warwick at the siege of Bamburgh. Somerset swore allegiance to Edward who, according to one contemporary account, "made full much of him." Beaufort gained Edward's trust; however, as the same source indicates, "the duke thought treason under fair cheer and words."[7] His unexpected rebellion in late December of 1463 triggered a new Lancastrian rising, culminating in the battle of Hexham (15 May 1464) — where Somerset was recaptured by the Yorkists, this time to be executed. The hint that the bull (Edward) and the bastard play at "base" may be the clue for such an identification. The child's game of "prisoner's base" was played by two opposing sides, each occupying a "base," or home. If a runner was captured on his way to his own base, he was made prisoner by the opposing side.[8]

The reference to a bear who "shall make the lyon meke" (l. 12) is undoubtedly another allusion to Warwick, since the bear was the other figure on the badge of the earls of Warwick.[9]

Further into the prophecy, a boar and a "yonge bull" appear (l. 21), along with a female griffin and an antelope. Kingsford identified the boar as the Lancastrian earl of Oxford, the young bull as George, duke of Clarence. The griffin must have been an allusion to Queen Margaret, and the antelope, a Lancastrian device, to Prince Edward. According to Kingsford, then, the reference are to the events of 1470 and 1471: the turning of Warwick (the bear) to the Lancastrians, Clarence's desertion of his brother Edward, Henry VI's brief restoration, Warwick's fall, and the defeat of Margaret and her son at Tewkesbury. The fleur-de-lys and the red lion (l. 24), traditional prophetic designations for France and Flanders, play an important part in the events thus "foretold" in the poem — as they did in the events of 1470–71.[10]

In the one fifteenth-century version of the "Marvels" that has survived, nothing clear emerges from the rest of the piece, not even whether it is Yorkist or Lancastrian in its sympathies. By the 1530s, however, the obscure predictions of the prophecy had taken on a new meaning. The line "predicting" a conflict between Flanders and England (l. 25) may be an oblique and topical reference to the war England had declared on Flanders in 1528 and to

[7] *Gregory's Chronicle* as quoted by J.R. Lander, *The Wars of the Roses* (New York, 1966), p. 140.

[8] *OED*, "base," sb[2].

[9] For a contemporary poem using heraldic devices to identify Edward IV (earl of March); Richard, duke of York; Richard Neville, earl of Salisbury; and Richard Neville, earl of Warwick, see "The Twelve Letters that shall save Merry England," printed by Frederick J. Furnivall, ed., *Political, Religious, and Love Poems*, EETS, OS 15 (1866; rpt. London, 1965), pp. xi–xii and 1–3. See also Robbins, *Historical Poems*, pp. 218–20 and notes, 379–81.

[10] For a general survey of the very complicated relations of the Lancastrians and Yorkists with France and Flanders, see Jacob, pp. 532–68.

the resultant fear about how the declaration of war would affect the cloth trade.[11] Since the action was a result of Wolsey's advice (and one of the factors contributing to his fall), the Cardinal may be the cause of the "treason vntrewe" that leads to the dissension between the two countries.

The reference to a young prince "faire off face and lyffe forsothe" (l. 41) who unites lords and commons and who then calls "prelates to his presence and spetiallye / The primate" and then sets "the churche and lawe in peace / And the realme in tranquilite" is most interesting. It is not hard to see in these lines a hope for the restoration of the Church in England.

The cryptic final lines of the prophecy are also striking:

> When the childe smytes the mother,
> The father shall hym distroye;
> The fluddes floing in Brettyn
> Shall cause an Interdiction.

This image of the unnatural child is a reminder of the prophecy said to have predicted Becket's death: "the son [Henry II, a son of the Church] shall slay the father [Becket] in the womb of the mother [in front of the altar, the Mother Church]."[12] It is easy enough to understand the sixteenth-century use of these lines: when the child (Henry) attacks his mother (the Church), the father (the pope) would destroy him.

The extraordinarily heavy rains of 1535, viewed by many as a sign of God's vengeance in England, make the references to floods in these lines particularly topical.[13] Also significant is the mention of interdiction. Although Henry was threatened with excommunication as early as 1533, by 1535 a bull interdicting all religious services had also been formulated. The reference to interdiction may thus have been regarded as more than mere prophetic fantasy and may, in fact, account for the popularity of "The Marvels of Merlin" at the time.[14]

Many references to this prophecy are to be found in the state papers. Mistress Amadas, in her garbled style, referred to Essex and Kent in her prophecies, and the "Marvels" predicts "Then shall Kent laughe and Essex make good chere" (l. 37) when the young prince restores order and peace in the land.

William Neville might also have been familiar with a version of this prophecy, considering his identification of himself as a bear, and remem-

---

[11] Mackie, pp. 318–19. Scarisbrick discusses this "cold war" and its contribution to Wolsey's fall, pp. 230–31.

[12] Dodds, "Political Prophecies," p. 277 and Thomas, p. 399.

[13] See Chapter Two, p. 36.

[14] See Chapter Two, p. 23. Some versions of the text refer to "insurrection" rather than interdiction, perhaps indicating they were revised or copied after the northern rebellions of the Pilgrimage of Grace.

bering his aspirations to the earldom of Warwick. Significantly, one of the contemporary versions of "The Marvels" appears in the same sixteenth-century commonplace book that contains another prophecy of a bear — quoted directly by Neville.[15]

During the investigation of the monks of Furness in 1537, John Broughton had prophesied, "in England shalbe slaine the decorat rose in his mothers bely." The monks had supported the rebels during the Pilgrimage of Grace, and the similarity of this image to lines of the "Marvels" is clear enough.

The most striking contemporary reference to this prophecy occurs in the 1538 examination of Richard Swann. According to one of the witnesses against him, Swann had repeated the prophecy "that he should bee killed that neuer was borne," a charge that Swann admitted: "he saieth that he founde in the said prophecye that 'a stoute knyght in a stowre hys bugle did blowe hys raches to reche to sle hym that neuer was borne.' " Swann was quoting directly from the "Marvels": "And a stoute kynd knight in a stowre a bugle shall bloo / To reire vpe his rachettes to ren with opyn mouthe / And slee hym that neuer was borne" (ll. 5–7). Swann had added that he had "founde a prophecie in London that 'the bore and the bere should play at the base and sette all Ynglond in a chace' "; a bore and a bear appear in the "Marvels," as does the prediction "The younge bull and the basterde shall pley at base" (l. 11). G.R. Elton, in his reference to Swann's examination, concludes the man wasn't making much sense: "what it [the prophecy] meant he no doubt could no more tell than we."[16] But Swann was clearly making sense, *prophetic* sense anyway, and certainly knew what he was saying and what the lines he was quoting meant. Now that we can compare the text of the "Marvels" to the record of his examination, we too can see what Swann meant in his confusing testimony.

[15] The manuscript is BL MS Lansdowne 762. For the other prophecy of a bear that interests Neville, see Chapter Two, p. 31.

[16] See above, pp. 52–53.

TEXT

Off all the merveles off Merlion, howe he makys his m[one]
Take tende to his talking in talys wher he tellys
Howe a lyon shalbe baneshed and to Berwyke gone,
By the roose and the ragged staffe, by frith and by fellys.

And a stoute kynd knight in stowre a bugle shall bloo   5
To reire vpe his rachettes to ren with opyn mouthe
And slee hym that neuer was borne; and the blake croo,
By cause off a vengeance shall falle in the southe;

A white lyon vnder the mone shall rampe in a reise
And saile to the see his owne dethe to seke;   10
The younge bulle and the basterde shall pley at base,
And bothe the bull and the beire shall make the lyon m[eke].

An wolffe shall waxe wrothe and wander on the felde
To seke a bore that is putt to grett dirision;
The same boore shall whette his kene tusskes on his owne side 15
To bringe a boore out off bale, his foome to conffuse;

A boore, a beire, and an wolffe shall semble to geder
And bringe wheite into Britten on a horse off tree.
Then shall a king flee for feare and he wiste whidder,
For a dragon that shall distroye a cyte;   20

1–4 The earliest version of "The Marvels of Merlin" is found in BL MS Harley
2382, where it is copied into regular cross-rhymed quatrains. This pattern is clearly
visible in some but not all of the later versions of the prophecy. Regular or not, the
lines have been printed here as quatrains. Notice also the use of alliteration. The
phrase *by frith* and *by fellys* is an alliterative phrase for "by fields and woods."
   While the meaning of these lines in the fifteenth century can be ascertained fairly
specifically (see "Commentary"), their sixteenth-century meaning is less certain.
They are perhaps best understood as a general prediction that the king will be
overthrown.
5 *stowre* battle
6 *rachettes* ratches; dogs
9 *rampe in a reise* rear in battle array
11–12 On these lines, see the "Commentary." "Bastard" may also be the title borne
by the acknowledged illegitimate son of a nobleman.
16 *foome* foam; foaming saliva or perspiration
17–20 Notable is the use of *horse off tree* as a metaphor for a ship, but here it may
also be an allusion to treachery (like a wooden horse) since this *horse off tree* is said to
bring *wheite* into Britain. The word *wheite* may be intended as a punishment or
penalty. But there may be less sinister meaning, since *wheite* may simply mean
"wheat," often imported from Denmark in times of scarcity. See Keith Thomas, p.
421.

95

A boore shall come with them and a yonge bull,
And bringe a foxe out off his denne that ligges in a bowre;
A female griffen and a anteclappe shalbe putt downe
Throughe the socoure off a lyon and the lille floure;

Flanders and Engelond shall fall at dissention   25
Bycause of a falsenes off treason vntrewe;
Therfore a dragon shalbe the confusyon.
A king to weire a Fleminges flese, a foxe minter shall rewe;

Then shall rere full off blode as redde as a rose,
And all starres aboute wepe shall and crye   30
For shenderring off the elephant with his longe nose;
The rowse female with hur floures dulffullye shall dye,

The folke downe shall falle and a gose faire shall flye,
Then shall come ageyn to Julius Sesare place,
And a beire shall shake his cheen a false megre to distroye,   35
And shireffes and ther affinite shall haue noo maner grace.

Then shall Kent laughe and Essex make good chere
And other diuerse shires moo then I can tell,
In trust of a yonge prince that then shall supporte
All the lordes and commens in peace and love to dwell;   40

22 *ligges* lies

23–24 The statement here does not seem quite justified in light of history if the references originally referred to the events of 1470–71. Certainly Edward IV had fled to Holland in 1470 and had received aid from Charles the Bold, duke of Burgundy, to mount a campaign to return to England (Jacob, pp. 560–67). Thus Margaret and her son might justifiably have been put down through the *socoure off a lyon*. But Louis XI of France supported Margaret and the Lancastrians. It is difficult to see how he might have helped in her defeat.

25 The significance of these predictions in the 1520s and 1530s is noted in the "Commentary."

28 The phrase *a foxe minter shall rewe* is something of a problem. The *OED* defines "minter" as a coiner of moneyer, but this does not seem to clarify much. It may be that *minter* is a miscopying of "winter," which is not much more helpful but which does seem to be more in keeping with the other references.

31 *shenderring* destruction

35 This line is absolutely perplexing, perhaps best rendered, "a bear shall shake himself to clear his head." Thus *cheen* for spine or backbone, and *megre* for dizziness or fantasy.

Then the same lorde, faire off face and lyffe forsothe,
Shall call prelates to his presence and spetiallye
The primate to sett the churche and lawe in peace
And the realme in tranquilite, the churche to giffe

Good insample to poore and grett estate;   45
Then Bede and Merlion and Arsaladone
And Seint Thomas off Canterburye and Bridlynton,
All these shall fall to on conclusyon:

When the childe smytes the mother,
The father shall hym distroye;   50
The fluddes floing in Brettyn
Shall cause an Interdiction.

41–45 Clearly these lines support the old Church and predict its restoration.
49–52 On these lines, see the "Commentary."

3. "The Cock of the North"

COMMENTARY

"The Cock of the North" derives ultimately from the fourteenth-century Latin prophecies of John of Bridlington. As with "The Marvels of Merlin," the earliest English versions of this political prophecy date to the mid-fifteenth century, probably referring to the Percy-Glendower rebellion of 1402. At that time, the cock was identified as Hotspur, the moon as the Percies, the dragon as Glendower, the bull as the Nevilles, and the lion as the Scottish king, all from various heraldic devices. The poem was later reinterpreted to suit the needs of the opposing factions during the Lancastrian-Yorkist civil wars.[17] It should not be surprising to find it proving itself useful during the 1530s as well.

By now we can begin to see the way the prophecies parallel and overlap. In its loose narrative structure, "The Cock" resembles "The Prophecies of Rhymer, Bede, and Merlin" — the poem recounts a series of battles, including those traditional battles of political prophecy, at Sandiford and between Seton and the sea (ll. 1–59), and the ultimate triumph of a young knight that "Fortune hath chosen" (ll. 60–68). After his victories, this "same barne" travels to Jerusalem, wins the Holy Cross and, in the end, dies in "Iosaphath" (ll. 69–80). The young knight, like the Child in "The Prophecies," has help to establish his place in England, though in "The Cock" his help is even more mysterious than the prophetic norm. Here, a dead man rises to help him: "he that was dede and buryed in sight / Shall ryse ageyne and leve here in londe / In strength and in comfort of a yong knyght" (ll. 61–63).

In many ways this poem has a great deal in common with "The Marvels of Merlin," too. That prophecy, as we have seen, does not have much of a narrative structure, but it does have many sharp images. The "Marvels" and "The Cock" seem to share these images, animals, even lines: the lion, the bull and the bastard, and the antelope, for example, appear in both prophecies. Given these parallels, repetitions, and echoes, tracing the history and transmission of individual texts is difficult.

With "The Cock of the North," as with the other political prophecies, simply trying to understand the text in literal terms is a problem. As R.H. Robbins said about one of the fifteenth-century versions of "The Cock," "The . . . text shows the difficulty, not of explaining the prophecy, but merely of getting a

---

[17] For a discussion of the origins of "The Cock of the North" and for a text and interpretation dating from the York-Lancaster wars, see Robbins, *Historical Poems*, pp. 115–17 and notes, 309–12.

correct reading which is not nonsense."[18] Still, it is perhaps best not to try to make too much sense of the details but to see the general aim of the prophecy. The "cok in the north," aided by Fortune, will have "his free entre," presumably into England. The moon also rises, in the northwest, as do a lion and a "dredefull dragon" that will "dreffe from his dene" to help the lion, who eventually emerges victorious from the terrible battles of Sandiford and Seton and the sea.

If we look at such a prediction in terms of the hopes and fears of the 1530s, this seems once again to be a strong piece of anti-government propaganda, looking foward to a rebellion in the north and the arrival of a conqueror, or, more correctly, a deliverer, of some sort. As the north grew increasingly restive, such a prophecy would have been especially appropriate.

The prophecy then moves to its vision of the return of the dead man and the coming of the young knight. Here the prophecy defies logic; if the lion has already saved England from the mole and the mermaid ("Cryst that is our creatour hath cursed them by mouth," l. 16), then who are these new saviors? But logic is clearly not a necessary characteristic for such prophetic visions. The predictions of invasion and salvation are what mattered, the more and the more often, the better.

Many of the documents in the state papers record details from "The Cock of the North." References to the cursed mole are many, and one of the details all the "prophets" managed to agree on was that the mole was none other than Henry. Mistress Amadas explained "that the Kynges Grace is called in her boke of profecyes the moldwarpe and is cursed with Godis own mowth," and John Hale, executed for his prophecies in spite of his desperate plea for forgiveness and mercy, had agreed in that identification. Thomas Syson, examined later for similar predictions, also identified Henry as the cursed mole. By 1538, in fact, Thomas Gibson devoted part of his pro-government, "reinterpreted" prophecies to showing why Henry *could not* be the mole, the sixth king to follow King John.

Still, even without this agreement that Henry was the mole, we would know that the prophecy was aimed against the King and predicted his overthrow. But who are the conquerors? The best evidence for how this particularly prophecy was read in the 1530s comes from John Dobson. Along with other texts, Dobson clearly had a copy of "The Cock." Among the initial charges in his case was that he had prophesied "that the cocke of the north . . . shalbe billid in the nek and the hed and after that he shall buske hym and brushe his fethers and call his chekins togiddire," quoting the opening lines of this prophecy. Dobson, it will be recalled, was investigated after the Pilgrimage of Grace, and the cock, the crest of the Lumleys, was predicted "to

18 *Historical Poems*, p. 311.

do great adventures." The moon, from the badge of the Percies, was, in the words of "The Cock," to "arryse in the northwest." According to the charges made by Dobson's parishioners, Dobson had claimed "the mone shall kindle againe." Both George Lumley and Thomas Percy were active participants in the northern risings, and the vicar was thus using "The Cock" to encourage the rebels. Dobson does not say anything about the lion but, as we know, the lion was usually understood to be the king of Scotland.

William Harlock, examined in 1530, surely was familiar with "The Cock of the North," since one of the prophecies he spread was "off the dredfull dragon." He had discussed this prophecy with William Loweth, and the two had apparently agreed that "the seyd dragon sholde lande wythe the bare leggyd hennys," identifying the dragon as the earl of Desmond. They had identified the lion of the prophecy as the Scots king. Harlock had also talked to Thomas Larke about the same prophecy, but Larke had identified the lion as the King of Denmark — a new twist, but not altogether unique, since prophecies like "The Prophecies of Rhymer, Bede, and Merlin" foretold an invasion by a "duke of Denmark."

The return of the dead man prophesied in "The Cock" is intriguing. In some ways, William Neville's prediction of the arrival of the "issue" of some "issue" of a Prince Edward might almost been seen as the return of a "dead" man, at least in a metaphorical sense. Mistress Amadas, obviously well-supplied with prophetic lore, had included the return of a dead man among her "ungracious rehearsals." Many of the prophecies linked the returning stranger — whether he was the "childe withe a chaplett" or a revived dead man — with the British belief in return of King Arthur.[19] (During Mary's reign, however, the mysterious dead man who would save England was a miraculously resurrected Edward VI.[20]) In "The Cock" the connection between the ancient British hope and the prophecy is clear. The lion who becomes "lorde" is described as "the boldest and best / That was in Brytayne syth Arthure dyed, I trow" (ll. 7–8). In the midst of the crisis, the narrator of the poem adds, "They sey that the Saxons shall chese them a lorde / Which shall in shorte tyme them full sore bryng vnder" (ll. 57–58). The "dead man" then returns, obviously helps to subdue the English, and helps the young knight, favored by Fortune. We can only assume that all those involved in the defeat of the English signal the return of the British, perhaps in the person of someone like the Welsh Rhys ap Griffith.[21] The many references in

[19] See Keith Thomas, pp. 493–96 and S.L. Jansen, "Prophecy, Propaganda, and Henry VIII: Arthurian Tradition in the Sixteenth Century," in *King Arthur Through the Ages*, ed. Valerie M. Lagorio and Mildred L. Day (New York, 1990), 1, pp. 275–91.

[20] See Thomas, pp. 498–501 and Jansen [Jaech], " 'The Marvels of Merlin' and the Authority of Tradition."

[21] For Rhys ap Griffith and his connection to political prophecy, see Chapter Two, pp. 28–29.

the state papers to a dead man returning to save England emerge clearly as dangerous anti-government propaganda when these predictions are seen in light of prophecies like "The Cock of the North."

TEXT

Whan the cok in the north hath buylded his nest
And gadered his byrdes and busked hym to flee,
Than Fortune, his frende, shall the gates vp cast
And than shall he have his free entre.

Than shall the mone arryse in the northwest   5
In a clowde so blak as the byll of a crow,
Than shall the lyon be lorde, the boldest and best
That was in Brytayne syth Arthure dyed, I trow.

A dredefull dragon shall dreffe from his dene
To help the lyon with all his hoole myght,   10
A bull and a bastarde with speres to spende
Shall abyde with the bore to recouer his ryght.

A lebarde engendered of naturall kende
With the sterrys of Bedelem shall aryse in the south
The molle and the marmayde have moued in mende —   15
Cryst that is our creatour hath cursed them by mouth.

1–10 In his discussion of the original 1402 meaning of the prophecy, R.H. Robbins, *Historical Poems*, pp. 309–10, cites an interpretation of these lines referring to the Percy-Glendower rebellion: "explaining the Cock (Hotspur), Moon (the Percies . . .), Dragon (Glendower), Bull (the Nevilles), and Lion (Scottish king, Douglas)." Robbins also suggests an interpretation of this poem relevant to the Lancastrian and Yorkist wars. In the 1530s, the poem was re-directed, its references still amazingly apt. Rebellion would still occur in the north, the cock (George Lumley), gathering his forces and smiled on by Fortune. The moon (Percy) rises also "in the northwest." The lion still likely refers to the Scots king, the dragon supporting him. Notice also (l. 8) the linking of the lion to the legendary King Arthur.
    2 *byrdes* young birds or animals; *busked* prepared or readied (himself)
    9 *dreffe* drive
11 A *bull and a bastarde* These two figures also appear together in "The Marvels of Merlin," l. 11.
13–14 In its Lancastrian-Yorkist version, the prophecy is interpreted by Robbins (p. 310) to refer to Edward, duke of York, returning from Ireland in 1450.
    13 *lebarde* leopard
15–18 In its fifteenth-century life, according to Robbins, these refer to the leaders of the two royal houses: "the Lancastrians, cursed by Christ — the mole (Westmorland) and the mermaid (Queen Margaret); the Yorkists — the eagle (Salisbury) and

The egill and the anthelop shall boldly abyde
A brydeled horse and a bere with helmes so bryght,
At Sandyforde forth on the sowth syde
A proude prynce in a prese lordes shall he alyght.   20

With bold barons and bushementes the batell to mete
There shall the prophecy be proued that Thomas of tellyth
And many a comly knyght shalbe cast vnder fete,
Causyng maydes and wyffes to wepe which in þe borow dwelyth.

Than shall the dolefull desteny dynne to the ryght   25
And many a wyfe and mayde in morenyng be browght,
There shall mete in the morenyng by the monelyght
Betwene Seton and the see shall sorow be wrowght.

The lyon shall bake and be hurte and not perisshed shall he be
But he shall brayed to the beste that hym wownde hath
   wrowght,   30
And many a sterne in that stowre shall folde from his free —
The prowdest in that preese in bales shalbe browght.

The fox and the fulmerde in handes shalbe tame

the bear . . . (Warwick)" (p. 310). In 1530, the terrible, cursed *mole* was Henry, the
egill the Emperor. The *marmayde*, *anthelop*, *brydeled horse*, and *bere* must also be
heraldic references, here supporting the emperor.
19 *Sandyforde* Another reference to the legendary battle of Sandiford. See Murray,
p. lxxxiv.
20 *prese* press; throng or multitude
21 *bushements* ambushments; troops
22 *Thomas* For Thomas of Erceldoune.
28 *Seton and the see* Another of the legendary battles.
29 *bake* for "break" or "back"?
30 *brayed* cry out
31 *sterne* for "stern one"; *stowre* battle
32 *preese* press; throng of battle; *bales* evil, harm
33 The *fox* and the *fulmerde* are probably heraldic references; they appear together
in "The Prophecies of Rhymer, Bede, and Merlin" (l. 430) as well. In the mid-
fifteenth century version, Robbins interprets the reference to the fox as meaning
Suffolk, who will be brought down along with his friends, including Lord Rivers. A
mid-sixteenth century prophecy of the fall of Charles Brandon (duke of Suffolk) and
his friends would be especially apt after their investigations of the northern rebels.
fulmerde foumart; polecat

And to the lyon be lede both to abyde,
Both the pye and the pycard shall sofer the same   35
And all the frendes of the fox shall fall from ther pryde.

Troy vntrewe shalbe trobeled that day
For drede of a dede man whan they here hym speke,
And the commyns of Kent shall cast them the key
The buschment of Barkyng there with shall brek.   40

Where vermene and wedys are wasted awey wede
And euery sede in season kendly sett,
And all ryghyt in rule and falshed is flede —
We shall have plentye and pease whan law hath not lett.

All grace and goodnes shall grow vs amonge   45
And euery frute have his fusyon be londe and be see,
Than the spouse of Cryst with ioyfull songe
Shall thanke God highly that is in Trynitie.

The son and the mone shall shyne full bryght
That many a day full drake hath ben sene,   50
And kepe the corse kendely by day and nyght
With mo mirthes and melody than man can mene.

The lyon and the lyones shall than regne in peace —
This Brydlyngton, Bede, and Banastour in þeir bokes tellyth,
With Merlyn and many moo that thus do reherse,   55
The cowper of west Wallys and Thomas wyche with this thinge
   medelythe.

They sey that the Saxons shall chese them a lorde
Which shall in shorte tyme them full sore bryng vnder,
A dede man shall com and make them accorde
When they here hym speke yt shalbe grete [wo]nder.   60

35 The *pye* and the *pycard* are probably heraldic references as well; *pycard* is a heraldic device (a sailing boat or barge).
37–80 After the legendary battles and the triumphs of the lion, the prophetic material predicts the arrival of a mysterious dead man and the young knight he will help. The fifteenth-century version is a Yorkist prediction of Edward IV's deposition of Henry VI.
37 *Troy vntrewe* For London.
49–50 References to the bad weather of 1535? On the weather, see Chapter Two, p. 36.
54–56 References to acknowledged prophets; *cowper* cooper, perhaps cupbearer, but no meaning for "cooper," "copper," or "coper" in the *OED* helps here.

That he that was dede and buryed in sight
Shall ryse ageyne and leve here in londe
In streng[t]h and in comforth of a yong knyght
That Fortune hath chosen to be her husbonde.

The whele shalbe turned to hym full ryght   65
Whom Fortune hath chosen to be her fere,
In Surrey shalbe shewed a wonderfull syght
Which in Babylon shall bryng many a won in bere.

Fiftene dayes iorney from Ierusalem
Then the Holy Crosse wonne shalbe   70
And the same barne shall bere the beme
The which at Sandyforth wan the degree.

Feythfull Fortune hath graunted hym victory
Syth the first tyme that he gane armes bere
For any maner treason or trechary   75
No dolefull destyny shall hym ons dere,

Tyll that kynde age vnto hym drawe
For euery man on molde is wormys fee —
Make an ende he shall, holy in Crystys law,
And in Iosaphath buryed shall he be.   80

69–80 A typically prophetic destiny, the winning of the Holy Cross and
death in the Holy Land.

4. *"France and Flanders Then Shall Rise"*

COMMENTARY

The prophecy titled here "France and Flanders Then Shall Rise," after its opening line, is classified by R.H. Robbins as a Merlin prophecy, though there is no attribution to Merlin anywhere in the poem.[22] Even more than the prophecies we have seen so far, "France and Flanders" is garbled and confused. Unfortunately, it is far more typical of contemporary texts than "The Prophecies of Rhymer, Bede, and Merlin," which, by comparison, seems a marvel of lucidity.

Certain common themes of political prophecies do recur here, though. The piece opens with the threat of upheaval (ll. 1–4), the threats here offered by foreign invaders — France, Flanders, Spain, Denmark — rather than by internal rebellion from the north, as in "The Cock of the North." Following these opening lines, the piece repeats the familiar prediction of the rising of an eagle (l. 5), and a series of battles that will follow (ll. 7–25). A bull appears, "a prynce noble" (l. 22), who seems to be a figure of deliverance but who is, unfortunately, not fated to rule long (ll. 22–25). He is driven from the realm and travels to the Holy Land where he lives and ultimately dies "vertuously" (ll. 26–36). The vision of the prophecy then returns to England and predicts a bloody three-year fight for the crown between two children (ll. 37–48). A mysterious dead man arises to "agrement make, / A set acorde" (ll. 49–50). The dead man establishes the right heir on the throne (l. 53). This new king then travels to the Holy Land and wins the Holy Cross (ll. 57–60).

This general outline is at least clear, though the specific details of the piece make little sense. Still, we can undoubtedly see what caught the attention of contemporary ears. By the later years of the 1530s, threats of foreign invasion were real enough, and this prophecy begins with an expression of the fear of these invaders, as well as of the eagle, the emperor. A falcon, often used as a reference to Anne Boleyn, is to be pursued by the eagle and will "fle lyghtly ouer molde" (l. 7), though by the late 1530s a reference to her pursuit by the emperor would have been unnecessary.

Among the various participants in the battles that take place is the moon, who "but a lytill shall kepe his lyght / For at vij downes vpon a grete playne / He shalbe ouer throwe in that same fight" (ll. 18–20). If this is again a reference to Percy, this prophecy likely gained a special credibility right after Percy's participation in the Pilgrimage of Grace. The reference to the fall of

[22] *Manual* V, 278(c). Curiously, Robbins indexes this item by its fifth line. See Appendix.

105

the "cok of the north" who will "curse the tyme that euer he was so high, / He shall wysche that he had be on bore / For wode and sorowe he shall dye" (ll. 43–44), likely an allusion to George Lumley's execution, reinforces the reason for the appeal of this prophecy.

Most interesting are the prophecies about the two who contest for the crown: "Than ij childerne shall stryve for the crowne, / Thre yeres there battaylles shall leste and more" (ll. 37–38). Since there was so much doubt about Henry's legitimate heir before the birth of Edward in October of 1537, these lines may allude to the problem of succession. The prophecy certainly suggests no answer to the dilemma: "No man shall know who shall have the victory / For the stretys of London shall ron on stremes blody" (ll. 47–48). The mysterious dead man will "sett the ryght heire in his ryght" (l. 53). It may not be too far-fetched to suggest that this prophecy might have been compiled and circulated right after the northern rebellions but before the birth of Henry's long-desired son.

By now the usefulness and danger of such a prophecy should be easy to see. Many of the documents in the state papers show generally how a piece like "France and Flanders" would have been understood, but there is one very specific reference in the documents collected there to this text. Among the witnesses examined in the case of John Dobson was a prior named John Borobie. During his examination before the Council of the North, Borobie recalled having read a prophecy beginning "France and Flaundres shall arise." Having read the piece, Borobie borrowed it to copy, saying that he had transcribed it onto "ij shetes of paper." That fits our text exactly, with its opening line and its relative brevity. In the sixteenth century manuscript from which the text below comes, the poem occupies a little over two sheets, its length extended onto part of a third page by Latin lines inserted into the text. Without doubt, this is the prophecy to which Borobie referred and one of the prophecies used by the northern rebels.

TEXT

France and Flaunders than shall ryse,
Spane shall supporte them with all their myght,
The Danes will com to take enterpryse —
Nowght shall they do, but all abowght lyght.

An egyll shall ryse with a bore bolde   5
And sey, "Rychard, the son of Rychard";
Than shall a facon fle lyghtly ouer molde,
A spett bert egyll, for sowth, shall he be.

At Bushbery a gret battayle shalbe,
The dragon, the red rose there shall fyght   10
The milfote, the gryffen there slayne shalbe
The woodes, the water their shall lose their myght.

Now help, dere lady, þe lanterne of lyght
For forth shall they passe towardes London;
In þat way shall mete them þe bore sterne in fyght, 15
The mone and the molet shal sone gre in one.

The bore for all his pryde shalbe put to fight,
The mone but a lytill shall kepe his lyght

1–4 These lines are set off in the sixteenth-century manuscript as a cross-rhymed quatrain, most likely the rhyme scheme for the whole text, though it is not copied as such in the manuscript. The poem has been presented here in quatrains, though with some irregularities, as noted. These lines are preceded by one Latin line: "Flan. fran. consurgent albani limina linget." This line is a conflation of two lines of Scottish prophecy printed in Robert Waldegrave's 1603 *The Whole Prophesie of Scotland*: "Flan, fran, consurgent, hispani viribus vrgent, / Dani consurgent, Albani limina lingent" (rpt. by the Ballantyne Club, *Collection of Ancient Scottish Prophecies . . . from Waldegrave's Edition* [1833], p. 42).

The quatrain is followed by two Latin lines, indented in the manuscript: "Aquila consurget aperum sibi associabit / hic duo cum rosa virgo imunis[?] G coronabit."

5 Here again the eagle sparks rebellion in England. The prophecy contains many other heraldic references.

6 The reference to *Rychard, the son of Rychard* may go back to some earlier version of the poem, perhaps to a Yorkist text or to a version of the poem circulating during Richard III's reign. (Richard used a boar as a device.)

8 *spett bert* unknown

11 *milfote* unknown Both "millpick" and "millrind" are heraldic charges.

13 *their myght* from l. 12 actually appears in the manuscript as the first of l. 13, but to preserve the rhyme it has been moved.

16 *molet* for "mullet," or "molet," a star used in heraldry. The star is sometimes used as a mark of cadency for the third son.

17–21 An irregular stanza.

For at vij downes vpon a grete playne
He shalbe ouer throwe in that same fight
And on a more there beside shall he be slayne.   20

Than the bulle, a prynce noble, shal com þen agene,
Batelles no dowght of he shall geve them thre
But yet for all his myght and mayne
To the castell of care he shall flee.   25

Than shall a prynce, nobyll of high degre,
Sege to hym, "Lay on ouer syde,
He shalbe cosyn chosen to the, Iesse" —
That shall a bate the bulles pryde.

Than shall sorow a wake on euery syde,   30
Lordes shalbe slayne of grete degree,
The bull shall stele away at a tyde
And passe ouer the salte see.

Loke no more for hym, for founde will he not be;
To the Holy Lande he shall goo vertuously
And shall dye at Iosaphathe byside Calvery   35
Vpon whose soule God have mercy.

Than ij childerne shall stryve for the crowne,
Thre yeres there battaylles shall leste and more,
Than many lordes shalbe case in sowne
But styfly shall stonde the blewe bore.   40

The cok of the north shall repent yt ryght sore
And curse the tyme that euer he was so high,
He shall wysche that he had be on bore
For wode and sorow he shall dye.

Than shall these ij yonge lordes fight manly   45
Betwen Andrewe, Iacob, and Iamys —
No man shall know who shall have the victory
For the stretys of London shall ron on stremes blody.

39 *sowne* for "swoon"?
44 *wode* madness
48 After this stanza, three Latin lines, virtually impossible to decipher, are inserted
into the manuscript: "Sextus vir sanctus ter.. rex inter mori..t / de quo psallet... pro
mundi machnne m.... / anno ter quinq... regnabit p.. e... m..."

Than a dede man shall aryse and agrement make,
A set acorde betwene two men envious;   50
Þen shall Troy ontrewe trymble and quake
Whan this messinger comyth from Cryst Ihesus.

He shall sett the ryght heire in his ryght,
The blode of hym selfe crowned shall be,
So warre shall sett stynte thorowgh Godes myght,   55
Rest shall contynnew with pease and vnytie.

Than shall þis made kynge pase þe see
And so forth to the Holy Lande;
The Holy Crosse wyne shall he,
And brynge hyt into Crystene menys honde.   65

Amen, Amen, Christ Ihesu for charytie.

51 *Troy ontrewe* A reference again to London.
57–61 The lines are garbled in the manuscript:
      Than shall þis made kynge pase þe see lond
      And so forth to the Holy Lande; the Holy
      Crosse wyne shall he, and brynge hyt
      Into Crystene menys honde. Amen, amen,
      Christ Jhesu for charytie.

5. *"The Sayings of the Prophets"*

COMMENTARY

The text of "The Sayings of the Prophets" consists of a series of brief prose paragraphs, each paragraph a "saying" attributed to a reputed prophet. Versions of "The Sayings" differ considerably, since such lists are infinitely expandable. At the same time, however, the surviving texts all share a common theme, since they all describe a mysterious king who is destined to win the Holy Cross.

The structure of these expandable pieces is not complicated. Each series is unique, but each is basically a list of descriptive paragraphs, usually of a single sentence in length. The lists build on repetition and parallelism, each paragraph beginning "Merlin calleth him," or "Merlin sayeth." The roster of prophets in these "sayings" is long. Most of the names are by now familiar: Becket, John of Bridlington, Thomas of Erceldoune, Bede, and, of course, Merlin. Some are more exotic: the Sibyl, Saint Jerome, Solomon, Mohammed. But some are as mysterious as their prophecies: the "patriarch" of Armonie; William, the abbot of Ireland; "Mayfair de Bater of Furnay"; an anchoress of Sheffield, as examples.

Some of the individual predictions in such lists of "sayings" seem less politically relevant than the other prophecies we have examined, but when the whole of each series is examined, the over-all effect as anti-government propaganda is significant. In one series, for example, a "saying" (whose prophet has, unfortunately, been lost) predicts "þe blake raven, þe king of Scottes, with þe red hand shall ouer goo all England."[23] This quite specific prediction was in part responsible for Rhys ap Griffith's arrest and execution. The indictment against Griffith, as quoted above, had included a charge that he had spread the Welsh prophecy "that king Jamys with the red hand and the ravens should conquer all England." The "red hand" and "ravens" were both heraldic references to Welsh figures — the ravens Griffith's own charges, while the "red hand" was a reference to the charge of an ancient Welsh hero. The same series includes another familiar item in its list of sayings: "Thomas of Arysdowne sayth þat þe fathers of the mother church shall cause the rose to dye in his owne sen."

That Griffith seems to have gotten into trouble for his familiarity with "The Sayings of the Prophets" is not surprising in light of what these

[23] Bodleian Library MS Rawlinson D.1062. For further details, see Appendix.

predictions have to add about the heritage of the savior-king. In the series of "sayings" whose text is presented here, for instance, the young king is called the "rose of *Bretayne*" (l. 41, italics added). Again, the old predictions of the restoration of the British are revived: "the trew Brewet [Brutus] shall com agayne" (ll. 75–76). Further, this list of "sayings" goes on to predict the victory of the eagle, who will not only conquer England but restore religious unity: "the egle of the trewe Brute shall set all Inglond in peas and rest, both spirituall and temporall, and euery estate in thaire degree . . ." (ll. 84–87).

Aside from his heritage, the recovery of the Holy Cross by this young king is also an indication of his threat to Henry. In almost all the political prophecies we have read so far, the young man whose return to England sparks rebellion and causes Henry to flee his realm is the man who ultimately recovers this most significant Christian relic. "The Sayings of the Prophets" is thus a series of predictions about a conqueror who is destined to be Henry's successor — and replacement. And such lists undercut the Tudor use of Welsh heritage by predicting that *this* young conqueror, not the Tudor kings, will fulfill prophecies of the return of British blood to England.

By the end of the 1530s, at least one version of the "sayings" had abandoned Henry altogether. In a list dated to 1540, the "Sayings of the Prophets" has been reinterpreted to refer to Henry's son. The "king who will win the Holy Cross" is still the subject of the predictions, but appended to many of the brief paragraphs is the addition: "and he shalbe called Edwarde." As examples, "The doctor Saint Ierome callyth him the trew dragon wich was cristened in a font and so was neuer non other conquerowre and he shalbe called Edward . . . ," "Robert the scribe of Birlyngton callith him the cocke of the trew Bruttes the wich shalbe called Edward . . . ," and "Macomyte callith him the paynems delectable rose of Brytayne the which shall wyne the holy crose and he shalbe protector and defender of all wydows, orphens . . . , and maydens and he shall distroy all falsehod and mayntayne all trewthe and shalbe called Edward." Thus by 1540 at least one compiler of "The Sayings" is willing to accept the Tudor line as the fulfillment of British prophecy — but the compiler has looked beyond Henry to the promise of his son.

This 1540 version of the "Sayings" is interesting for more reasons than its focus on Edward as the longed-for deliverer to succeed Henry.[24] The manuscript copy of this text is exactly the kind described in so many of the documents in the state papers but otherwise unpreserved — a copy made to be easily carried by its owner. These "sayings" have been transcribed onto one large folio sheet (measuring approximately 42 cm in width by 31.5 cm in height), the sheet having been folded before the copyist began to write down the prophetic paragraphs. The sheet was then folded once more, into a size that could easily be carried, the perfect size to put into a pocket, for instance.

[24] Folger Shakespeare Library MS Loseley b. 546 (c. 1540); see Appendix.

The outer edges of the folded manuscript have crumbled away, the ink slightly faded and the paper worn at the folds, the text inside much cleaner than that on the first copied side of the folio (1r), which obviously had more wear. Such slight documents, like those mentioned by John Borobie in describing his own collection of prophecies, were obviously ephemeral, carried around or passed on until they wore out. This surviving copy of the "Sayings" is thus a rare find for its form as well as for its content.

One set of "sayings" indicates it was compiled about 1536, another indicates the predictions "shall fall at the date of Our Lorde God betwixt vj and ix," and the list that calls on Edward is from 1540. These dates suggest that series like these were circulating in the late 1530s. In his 1537 *The fall and evill success of rebellion*, the Yorkshire poet Wilfrid Holme had addressed himself specifically to propaganda like "The Sayings of the Prophets" that looked for the return of a young ruler of British blood. In Holme's argument, Merlin's prophecies had already been fulfilled by the Tudors. Henry VII had, according to Holme, "Cadwalladers bloud renued," and Henry VIII was himself the longed-for British king whose rule Merlin had foreseen.

But perhaps no evidence can more strongly prove the popularity of "The Sayings of the Prophets" than Thomas Gibson's reinterpreted version, which he so very helpfully sent to Cromwell in 1538. In his attempt to gain a place on Cromwell's propaganda team, Gibson collected his own series of "sayings," then glossed them to show that they all *really* referred to the King, who was himself the predicted savior of his people and the conqueror who would win the Holy Cross.[25] Prophecy, therefore, had already become reality.

The lengths to which Gibson had to go to interpret his "sayings" in Henry's favor are incredible but wonderfully ingenious. The full texts of both his letter to Cromwell and his prophetic efforts follow the text of "The Sayings of the Prophets" printed below.

---

[25] Using the abstract of Gibson's efforts printed in *Letters and Papers*, Fox, "Prophecies and Politics," p. 93, implies that Gibson's text followed the series of "sayings" printed as *Text 1* here (Fox says Gibson's sayings present "the same thirteen prophecies, in the same order"). When the complete texts of both sets are printed together, however, their differences in content and order are clear. Gibson knew of the general popularity of such lists, not necessarily of this particular list. Fox seems not to have consulted manuscript originals.

TEXT 1

Thes be the namys of the sayntes and doctoures
That speke of hym that shall wynne the Holy Crosse.

Furst Sent Thomas of Canterbery calleth hym
the virgyn kyng of bewtye.

Seynt Iohn of Byrlyngton callyth hym the most
prince of honour and he shall com by the meracle of God.

Wylliam of Ambrose callyth hym a booll threfull   5
naturys tha[t] ys to say Englond, [Wales], and
Skottlond and he shalbe called H, G, or I [and] shall
wyn the Holy Crosse.

Wylliam of Ambros namyth hym the kyng of the
brod sordes that is to say the kyng of the brod see   10
of all Crystyndome.

Wylliam of Syluester callyth hym the kyng of
wrechyde þat ys to wete þer shalbe so ma[n]y theves
the ijde [and] þe iijde yere of hys reinge þat he shall haue
moche to do [t]o corect hym.   15

The pa[tri]arke of Ermony callyth hym the westorn
best, þat ys to wete þe blake bull with gylt hornys,

1 *Sent Thomas of Canterbury* A reference to Becket's reputation for prophecy (see also l. 53).
3 *Seynt Iohn of Byrlyngton* A reference to John of Bridlington's reputation for prophecy (see also l. 50).
5 *Wylliam of Ambrose* A name that appears on occasion as a prophet (see also ll. 9 and 57), but many of the prophets named in this piece remain as mysterious as the mysterious young man who will win the Cross.
6 *[Wales]* The text reads "welone." The unification of England, Wales, and Scotland is a significant part of *British* hopes.
7 The sibyllic method of using initial letters in prophecy is seen here and in lines 25, 41, 56, 61, and 71.
12 *Wylliam of Syluester* After Geoffrey of Monmouth, the legend of two Merlins arose, one the Ambrosius Merlin of the *Historia,* and the other Merlin Silvester or Caledonicus (see Taylor, p. 15). Perhaps the confusion of prophets here — William of Ambrose, William of Silvester, Merlin "of Salodown" — reflects earlier confusion (see also l. 68).
16 *patriarke of Ermony* Probably a reference to Armenia (see also l. 73). For this, as well as for her help with many of the prophets on, as she described it, "this crazy list of names," I would like to thank Professor Kathryn Kerby-Fulton of the University of Victoria.

113

and he shall go into the Holy Lande and when
he must departe out of the worlde in hys tyme ther shalbe
moche spekyng of the commyng of Antecryst aswele by
    maracle   20
as by other thynges in hys tyme and he shall dye in the
Holy Land.

But Wylliam the a[b]bot of Irlond callyth hym the vj[th] that
shall com out of Ireland and hys name shalbe callyd
G or I.   25

Sybell the sage sayth and callyth hym the secunde lyon of Gret
Breton the wych wylbe rulyd by no man but by God and hym selfe.

Petuour the beddart of All mayne callyth hym the egell
that shall ouer com vj landes and he shalbe emperour and
    dessease   30
in the saindi for the fayth of God.

Mayfair de Bater of Furnay callyth hym þe vnicorne þat shall
neuer torne hys face for no man of wer.

Alffueck the profyte callyth hym in the sawter buk the
son of man.   35

Seynt Gerom callyth hym the trew dragon that was
crystned in hys fonte and he shall neuer be conquered and
he shall tred downe vnder hys feett the kynges of pride and fle
from thens into the Holy Land.

Makomyt saie to the paynyms that he shulde be the dilegatt   40
rose of Bretayne and he shalbe called V or H.

---

23 *Wylliam the ab[b]ot of Irlond* This figure is also called on as a prophet (see also l.
61).

26 *Sybell the sage* for the Sibyl.

29 *Petuour the beddart of All mayne* Another mysterious prophetic source.

31 *saindi* perhaps for Sinai?

32 *Mayfair de Bater of Furnay* Another mysterious prophet.

34 *Alffueck* The *Manual* refers (p. 1534) to fifteenth-century prophetic lines attributed to "Old Edfrikke," perhaps the prophet meant here (see also *Manual*, V.
304[p]).

36 *Gerom* for Jerome. Note, too, the reference to the Welsh dragon.

40 *Makomyt* for Mohammed

41–46 Familiar predictions in the prophecies we have seen. *Mamyvon* (?) and
Thomas of Erceldoune (here *Ashledon*) are the prophets cited (see also l. 84).

Bot Mamyvon the profet sayth that the dilecate rose shall
dye in his moders bely.

Thomas of Ashledon sayth the faderes of the moderes church
shall cause the roses bothe to dye in hys own fonte ther   45
he was cristened.

Merlyon of Salodown sayth when the rose and the grey
hound ys agoon of woo shalbe the byschopes song that euer
that take crose in hond.

Seynt Iohn of Byrlyngton sayth that the Danys shall   50
entre into the land of the mone and he shall lose hys
lyght the space of iij days and a nyght.

Seynt Thomas of Canterbery callyth hym the blake
dragon and he shall com out of Demark with the Danys
and he shall declyne the laweys the space of iij^d iij^w 55
and hys name shalbe callyd G.

William Ambrose sayeth þat the redd dragon shalbe
put vnder fote and cast his fome at Charyng
Crosse and ther the most parte of Saxvns
shalbe distroyed.   60

William the abbot of Irelonde sayeth that I or G
shalbe called kyng of the brode see thorowe all
Crystendome and he shall bere thre wylde bestes in
his armes and he shall com owte of the west;
the one of the bestes shall come owte of Irelonde,   65
another best in Wallys, and the thirde at Charing
Crosse.

But William of Siluester sayeth that iiij bestes
shall knyt their tayles togyther: a lyon,
a bere, a horse, a antelop, with a lybard and   70
they shall crowne G or I by the help of the egyll
and they shall set all in pease and in rest.

---

47 *Merlyon of Salodown* See note to l. 12.
50–56 Again, an invasion of the Danes.
   55 *declyne* decline; shun, avoid, refuse, abandon, or forsake
57–60 Again, an anti-*English* bent in this prophecy.
68 Four beasts are mentioned, but they are enumerated as a lion, a bear, a horse, an
antelope, and a leopard.

But the patriark of Armony wrytith in
his estryke and sayth the Saxons shalbe delyuered
and put downe and the trew Brewet shall come   75
agayne.

Salamon sayeth that the egill shall wyn
and conquer vj realmes of Crystendome and
he shall declyne the pope and his lawes and
they shall preche and teche the worde of God   80
and they shall go barfote and barlegged
for drede and love of God and they shalbe the
lanterne to the worlde.

Thomas of Asheldon sayeth the egle of the
trewe Brute shall set all Inglond in peas and rest,   85
both spirituall and temporall, and euery estate
in thaire degre and the maydens of Englond
bylde your howses of lyme and stone.

But Marlyn sayeth he that shall wyn the Holy
Crosse shalbe a virgin kynge that shall come of ij   90
virgins by the myrcle of God and he shall distroy
the bastardes blode.

Also these profettes concluden in one when that this
shall fall: at the date of Our Lorde God betwixt
vj and ix, wonders of Inglonde shalbe seen and betwene 95
ix and one all shall be don.

---

74 *estryke* perhaps for "estriche," eastern kingdom, but no usage so late is recorded
in the *OED*
75 On the return of the descendants of *the trew Brewet*, see "Commentary."
77 *Salamon* A reference to Solomon as a prophet.
85 See "Commentary."
89 *Marlyn* for Merlin

TEXT 2

I — beyng of that grete multitude which be most rude
and with whome few good thynges are worthely accepted
and that for lacke of grace, of which God is the only
gever, which grace is the encrease of all godlynes
which flowith in your Lordship, and in all other suche
which be Godes electe, whome God also wyllyth to
be rulers, gyders, and correctors of the ignorant
which doth nothyng consyder your greate paynes
and laboures takyn for there profites, and in especiall
at such tymes as this is whan sysmis begyn to
be spoken of, for than the comen perswacions of the people
are prouysions, be cawse they for the most parte iudge
most vntrewly — have here gathered to gether the
sayinges of dyvers prophecies that shewyth of a kyng
which shall wyn the Holy Crosse and also dyuers
realmes, ye, and also be cawse I perceave that those
who hath gyven them selfe to knoledge and wysdome
hath geven iudgement with the rude multitude and that
in those thynges which men owght least to medle
which be darke prophecies, which I well perceave they
have done it to avawnce the fame and glorye
of Charles there emperowre, the whiche also hath
occasioned me to enter in to this dawngerus
enterprise which in maner is fyt for no man to do
except he had grete speculacion therin and also many
propheces, of both I am destitute, which gatherynges
wyll shew planly hym whome honowre, lawde, and
glory owght to be gyven vnto, that is to hym whome
God makyth worthie therof, which is owre moste
gracious kyng, Kyng Henry the viij^th as shall apeare
in those my gatherynges and where the rude sort
thynkyth it over grete a wonder that this owre most
victorious Kyng to ouercome so many realmes His Grace
havyng so few nomber of people as in dede he hathe
to the regarde of those that all other prynces hathe
surely therin they declare them to be teachers of
greate errors tyll they make of Godes worde theire
mesure, which is a trew scole master to all nacions
of people and althoughe we seme to be soone ouer come
yet wyll God wyth a myghtie stretched owte arme
delyuer his electe and delyuer in to oure Kynges handes
his enymies, ye and wylbe his defence even as he was
Gedions who put to flyght with iij D persons a myghtie
host who ware in number as the sand on the see
bancke, ye and as God reased the swerdes of the

Madionites one agenst another, even so no dowte God
wyll rease the swerdes of the Kynges enymies one
agenst another, and as surely as pharao with his
grete hoste colde not have byn dystroyde but only in
folowyng to presente Godes electe, the Israelites, even
so shall the papistes seke there owne confucion and
sodenly shall fynde it or it once be thoughte lyke
to come and be drowned in theire owne bloode by
swerde, ye and what faythfull harte wyll once thynke
that God wyll not make one man strong enoughe
that fyghtyth in his quarell for x other that fyghtyth
agenst hym, ye, I dowt nothyng at all but that
God wyll fulfyll his promyse agenst them and
that we shall rewarde the papystes as they rewarded
vs, as is saide in the Apocalypes the 18 chapter
rewarde her as she rewardyd yow, which rewarde
shalbe wyth swerde and so dryven owt of this lande
for ever as is saide in the Proverbes, the ryghtwyse
shall neuer be ouer throwen, but the vngodly shall not
remaine in the lande and to be shorte the Lorde of
Glorie preserue your lyffe to preferre his wyll and
pleasure and who ever be your gyde, Amen.

By your humble harted seruant

Thomas Gybson

Saynet Thomas callyth hym the which shall wyn the
Holy Crosse the king of virgyns. Surely it semeth
very well to be owre Soveraygne Lorde, the
Kyng that now is, for in that His Grace hath
takyn vpon hym to set fourth the worde of God,   5
which worde ledith all men to lyve acordyng to
Godes will and pleasure, and as Saynet Poule
saith, now are we delyuerde frome the law
and ded frome it, whervnto we ware in bondage
that we shulde serue in a new conversacion of the spirite   10
and not in the olde conuersacion of the letter, agayne
he saith, which walke not after the fleshe but after
the sprite, which sprite Owre Savioure Christ saith shall

Text 2   Thomas Gibson's letter and "sayings" were sent to Cromwell. See Chapter 2,
pp. 58–59. Gibson does punctuate his letter and prophecies, and his punctuation is
followed here. Notice here Gibson's references to *that grete multitude, the ignorant, the
comen perswacions of the people, the rude multitude*, and the *rude sort* as those who
consult, misuse, and misunderstand prophecy.
1–22   See "The Sayings," Text 1, ll. 1–2.

lede vs in to all truth, which truth shall lede vs
to lyve as virgins, for that was the very cawse wh[y]   15
Oure Savioure Chryst came to redeme man to lyve in
the same virginycall lyfe which Adam lyved in
be fore his Fall, which lyfe colde to this tyme neuer
be set fourth, and the cawse wh[y] is, there was
never kyng which durst take vpon hym once to be   20
so hardye as to medle with the Scrypture, which is
the only rule of a virginicall lyfe.

Also Iohn Hermyte callyth hym the kynge of sourdes,
which is to say kyng of that realme where plenty
of waters are which is Englonde as apeareth well by   25
Toulions where he callyth hym the kyng of brode
passage which is to say full of havens rownde
abowte the domynyon of the saide kyng which
is Englonde for the see is a bowt it.

Marlyn and Sylvester callyth hym the kyng of worches   30
which is to say king of workes or of marvales and
what marvales and notorious workes hath His Grace
done which neuer kyng was yit able to do savyng
only His Highnes, who hath folowed the cownsell
of Salamon and hath adwyned hym selfe with wysdome,   35
which wysdome cawsith an vncorrupte lyffe whiche
makyth kynges famyliar with God and as it is saide
in the Proverbes a wyse kyng distroyth the vngodly
and bryngyth the whele ouer them, who also saith
marcie and faythfulnes vpholdyth a kyng, and as Saynet   40
Poule saith seyng God is of the Kynges syde who
shall be a geynst hym, and whome shall he fere
seyng God is his shelde?

Albanus Monacus callyth hym the lion of the acre
the which shall take his wynges and fle vnto Rome   45
where he callyth hym the lion of the acre. It may

23–29 See "The Sayings," Text 1, ll. 9–11.
      23 *Iohn Hermyte* A reference to a prophet named John the Hermit appears in
Robert E. Lerner, *The Powers of Prophecy*, p. 94. A Latin prophecy of John the
Hermit, beginning "Quam videt in Caucaso Monte," appears in Cambridge University Library MS Mm.I.16 (not an English manuscript). For this reference, I wish to
thank Professor Kerby-Fulton.
      26 *Toulions* unknown
30 *Marlyn and Sylvester* On Merlin Silvester, see Text 1, note to l. 12.
35 *Salamon* See Text 1, l. 77.
44 *Albanus Monacus* unknown

welbe saide it is oure Kyng, when he well declared
hym selfe to be only gouerner of his subiectes and
bet the bysshope of Rome with Godes worde frome
his vsurped powre, which lion also sygnyfiethe   50
to vs, that as Saynet Marke the evangelist treatyth
of the kyngdome of Christ of which kyngdome
owre Kyng is mynyster, wherfore he is lyckned
to a lyon of the acre whiche is the badge
of an invincible kyngdome, which owre Kyng sent   55
vnto Rome and ouer came the pope with all papistes
which yit sease not to worke there owne confucion.

Malangaly the abbot of Irelonde callith hym the
vj^t of Irelonde the which wylnot be gouerned by
no man but by God and hym selfe, and truthe   60
it is owre Kyng, Kyng Henry the viij^t is the syxt
of Irelonde that is to saye the syxt of that name
synce it was conquered, for Kyng Henry the Seconde
wan Irelonde, and owre Kyng is the viij^t of that
name which did conquere it and also is the syxt   65
sence it was conquerde, and where he saith he
wylbe governyd by no man but by God and hym selfe,
how well was this prophete aquaynted with that
godly kyng Salamon which saith the harte of the kyng
is in the hande of the Lorde and turnyth it whether   70
soeuer that he lystyth, who also saith the iust delityth
in those thynges which be iust, and as Saynet Iohn
sayth the anoyngtyng which ye have receaved of
God the Father which dwellyth in yow, and that anoyntyng
shall teach yow althynges, so that this prophete   75
well declarith it to be owre Kyng Henry the viij^t both
in that he callyth hym the syxt of Irelonde and
also where he sayth God and all godlynes shalbe
his only gyde and cownselowres.

Also Ampho the patriarke of Armonie callyth hym the   80
weste beast the which shall put downe a parte of the
freare preachers and wyn a grete parte of the
worlde and make a fre way vnto the Holie Lande
and in that tyme shalbe many marvayles of Anty-
Chryst, where he callyth hym the west beast, me   85
thynke the prophet Ieromie also doith afirme it to

58–79 "The Sayings," Text 1 indicates "William" is the "abbot of Ireland." See ll.
23–25.
80 Here the patriarch of Armenia is called Ampho; see Text 1, ll. 16 and 73.

be of Englonde, where he spekyth in the person of God,
Lo I shall bryng them agayne frome the north
regions, meanyng of Godes electe and Englande is
north, and west frome the place where these prophettes   90
prophecied of it, and in that he saith he shall put
downe a parte of the freare preachers it is a manyfest
tokyn to be owre pryncely Kyng, for he hath
lefte none, which freares hath alwayes deludid
all people. And in that he saith he shall wyn   95
a grete parte of the worlde and make a fre way
vnto the Holy Land, I thynke it is to wyn the
whole worlde to Chrystes true religion and to
make a fre way to the Holy Lande is to set
the Scryptures at lybertie for every man to   100
looke on it, for the Holy Lande which is called
Iewry is no holier then other places be, no not
for all the myracles which ware there done.
Also he saith here shalbe many marva[les] of
Antichrist, this saying declarith playnly that   105
owre Kynges Hyghnes in stablysshyng Chryst must
nedes declare the dedes and craftes of hym
which is agenst Chryst who also is named
or called Antichryst whiche is the bysshope of
Rome.   110

Sybyll callyth hym the seconde lion of mykell
Bryton, which is to say he shalbe the seconde
son of a kyng of Englonde which holdythe his
kyngdome by succession, as whan it pleased God
the maynteyner of all godly kynges to take awaye   115
Prynce Arthur and wolde that Kyng Henry the
viij^t to worke his wyll.

Petrus Balswell callyth hym the egle that
shall ouer come vj kyngdomes, where he callyth
hym the egle I remember that famoose clarke Jeffray   120
Chawser saith in the *Roman Drose*, "whyll Peter
bearith mastrye, Iohn shall never well shew

111–17 See "The Sayings," Text 1, ll. 26–28. In l. 16 is also an overt reference to
Prynce Arthur, perhaps a reference to Henry VIII's older son (and Henry VIII's older
brother), but also an interesting possible allusion to the British Arthur.
118–45 See "The Sayings," Text 1, ll. 29–31 and 76–83.
    Although not explicitly cited as a prophet here, Chaucer is occasionally used as a
prophet in political prophecy (see *Manual* IV.11 for the apocryphal "Chaucer's
Prophecy."). Lines 121–25 are quoted from Chaucer's *The Romaunt of the Rose* (ll.

his myght, now (saith he) I have shewed yow
the pythe and rynde that makythe the intencion
blynde" meanyng herby that so long as the   125
bysshope of Rome kepe his vsurped powre and
awtorite the which he clamyth by succession of
Peter, which (saith he) had only gyven to hym and
to his successors the kyes of the kyndome of God, so long
shall not the dyvinitie of Saynet Iohn be knowen.   130
So to my purpose this Peter Balswell callyth
hym the egle meanyng therby he shall have
such devyne knoledge that by it he shall ouer come
vj kyngdomes. And be cawse he shall excell all other
kynges in knoledge even as Saynet Iohn dyd excell   135
all other the apostles and evalgelistes in that Owre
Savioure Chryst shewed and reveled to hym suche
mysteries which were kepte secrete frome all the
other apostles and evangelystes, wherefore he is lyckned
to an egle which byrde fleith most hiest, and   140
therfore this prophet callith him the egle which shall
ouercome vj kyngdomes. And I remember I red in a
Walshe p[ro]phecie which callyth him the egle ouer
irire, which is to say ouer owre eglees.   145

The Doctor Saynet German call hym the trew dragon
that shall ouercome the lande of pryde and than
shall take his wynges and fle vnto Rome, in that he
callyth hym the true dragon, it semethe that
theire shalbe some which falsly wyll take vpon them   150
to theire confucion to be dragons which shall thynke
to do grete feates. And where he saith he shall ouercome the
lande of pride, was whan he ouer came the adherentes
of Antychryst, the clargie I shulde have saide, which
myght better be saide a worlde than a lande seyng   155

7165–67), where Fals Semblant is speaking: "Petre" stands for the secular clergy and
"John" for the friars. Gibson has here re-interpreted the references.

146–60 See "The Sayings," Text 1, ll. 36–39, where the reference is clearly to
Jerome. Gibson's *Doctor Saynet German* may be an altogether different figure, a
reference to the contemporary and formidable Tudor lawyer and propagandist,
Christopher St. German. See John A. Guy, *Christopher St. German on Chancery and
Statute*, Selden Society supp. ser., 6 (London, 1985) and his "Thomas More and
Christopher St. German: The Battle of the Books" in *Reassessing the Henrician Age*,
pp. 95–120. Gibson may have deliberately changed the reference, or he may simply
have misunderstood the likely references of his sources to Jerome. If Gibson does
intend *Doctor Saynet German* to refer to the Tudor lawyer, it is an unprecedented
inclusion of a contemporary figure as a *prophet* — certainly a diminution of prophetic
authority.

theire abus is so grete and manyfest and they once
ouer come by his godly policie then shall take his
wynges and fle vnto Rome, the which His Maiestie did
and theire ouercame that grete hore of Rome with
the toche stone of owre faythe, Godes worde.   160

Robert of Surrey callyth hym an vnycorne that
shall never be ouercome, what fame and glorie
shall it be vnto this yle of Englond after owre
dayes, whan it shalbe said Kyng Henry the viij^t
was neuer ouercome, ye whan he toke that in hand   165
to do, ye and also did it, the which all kynges
chrystened doist not once seme to medle wyth.
Wherfore it is well saide of Salamon that
a kyng wythe true iudgement exaltyth
his lande, what region in this worlde   170
is their but it may muse at the hyghe
felicitie of Englonde for surely it is a kyng
that ether makyth a realme faymose or that obscurith it.

Saynet Davy callyth hym the very bore of Clyffordes
which is that he shalbe of the howse of Yorke.   175

Robert scrybe docter of Bredlyngton cally[th] hym the
cocke of Brytayne which cannot be aplied to no other
then to the Kynges Maiestie, for even as a cocke
hatyth darknes even so hath His Grace hated
all darknes, ye and hath set the lyght vpon the   180
howse top for all kynges to se lyght by.

Macamyte saide vnto the paynems and called
hym the very delicate rose of Brytayne, yf
this ware Macamyte, the which set vp that secte
which the Turkes is of, than had he his knoledge by   185
the dyvell the which was awter of his religion

161–73 See "The Sayings," Text 1, ll. 32–33. The reference to a unicorn is the
same, but not the prophets cited.
174–75 *Saynet Davy* is unknown; also interesting is the reference to a Yorkist heir
— particiularly timely in 1538, when Henry was eliminating all possible rival claim-
ants among the Courtneys, Poles, and Nevilles. See Chapter Two, p. 52 on Henry's
efforts and the executions that resulted on 9 December 1538.
176–81 *Robert scrybe* is here identified with Bridlington; see Text 1, ll. 3–4 and
50–52 for references to Bridlington.
182–88 See "The Sayings," Text 1, ll. 40–46.

who be lyke shewed how long his secte and all
other such lyke sectes shulde indure.

And now forasmoche as all thees aforesaide prophetes
shewyth that this owre most victorious kyng, Kyng
Henry the viij^t shall wyn the Holie Crosse with so
many realmes as is aforesaide which hapely semyth
to some but a vayne thyng once to thynke that
he shall go to Ierusalem for to fetche the Crosse
which Owre Savioure Christe sufferde payne and
passion on. Thees prophetes meane nothyng lesse
then so, but goith abowte to shew that His
Magestie shall wyn victory of the dyvelles
mynyster the bysshop of Rome and shalbe vnto
all realmes a lanterne of lyght wherby they
may truly and faythfully se the cencerenes of
the Gospell, whiche is the glorye of God the
which glorye, the dyvell by his mynysters the
papystes hath byn darkned with beggarly bagage
wherby the prophecie of Amos is fulfilled
that an hunger shulde come on the erth for lacke
of Godes worde the which now is set owte by
the true mynyster of God, Kyng Henry the viii^t
and the only setter fourth of Chrystes fayth
which is the very same Crosse which the prophetes
meane and hath spokyn of, as Owre Savioure
Chryst saith he that takyth not his Crosse and
folowith me is not worthie of me, agayne
Saynet Paule saith Christ sent me to preache
the Gosspell, least the Crosse of Chryst shulde
have byn made of none efecte, for saith he
the preachyng of the Crosse is to them that
peryshe, folyshenes, thus owght thies prophetes
to be vnderstande who saith that the Kynges
Maiestie shall wyn the Holy Crosse owt of the
landes of the heathen, whiche
heathen may be saide is Gog and Magog that
Ezechiell spekyth of which shalbe distroyde.

Amen

6. *"The Prophecy of the Lily, the Lion, and the Son of Man"*

COMMENTARY

It is almost a relief to come across "The Prophecy of the Lily, the Lion, and the Son of Man." After the confusion and ambiguity of prophecies like "The Marvels of Merlin" and "France and Flanders Then Shall Rise," this Merlin prophecy is clear: it is a prediction of the conquest of France by the king of England.

The sixteenth-century versions of this prophecy are variations of a very popular fourteenth-century text. M.E. Griffiths, discussing early Welsh and Latin versions of the prophecy, notes that they told the story of the Son of Man (Edward III), who allied himself with the Eagle of the East (the emperor), and then defeated the Lily (Philip of France) and his ally, the Head of the World (the pope), in the land of the Lion (Flanders).[26] The Son of Man then claimed the crown of the Lily. The symbol of the "son of man" derived from the Book of Daniel, but by the fourteenth century it was used frequently in political prophecies.[27]

Two versions of "The Prophecy of the Lily, the Lion, and the Son of Man" are included here, the first in prose and the second in verse. Both versions are accompanied by keys that identify their animal symbols. Briefly, these sixteenth-century versions of the prophecy predict that a lily (the king of France) will invade the land of the lion (Flanders) and overthrow the son of the lion. The prophecy continues by foreseeing that "the son of man bearing in his arms wild beasts" (the king of England), whose kingdom is the land of the moon (England, Wales, and Ireland), will come to the aid of the lion.

In the same year, an eagle (the emperor) and his "chickens," with the help of the son of man, will invade the son (France). There will be a great battle, and both versions of the prophecy agree that there will be a bloody flood. The lily will lose his crown. The prose text says that the crown will be taken by the eagle, while the verse text gives the crown to the son of man. This discrepancy is the only difference between the two versions of the prophecy, and it is resolved when the prose text continues by saying that the son of man will be crowned within four years. Both versions then foretell the fall of "the

---

[26] Griffiths, *Early Vaticinations in Welsh with English Parallels*, pp 170–71. See also Scattergood, p. 77, and Thomas, p. 468. (Thomas does, however, indicate this prophecy is an example of a text derived from *The Prophecy of Thomas à Becket*).

[27] On the symbols, see Griffiths, p. 170. On the larger issue of the relationship between religious and political prophecies, see Chapter One, p. 13, and note 10.

head of the world" (the pope), the son of man's crusade and recovery of the "sign marvelous" (the Holy Cross), and the peaceful reign of the son of man and the eagle.

Throughout the 1520s and into the 1530s, England was clearly concerned with the activities of the emperor, France, and Flanders, and these concerns were reflected, as we have already seen, in political prophecies. One of the recurrent themes in nearly all the prophecies we have read thus far has been either support for the emperor (usually represented, as he is here, by the heraldic Hapsburg eagle) or fear he would invade England. "The Marvels of Merlin" predicts a conflict between Flanders and England, and in "France and Flanders Then Shall Rise" we see again the theme of international dissension. "The Prophecy of the Lily, the Lion, and the Son of Man" thus covers familiar territory.

Also familiar is the theme of the victorious king who recovers the Holy Cross. We have seen this incident in "The Prophecies of Rhymer, Bede, and Merlin," most notably, and as the conclusion of "The Cock of the North" and "France and Flanders." And the figure of the king who recovers the Cross is the whole organizing principle for "The Sayings of the Prophets."

What makes "The Prophecy of the Lily, the Lion, and the Son of Man" unique among the sixteenth-century political prophecies presented here is that there is no overt or, apparently, covert anti-government sentiment. In fact, though the prophecy foretells the fall of the pope, it predicts the emperor and the king of England will cooperate to produce harmony and peace. The prose text speaks only of "the son of man" as the king of England, but the verse text identifies him specifically as "Kynge Henry."

Although this text is found in the company of the vigorous anti-government prophecies we have so far read, it is difficult to see how it can be reconciled with the political and religious events of the 1530s. It would have been much easier to see this as a piece of political flattery dedicated to Henry in an earlier decade, say the 1520s, or even to early 1530. Yet both texts included here keep company with anti-government prophecies of the 1530s like "The Prophecies of Rhymer, Bede, and Merlin," "The Marvels of Merlin," and "The Cock of the North." It is included here to show the full range of prophetic interests in the decade.

TEXT 1

A lille rayning in the best parte of the worlde shalbe moved
lyke vnto the seede of a lyon and he shall come into his lande
and stande in the felde amonges the thornes of his kingdom
and vnbesett the son of a lyon. In that yere the son of a
man bering in his armes wilde bestes whose   5
kingdome is in the lande off the mone that is to
be drede in the vniuersall worlde bicause of his principall
power and shall passe ouer the waters with a grett
cumpanye and shall entre into the land off the
lyon ther waitting helpe for whye the bestes off
his region then with ther tethe shall rent his skyn.   10
Nowe the same yere shall come an egle from the
costes off the est with his winges extending abroide
vppon the son with a grett multitude of his chekyns
into the arde and with the helpe of the son of man the
casteles shalbe distroide and grett feire shalbe in the worlde   15
and in on daye in a parte off the lande of the lyon shalbe
a battell amonges monye more cruell then euer men
see vnto þat daye and in ther blode shalbe a flode. The
lille shall lose his croune whiche the egle shall
take and therwith afturwarde the son off man shalbe   20
crowned within iiij yeres ther following. Then in
the worlde shalbe many batteles done amonges suche
as strive in ther feithe for in that tyme all these
thinges shalbe to be beleved. The more parte off the
worlde shalbe distroyed. The heede off the worlde   25
shalbe cast downe vnto the gronde. Then the son
off a man shall ouerpasse the waters and shall beire
a signe mervelous vnto the lande of promission for
the furst cause committed shall remayne to hym selffe
butt the son off man and the egle shall priuelye concorde   30
and peace be over all the worlde and grett plentye off
frutes.

Text 1 The key appended to this prophecy identifies all the figures mentioned in
the text, though no historical events in the 1530s seem to correspond to the
prophetic visions. The symbol of "the son off man bearing wild beasts in his arms" is
used also in contemporary versions of "The Sayings of the Prophets"; see above, p.
115.
12 *abroide* abroad; broadly, widely
13 *chekyns* chickens; the young of any bird
14 *arde* yard

The lylle is the kynge off France
The lyon is Flanders
The son off the lyon is the egle of Flanders   35
The son off man bearing wilde beastes in his armes
     is the king off Engelonde
The lande off the mone is Inglande, Wales, and Ireland
The egle is the armes off the Emperour
The son is France
The heede off the worlde is the pope   40
The mervelous signe is the token off the
     Hollye Crosse

TEXT 2

Declaratio signorum infra scripter

The lylie that faire flowre
     is the kyng of Fraunce that socour.
The lyon that ferefull is
     is the londe of Flaunders.
The lyons son, I saye certayne,
     is the duke of F[l]aunders, P. Burgeyn.
The man son with the wilde bestes
     is the kynge of Inglonde by conqueste.
The londe of the mone, I vnderstonde,
     is Englonde, Wales, and Irelond.
The egill with the birde in bowre
     is the nobyll emperour.
The son that so high is
     is the londe of Flaunders, iwis.
The hed of the worlde also
     is the pope withouten woo.
The mervelous signe is, parfay,
     the Holy Crosse that God died on Good Fryday.

When a m^l ccccc togyther be knett
And xxiiij with them be mett,
As Merlyon sayethe in his story of Bryttayne,

Text 2 Because of the key's reference to the "duke of F[l]aunders, P. Burgeyn,"
whom he identifies as Philip of Burgundy, Scattergood (*Politics and Poetry*) contends
that 1524 is a mistake for 1424 and that the prophecy refers to the battle of Verneuil.
There are inconsistencies with such an interpretation, as Scattergood himself notes
(pp. 78–79). More likely is that the date of 1524 represents an *up*-dating of an earlier
prophecy.
     In the *Manual*, Robbins (p. 1520) indicates that the key reads "the duke of

128

Of Kynge Henry of Englond, certayne,
And themperoure, and the kynge of Fraunce and
    Flaunders als[o]   5
And other lordes many moo,
By trew prophecy that sholde befall
Off diuers meruaylis amonges them all —
Thuse sayeth Merlyon in his prophecye
That in no wise kepyth to lye.   10
First the lylie, that faire flowre
That many yeres shall kepe his colour,
After that he shall sprede into lyons land
And grow amonge the thornes, I vnderstond;
After that a mans son shall mete with mone   15
Bryngyng in his armes bestes many oon;
Thus mannys son all nations hym shall drede
Above all the worlde in euery stede;
With many a creature the lyon shall mete
And enter in to his londe that socourles shalbe lefte,   20
With them they shall bere both flessh and fell
With wylde bestes of the region full cruell;
The same yere shall com an egill oute from the east
Spredyng his winges abowte the son in hast,
Many of his chekyns with hym will he bryng   25
To helpe the manys sone with grete ioying;
First many a castell they shall ouerthrow
With pillers and townes that shalbe full low,
Also in one parte of the lyons londe
Shalbe a grete battaile, I vnderstonde,   30
For many kynges shall fight there so
That of red blod a grete flode shall goo;
There shall the lylie lose his crowne so gay
With the which the mans son shalbe crowned, perfay,
So great a battayle shall then there be   35
That fewe of on lyve men shall see;
The most parte of the worlde deth shall tast —
Welbe he þat shall scape in haste;
Then after this grete battayle
The hed of the worlde, his myght shall faile,   40
To the erthe with hed makyng incluacion
Praying to God for manns salvasion;
After this the egill and the mans son

Flaunders & Burgeyn." This reading makes more sense, but the mysterious letter isn't clearly either a P or an ampersand.
25 *chekyns* chickens; the young of any bird

Shall reigne together withouten mone;
In all the worlde then shalbe pease   45
With Christen and hethen dowtles,
Also of frutes grete plentie —
Ioy may they that thus ioy may see;
Then shall manns son for Christes sake
A mervelous thing vpon hym take   50
And take his way to the londe of promission
And thus God hath prouyded for Kynge Henrys salvacion.

7. "A Prophecy of a New World Emperor"

COMMENTARY

Each of the prophecies we have so far examined presents its own unique set of complications and confusions. "A Prophecy of a New World Emperor" is no exception, the question here being not so much the aim of the prophecy as just *whose* prophecy it is.

The manuscript version of "A Prophecy of a New World Emperor" clearly attributes the piece to Bishop Methodius: "Here followethe the reuelation whiche was shewede to Seynt Methedius, bisshoppe, when he was in prison and itt pleased Almightye God to reuelate secrettes to hym that were comming to the churche off Rome." During the Middle Ages, prophecies falsely attributed to Bishop Methodius (d. ca. 300) were widely circulated, and they greatly influenced popular expectations about the end of the world. These Pseudo-Methodius *Revelations* actually date to the late seventh century and are a series of apocalyptic predictions that detail the events of the last days.[28] The visions generally foretell cosmic signs of the approaching end of the world, foresee the conversion of the Jews, and warn against the imminent danger of the rise of the Antichrist. "A Prophecy of a New World Emperor" is similar to the *Revelations* in its predictions of worldwide tumult, but despite its attribution, the piece fathered here on Methodius is, in fact, a sixteenth-century version of the fourteenth-century prophecies of John of Bassigny. Not much is known about this obscure French "prophet," but his predictions of devastating universal turmoil and the coming of a young hero and a new pope spread rapidly. By the sixteenth-century, Bassigny's prophecy was included in the prophetic anthology *Mirabilis Liber*, printed in France in 1522. The original predictions of Bassigny referred to dates from 1345 to 1382; the sixteenth version re-dates the predictions, 1490–1525.[29]

[28] Selected translations of the pseudo-Methodius *Revelations* are in McGinn, *Visions of the End*, pp. 70–76. The text of the *Revelations* in its entirety is available in Sackur, *Sibyllinische Texte*.

The influence of the legends of Methodius is discussed in Cohn, *The Pursuit of the Millenium*, pp. 71–73. Concerning the wide-spread influence of the pseudo-Methodius *Revelations* in England and the availability of the text there, see Charlotte D'Evelyn, "The Middle-English Metrical Version of the *Revelations* of Methodius; with a Study of the Influence of Methodius in Middle-English Writings," *PMLA*, 26 (1918), pp. 135–203.

[29] On Bassigny and his text, see Robert E. Lerner, "The Black Death and Western European Eschatological Mentalities," in *The Black Death: The Impact of the Fourteenth-Century Plague*, ed. Daniel Williman (Binghamton, New York, 1982), esp. pp. 89–90. On the *Mirabilis Liber*, see Jennifer Britnell and Derek Stubbs, "The *Mirabilis*

The English "A Prophecy of a New World Emperor" is a fairly close translation of the Latin *Mirabilis Liber* text, but it predicts the date of 1534 for the beginning of the last days. It foresees a time of general turmoil and civil upheaval: men will make insurrections, the commons will abandon towns, castles will be destroyed, women will be left widowed, neighbor will turn against neighbor, and all men will be deceitful and unfaithful. It also predicts dissension between the Spaniards and the Aragonese (ll. 32–36). Long-lasting and disastrous wars between Castile and Aragon in the fourteenth and fifteenth centuries had been resolved by the dynastic marriage of Ferdinand and Isabella; it is possible that this part of the prophecy incorporates earlier fifteenth-century material written when the affairs of Aragon and Castile were of pressing importance.

By the year 1535, according to the English prophecy, disaster will engulf the world. Rome will fall: ". . . all Cristendome shall sorowe for the distructyon, robbing, and wasting off the most noblest cyte, whiche is the heede off all Cristondome and ladye off all Cristen faithe" (ll. 37–40). All religon will cease. Nuns will be turned out of convents and defiled; prelates will be "pursuyed cruellye," and priests will deny that they were ever priests. The pope will flee from Rome (ll. 60–66) to safety and will endure more than twenty-five months of exile and persecution.

These lines might well reflect what was known about the sack of Rome by Charles V in 1527 and about the capture of the pope, who had had to secure his freedom by the payment of a heavy ransom. The impact of such an event on the European mind had been enormous. Judith Hook says, "It is impossible to ignore the sack of Rome. That in 1527 the city of the popes was

Liber: Its Compilation and Influence," *Journal of Warburg and Courtauld Institutes*, 49 (1986), 126–49. The prophecy of Bassigny is listed as Item 11, described on pp. 136–37.

Robert E. Lerner has very kindly proided me with a photocopy of a nineteenth-century edition of Bassigny's prophecy, as recorded in the *Mirabilis Liber: Prophétie Recueillie et Transmise par Jean de Vatiguerro* [for John of Bassigny]; *Extraite Du Liber Mirabilis . . . de l'edition de 1523* (1814).

A copy of Bassigny's prophecy had reached northern England within a few years of its composition — the Augustinian friar John Erghome had access to a copy (Lerner, p. 90 and note 42). The English version printed here most likely derives from the *Mirabilis Liber*, however (my thanks to Professor Lerner for his conclusions about the text). Since the first item of the *Mirabilis Liber* anthology is a version of the Pseudo-Methodius *Revelations*, that may account for the attribution of "A Prophecy of a New World Emperor" to Methodius here.

This unique sixteenth-century English version of Bassigny is collected in Bodl. Libr. MS Rawlinson C.813, which also contains "The Prophecies of Rhymer, Bede, and Merlin," "The Marvels of Merlin," and "The Prophecy of the Lily, the Lion, and the Son of Man." These same items are also collected in BL MS Lansdowne 762 (see Appendix), which also contains a version of Bassigny's prophecy, in Latin, however, and independent of the printed *Mirabilis Liber*.

subjected to one of the worst sacks in recorded military history at the hands of the army of Charles V is a fact which sooner or later faces the general historian of the sixteenth century. Not only was it 'one of the most frightful and dramatic events of the century,' of a century which was not lacking in frightful and dramatic events, but the effects of the sack were to be felt throughout Europe for years."[30] The decimation of the imperial armies in Naples by the plague was considered a "divine punishment" and such a belief may have accorded well with the note of doom in the prophecy.[31] The prophecy states, "then the herdman off the Churche and dignyte shalbe expulsed" (ll. 52–53). This could refer to the absence of Clement VII who was away from Rome for almost a year, fleeing in December 1527 and returning in October 1528.

In addition to these references to continental upheavals, the prophecy does seem to allude to problems closer to home. Early in the prophecy (ll. 9–13), there are references to insurrections, new constitutions, and new laws; in addition, there is a passage which refers to the destruction of holy authors, the defiling of churches, and "monastories spoilled and robbed" (ll. 75–77). The results of the new legislation are predicted to be utter ruin, and the passage may well refer to the parliamentary acts taken between 1532 and 1534, a date consistent with the opening reference in the prophecy. The fears for the church and monasteries could well allude to the growing secularization and confiscation of religious houses in England during the same period. Although suppression of the monasteries under Wolsey's direction had begun as early as 1518, Cromwell greatly accelerated the process, and in 1535 a general visitation of all churches and monasteries had begun.[32]

The prophecy then moves to a series of omens signalling man's coming destruction: a great earthquake will appear, crops will fail, marvelous signs will appear in the heavens. During this period of universal destruction, "Ireshemen" and "Scottishmen" will invade England (ll. 114 ff.). A young man, long in captivity, then will arrive, but his role is ambiguous, at least from the British point of view:

> . . . Then Ireshemen and
> Scottishmen shall invade Grett Bretten and muche distroye
> and waste, in the helpe off whome shall come a yonge
> kyng or yonge man whiche hathe be longe captiuat
> the whiche shall recouer the crowne off the lillye and
> shall beire rule throughe the worlde and be rooted and

---

[30] *The Sack of Rome* (London, 1972), p. 279.
[31] Hook, p. 287.
[32] Mackie, pp. 275–79.

gronded and he shall distroye the childerne off Brute
and all ther ilande insomuche hytt shall neuer
more be hadde in memorye. (ll. 114–22)

After this general destruction, God will appoint a new pope, a man who is
holy and who reforms the Church by his example of purity and humility. God
also will ordain an emperor "off the most holliest blode and off the Frenche
kinges blode" (ll. 141–42). This emperor will help and obey the pope, and he
will deliver all Christendom from its enemies. Thus there will be one law and
one peace in the world until the coming of Antichrist.

This example of political prophecy is notably different from the other texts
we have read so far, but our purpose here is to survey the varied kinds of
prophecies popular during the decade. Clearly "A Prophecy of A New World
Emperor" was circulating throughout England in the 1530s. In 1537, for
example, the prior of Malton, William Todd, was investigated and ultimately
executed for his part in the northern rebellions. Along with a scroll of
painted prophecies, Todd admitted owning a book of prophecy "called 'Metodius.'" According to his testimony, he kept it lying "vpen in his chambre for
euery man to loke on." He had showed both scroll and "the prophecy" to Sir
Francis Bigod as well "as to diuers other" during the Pilgrimage of Grace.
Todd's prophecy may, in fact, have been similar to "A Prophecy of a New
World Emperor," which could be attributed, as we have seen here, to Methodius.

Among other references that help to date this item, the prophecy refers to
a "commotion" of the planets, most likely dated to 1529.[33] The use of the
word "commotion" here jumps out of the text. In the astronomical situation
described by the prophecy, the word likely refers to a conjunction of the
planets, but after 1536, the word was widely used to refer to the northern
rebellions of the Pilgrimage. Todd himself used the word to refer to Bigod's
rebellion. In spite of its obvious astronomical context and meaning here, the
word "commotion" must also have sent a shock of recognition throgh its
readers, familiar with its current political use as well.

[33] See the note to ll. 42–44.

TEXT

Here followethe the reuelation whiche was shewede to
Seynt Methedius, bisshoppe, when he was in prison
and itt pleased Almightye God to reuelate secrettes
to hym that were comming to the churche off Rome
and in espetiallye to all other churches and monastories   5
through all Cristendome in generaltye aboute the
yere off our Lorde God a mille v c and xxxiiij. All
maner of people for the more partye shall dispoose them-
selffe to make insurrectyons, on ageynst a nother, and in ther
ranker and invye on to slee another. Many grett men   10
off townes and cities shalbe moved to make newe constitutions and lawes for the whiche the comens shall forsake
and leave townes disolate. Castelles that ar most stronge
shalbe taken and ouerthrowen and vtterlye distroyed and manye ladyes and gentilwemen shalbe made wydowes and be   15
forsaken and euery neibure shall robbe, spoile, and slee other
most theveslye and cruellye and noo man shall kepe his
faithe trulye and iustelye butt rather on man disceyve
another treterouslye and maliciouslye and the commenwaile
shalbe layd downe. Ther shalbe noo comminalte butt   20
partialite and singularite, and partialite shal be stronge and occu-
pye the place. Wherefore Almightye God shall take vengeance
generally and spetiallye vppon all maner off people. Turkes
and infideles shall distroye manye landes, provinces,
cities, and townes off Cristendome. Iarmania, Francia,   25
Dacia, Norwigia, Crissina: all these shalbe ouerthrowen off the Infideles and enymyes and shall nott be
able to recouer but be wasted and ther cuntrey lafte
dissolate many yeres and many cities, casteles vppon
Damen and Redam and Legerum shalbe turned vppe   30

10–13 The prediction that great men will make new laws and constitutions that
alienate the commons may refer to the parliamentary acts taken between 1532 and
1534. See Chapter Two, pp. 22–23.

13–22 General civil strife and turmoil are predicted.

   20 *comminalte* commonality; community

25–26 *Dacia* is the Latin name for a region of central Europe including northern
Hungary, Transylvania, and Rumania. *Crissina* is unidentified. The *Mirabilis Liber*
lists "Armenia, Frigia, Dacia, Norvagia"; *Crissina* may be a mistranslation of the next
Latin word, "tristissime."

30 From the context, these seem to be rivers. *Legerum* is the Loire, the medieval
Latin name for which was Liger. *Damen* may refer to Damme, the port of Bruges at
the mouth of the Scheldt, but in the *Historia* Geoffrey refers to a battle at Mount
Damen (VII.18). *Redam* is unidentified. The *Mirabilis Liber* here lists "Padum et
Thiberum" (Po and Tiber), "Rodanum" (Rhone), "Ronum" (Rhine), and "Ligerim"
(Loire).

135

and ouerthrowen and grett abundance off water and erthe-
quake. Betwixt the Aragons and Spaynyerdes shalbe grett
tribulation and discention and shall feght togeder with
grett cruelte and shall neuer be pease betwixt them
tyll on realme haue vtterlye distroed the other. Vasconia   35
shall wepe for woo therof, and before the yere off our
Lorde God mille v c and xxxv, all Cristendome shall sorowe
for the distructyon, robbing, and wasting off the most
noblest cyte, whiche is the heede off all Cristondome and
ladye off all Cristen faithe. Euery churche by all the vny-   40
uersall worlde shall lamentablye and sorooffullye be disp[oi]

32–35   The conflict between Aragon and Castile had been settled in 1479 by the
marriage of Ferdinand and Isabella. Trouble flared again after Isabella's death in 1504
and revived once more in 1516 after Ferdinand's death.

   35   *Vasconia* is the medieval Latin name for French Gascony, but here the
more likely reference is to the Basque provinces, the Vascongadas, now Navarre. The
Basques were known as the "Vascones" and the Spanish reference seems more likely
than the French since *Vasconia* will weep for the destruction of Spain and Aragon.

36–40   Before 1535 Rome will be destroyed. Rome was sacked in 1527, and its
destruction then may have provided the prophecy with the images that appear in ll.
44–81.

42–44   The astrological reference does not appear in the *Mirabilis Liber*. A conjunction of Venus and Saturn occurs fairly often, but "commotion" of the two must be
something special. For the following I am indebted to S.S. Jacobsen, Professor Emeri-
tus of Astronomy, University of Washington:

   ". . . all our difficulties are caused by the lack of an astronomical meaning of the
word 'commotion.' I have assumed that it entails a somewhat spectacular aspect of
the sky. . . . For fifteen or more years before and after 1530 there is no total solar
eclipse visible anywhere in Europe which could come under consideration. There are
partial eclipses, but these are never spectacular to the unaided eye. I will not now
outline my search for phenomena but merely point out that a 'commotion' must
probably be something more spectacular than an ordinary conjunction between
Venus and Saturn. Saturn being at all times more than about six times fainter than
Venus, when both are at sufficient elongation from the sun to be good evening or
morning stars, a conjunction between the two would not be particularly striking,
unless it were so close that they looked like a close pair or merged into one star image
to the naked eye. Nothing like this happened during the period we are considering,
even though there were conjunctions about every 378 days, on the average. . . .

   "What did happen March 12 1529, 5:35 pm was a geocentric conjunction in
celestial longitude of the Moon with Venus, in Taurus, so close as to suggest an
occultation of Venus by the Moon. (Note the meaning of the word 'occultation';
namely, an eclipse of one body by another, when the eclipsing body [the Moon] is of
much larger angular size than the eclipsed body [Venus]. In order to be certain that it
was an actual occultation and not merely a very close approach of the Moon's edge to
the bright image of Venus, I would need to consider a definite geographical location,
as a city or a country. But in this case, what happened would be far more spectacular
than the general run of conjunctions. The ingress would be seen in the western sky,

led and depriuate in all ther temporall tythes, and then
shalbe a commotion off Saturne and Venus in the taile
off the dragon, whiche is a mervelous signe, and then
ther shall not be soo grett a man in the vniuersall 45
churche that shall haue sufficient lyving, for
whye the churche shalbe maculate and defiled. All reli-
gyon shall cesse by cause off the woodness, grett cru-

slightly before sunset, and the egress could be seen an hour or less afterwards, when the Moon (and Venus, and Saturn further east) had not yet set on the western horizon . . . in other words during twilight for an observer anywhere favorably situated. Here is what would happen: The three-day-old Moon would 'swallow up' Venus at its dark edge, and then 'disgorge' the planet at the bright edge, perhaps an hour later. This would occur about 1 degree north of the ecliptic. The Moon being at its descending node would then seem to 'swoop down' upon Venus from the North, it would then continue in its southern course, overtaking Saturn in celestial longitude some hours later. (This would not be visible, as Moon, Venus, and Saturn would have set earlier on the western horizon.) The Moon would miss occulting Saturn, since the latter was about 2 degrees south of the ecliptic, when the Moon overtook Saturn in celestial longitude (i.e. at the time of exact conjunction between Saturn and Moon). Using the flowery language in which our problem was originally stated, an exact description of what I have here outlined would be: 'a commotion of Venus, Saturn being near the tail or the dragon.' Or, if the Moon, after passing Venus, is considered to be 'chasing' Saturn (although missing it) we might perhaps have 'a commotion of Venus and Saturn in the tail of the Dragon.' The Moon is thus causing the commotion. . . . Of course all three bodies would be near the tail, or 'in the tail of the Dragon. . . .'

"Although an occultation of Venus by the Moon is very spectacular, it is not too rare an occurrence. . . . To have the phenomenon happen when near Saturn, and when all the bodies are 'in the tail of the Dragon,' is vastly more rare. I cannot say how rare, as I am not a theoretician. However, since Saturn passes the same node every 11.4 years, I should guess that it may occur a few times each century. Saturn passed the 'tail of the Dragon' in 1518, 1529, and 1540. So the information . . . seems to make the March 12, 1529 phenomenon the distinctive one." Personal letter, 21 January 1981.

Astrological phenomena are frequently mentioned in prophecies, and such planetary conjunctions are often regarded as ominous signs. For an extended discussion of the reactions to such conjunctions, in particular an especially notable conjunction of Saturn and Jupiter in 1524, see Lynn Thorndyke, A History of Magic and Experimental Science (New York, 1941), Vol. 5 [and 6]: The Sixteenth Century, pp. 178–233 ("Chapter 11: The Conjunction of 1524").

43 A stroke over the second -o in commotion seems to be a flourish and not an abbreviation. The earliest recorded use of the word "commotion" in the OED (1471) refers to a public disorder. "Commotion" as a continuous motion or an up-and-down motion appears in 1526. The earliest recorded use of the word to describe a violent physical disturbance (such as of the sea) is 1592, but this seems to be the sense of the prediction here.

47 maculate The antithesis of "immaculate," and thus stained or defiled

eltye, ire, and mischeffe sowen betwixt man and ma[n].
And women off religion shall forsake ther monas-   50
toryes and flee all about, her and ther, defiled and vyolate,
and then the herdman off the Churche and dignyte
shalbe expulsed and eiecte from ther dignites, and all prelates
off the churche shal be pursuyed cruellye and shall flye
further and ther parishons and subiectes shalbe without
     doctrine   55
and dispertyll abrode and prestes shall haue soo gret vexation
that many off them shall denye that ever they were
prestes or weare crowne. And trulye the malice off all
men commenlye shall turne ageynst Hollye Churche.
Then shall the gouernour and ruler off Hollye Churche,
     that is to   60
saye our hollye father the pope, with many other good prelates
and well disposed men, flee from Rome to seke them a
place, the whiche they may abide in in saffegarde and
in þat waile, weping and waylyng, and shall ayte ther
bred with grett feare and mourning. And grett mischeff   65
and persecution shall indure xxv monthes and more and in all
thys space shall noder be pope off Rome nor Imperour
nor rightwayes king off France, and ther shalbe noo
man for the most parte off the worlde lyving butt he
shalbe redye to doo evyll and vengance ageynst Holly Chur- 70
che through sclandering, crueltye, and other vengeable
dedes. Alas! for sorowe and petye, for all tirrannes and
crueltye shall reigne amongest Christian men in persecu-
tyng Hollye Churche and all miserrye and dolorous
pestilence is liklye to come to Hollye Churche shortly for   75
whye the hollye auters shalbe distroyed and the Hollye Churche
pavement shalbe polluted and monastories spoilled and robbed.
For the ire and wrothe off God shalbe moved ageynst the
worlde for the multitude and besines of false iuges and
iugements and per[rit]ours covetousnes and pride inordinate, 80
lecherye, oppression of pore people, and other vnhappye beings.
Then the elementes shalbe changed. Therfore itt folowethe
off necessite that all the states off the wo[r]lde be changed
for the erthe shalbe moued with mervelous drede in
many places and men shall synke into itt alyve   85

52–55 Clement VII was exiled from Rome, leaving in December of 1527 and
returning in October of 1528.
    55 *parishons* parishioners
80–82 *per[rit]ours* Summoners (paritors) are one of the targets of God's wrath for
their covetousness, inordinate pride, lechery, and oppression of the poor.
82–108 The cosmic signs of the last days.

as they goo and many casteles, cities, and townes the most
strongest shalbe caste downe for the grett erthe quake
that shall falle att þat tyme and the frutes off the erth[e]
shalbe made lesse and ther shall no moystre be in the
rootes. Seedes shall rotte in the felde and corne shall beire   90
noo seedes and the see shalbe crying and roring ageynst
the worlde and shall swallowe many shippes into hym
and the aire shalbe made foule and corrupped for the grett
malice and wiked lyving off the peopple. And heyvon
shall showe many mervelous and wonderffull tokyns to   95
be merveled off: the son shalbe made blake and in
many places apere blodye and twoo mones shall
apere togeder att on tyme and soo shall laste iiij houres
and more, the starres shalbe seen feghting togeder, whiche
is a token off distruction and sleing almost off all   100
mankynde throughe the worlde. And the naturall
course of thinges shalbe changed and turned vp-soo-doune
and many diuerse and vniuersall passyons and infirmities mortall
and soden shalbe as well in man as in beste and vniuersall
pestilence and hunger most cruell with miserable
derthe, suche   105
and soo grette by the vniuersall worlde and most strongest in
the west partye that from the beginnyng off the worlde hathe
neuer be harde off. For suche another grett pompe and pride off
the noble estates shalbe assessed and all disciplyne and loore
shall perishe and breflye, all the estate and clergye shalbe   110
putt vnder and Loringiam shall wayle and wepe and be
dispoiled and Cumpna shall wepe for lake of his ney-
bures to whome noo helpe shalbe geven, butt spoiled and robbed
and the realme dissolate and wasted. Then Ireshemen and
Scottishmen shall invade Grett Bretten and muche distroye   115
and waste, in the helpe off whome shall come a yonge
kyng or a yonge man whiche hathe be longe captiuat
the whiche shall recouer the crowne off the lillye and
shall beire rule throughe the worlde and be rooted and
gronded and he shall distroye the childerne off Brute   120

111 *Loringiam* for Lorraine
112 *Cumpna* for Champagne
114–22 The prospect for England is certainly not good. The prophecy says the
childerne off Brute will be overrun and destroyed by the Irish and the Scots. The
phrase *in the helpe off whome* (l. 116) is, in itself, somewhat ambiguous, but it is clear
the young king, long a captive, helps to destroy the English. The young king is
strikingly reminiscent of the young king whose career is chronicled in "The
Prophecies of Rhymer, Bede, and Merlin." The victorious young man recovers the
crowne off the lillye, presumably France.

and all ther ilande insomuche hytt shall neuer
more be hadde in memorye. Butt aftur all these
persecutions and tribulations off the churche, Almightye God shall take and choyce a pope aftur his blessed
wyll whiche shalbe on off the lyving off the persecution off   125
the churche, and he shalbe soo hollye a man that the
angeles off God shall crowne hym and leyde hym with his
bretherne off his affinite to the hollye faithe. This
man alwey shall refforme all the worlde into better
lyving by his hollynes and good lyving into the furst   130
maner and forme of lyving as the disciples off Crist did,
and he shall reduce all men off Hollye Churche and
all they shall drede hym and followe hym for his
grett hollynes and vertues and he shall preche barefoted
euery where and he shall nott dred the power off princys   135
nor ther malice and he shall turne many men
from ther evyll errours and evyll lyving and spetiallye
he shall turne many Iues to the Cristen feithe.
Also our Lorde God shall ordeyn with hym an Imperour most hollyest whiche shalbe off all men ly-   140
ving and off the most holliest blode and off the Frenche
kinges blode and he shalbe ordined to helpe the pope and to
obaye hym in all his commandementes and shall reforme
the vniuersall worlde to the better. And this Imperour shall deliuer all Cristen peopple from ther ene-   145
myes as Almightye God deliuered Ionas from the
bellye of the whalle. Nowe vnder these twoo, that
is to saye the pope and the Imperour, all the worlde
shalbe gouerned and rulyde and soo then shall ceasse
the wrothe off God and then shalbe on faithe and on   150
lawe throughe the worlde and vnyte and peace betwy-
xte all men foreuermore vnto the cummyng
off Anticriste.

Anglia, Scotia, Flandria, Francia rege sub vno   155
fartilis inculta diues breuis absque tribuno
gaudet flet flevit fallit cum ducit ad vnum.

148–54 The prophecy ends with an apocalyptic view of the coming of Antichrist.

8. "When Rome Is Removed Into England"

COMMENTARY

"The Cock of the North," discussed above, is sometimes referred to as "The First Scottish Prophecy"; "When Rome Is Removed Into England" is at times labelled "The Second Scottish Prophecy." Developing symbols originally used by Geoffrey of Monmouth, the texts of this prophecy are amazingly varied. The two separate items included here are both representative versions of the prophecy, yet they are nothing alike.[34]

Like other prophecies we have seen, this one seems to have originated in the fourteenth century in response to ecclesiastical and social disputes. As the "second Scottish prophecy," it was obviously sympathetic to Scottish interests, but it is difficult to see the original intention in the two sixteenth-century versions discussed here.

The first version of "When Rome Is Removed" printed below is not at all difficult to understand in sixteenth-century terms, however. In fact, it is amazingly appropriate for the religious revolution of the 1530s, since Henry's claims to religious supremacy seem obviously to have "removed" the authority of Rome to England — in the words of the prophecy, the "popis power" had been taken "in hande" (l. 2). Both church and justice are "lawles." When all these disasters occur, the prophecy warns, in shattering anti-climax, "Than England take hede sone after."

The second version of the prophecy consists of prose and some very bad alliterative verse, and it purports to be a prediction for the year 6,508 (counting from the year of creation). Astrological references to the "tayle off the somertyme in his lappes" (ll. 3–4) and the "taylle off wynter" (l. 5) are intended to help fix the dating of the coming great war. The prophecy predicts a time of wickedness and falsehood, and it foretells the ultimate fall of England "within ij dayes off the feaste off Seynt Martyn" (11 November). The victorious enemies of England are figured as a lily and a lion who comes "to helpe a liones to bringe forthe hur briddes" (ll. 10–11). While there is no clue here to explain the lily or the lion, the lily is usually meant to stand for the king of France, while the lion, as we have repeatedly seen, refers to the king of Scotland.

The prophecy next addresses Berwick, the "true towne vppon Twede" that will remain loyal to "the king that is kynd heire" (l. 14) evidently the lion.

---

[34] On this prophecy, see Reinhard Haferkorn, *When Rome Is Removed Into England: Eine Politische Prophezeiung des 14.Jarhunderts* (Leipzig, 1932).

141

From this place those loyal to the "rightwes king" call upon their neighbors to condemn all traitors and to recognize the true king.

TEXT 1

When that Rome remeueth into England
And euery prest hath the popis power in hande
Bytwene xvij and oon whoo wyll vnderstande
Moche care and sorough shalbe brought into England.
When that the lambe is lowys that Holy Church kepyth   5
And cheyf covytes in theyr handes and lechery
And none spare oother but playn occur
The church lawles, iustes lawles
Knyghtes and knavys booth bee clothyd in a lyke clothinge
Godes fleshe and his blod ys sworne in euery mans heryng   10
Lordes and knightes bee made that neuer wane armys
Marchaunte strayngers beryth the rowme
Englishmen wot neuer howe for to goo but aftir
   oother landes fashyonys
And euery man fayne to begyle oother —
Than England take hede sone after.   15

3 The specifics of the dating indicated here, "Bytwene xvij and oon," are unclear.
5–14 These lines follow an "abuses of the age" formula.
    5 lowys from "lowis," an obsolete form of loose, meaning here unrestrained?
    7 occur ocker; usury

TEXT 2

From the making of the worlde vj mille v c and viij all this
shall begyn. Aftur the heght off the heyte the warre
shall begyn during to the tayle off the somertyme
in his lappes tyll aftur the heyte off the herwest bekinde
off the yeres to the taylle off wynter.   5

Wiked dedes shall vndoo and drawe them to light;
falsehede shall falle and vasels, and Ingelonde shalbe
ouer comyn with a newe victorye within ij dayes off
the feaste off Seynt Martyn. A lille and a lyon to geder
shall layne, come with ther grett names to helpe   10
a liones to bringe forthe hur briddes.

Buske you well, Berweke, in wordes thou be blithe,
thou true towne vppon Twede with towres soo faire,
thou shalt leyn with the king that is kynd heire.
All the burrowes therby with ther brode wallys   15
shall leyn with the olde lyon and lenge with hym for euer.

From the stremes off Twede to the stremys off Temmys,
this shall they calle vppon ther neghburs
to noye, to iuge, to deme, to hange and drawe,
all false commen trayto[r]s ther rightwes king to knowe,   20
by lieffe and by good lawe.

The title here echoes the Gospel of John.
1–2 Although the events described in the prophecy are said to occur in the 6,508th
year after creation, this does not seem to be of much help in dating the year of the
predictions. The traditional dating of creation was 3760 B.C. Ussher was to revise
the figure to 4004 B.C. Neither of these dates puts us in a likely year.
    2 *heght off the heyte* height of the heat
3–5 These are evidently astrological references intended to help fix the date of the
impending war.
9–11 The lily is a traditional symbol for the king of France (for the fleur-de-lis), and
the lion is a traditional designation for the king of Scotland. The identity of the
lioness is unknown.
    9 *the feaste of Seynt Martyn* 11 November
    10 *layne* lay
    11 *briddes* birds; young birds, or the young of any animal
12 *buske* prepare or ready (yourself)
14–16 Berwick is addressed as the *true towne* that will, evidently, be the refuge for a
deposed king and that will become the center of a movement to persuade traitors to
recognize their rightful king. The implication seems to be a Scottish king.
17 *the stremys off Temmys* may refer to the Thames; thus *From the stremes off Twede
to the stremys off Temmys* may be intended as "from one end of England to the other."
However, *Temmys* may also refer to the river Teme, near Ludlow Castle.

9. "A Prophecy by the Dice"

COMMENTARY

Prophecies that predict the future based on rolls of the dice are found in many manuscripts, the earliest texts dating from the fifteenth century. These are curious items, often, as in the first text printed below, accompanied by sketches of dice.

The prophecy seems somehow to identify the throws of the dice with the various estates. One fifteenth-century text glosses "ace" or one as "rex," "cater" or four as "domini," and "syse" or six as "vulgus." The number "sink" or five is glossed as "religious," or clerics, but probably more specifically meaning monastic clergy. Much less clearly, "dowse" or two signifies the "bilingue." This could literally mean those who speak two languages, but in a more figurative sense could mean those who are "double-tongued," and thus hypocritical. The cast of "trey" or three is glossed as "proditores," traitors or betrayers. In spite of the difficulty in understanding what exactly all the throws may mean, they seem to point to the victory of the people over the king.

Noteworthy in the two texts printed here are the references to the "newe parliament," particularly appropriate for the 1530s, and the familiar prediction of the rise of a dead man. Also significant is any prophecy that foresees the victory of the people over Henry and his government.

TEXT 1

Whan ⚅ ys the best caste of the dyesce
And oon beryth vppe ⚃
Then England ys paradysce;
But when ⚁ and ⚂ bee set a syde
The worde of ⚅ shall sprynge full wyde;   5
But when ⚁ put owte ⚂ then ys all shente,
For than we shall haue a newe parliament;
Yet ⚅ shall vppe and ⚀ shall vndre,
When dedde men ryese it shalbee greate wonder.
The lyon, the redrose, and the flower de luce,   10
The locke shall vndo ⚁ ,
Yet ⚅ shall bere the price
And ⚀ shall help therto.

TEXT 2

Syse is euer the best chaunce of the dyce.
When ace bereth vp syse, ther is Englend paradyse;
Butt ace wyll be vp and syse wyll bee vnder,
Then the dedd man shall ryse with grete wonder;
The lylly and the lyon the locke shall vndoo,   5
Than syse shall bere the pryce and ace shall help therto;
Butt when synk and cater bee putt asyde,
Then the name of syse shall spryng full wyde
And dowse putteth vnder trey then all is shent
Then shall wee haue a newe parlyament.   10

Text 1

1–3 Here England seems to be in its proper state (*paradysce*) when the King (*oon*) supports the people (the roll of six).

4–5 When true religion (represented as the rolls of four, the church, and five, clerics), is displaced, then it seems that the people are justified in their challenges to authority.

7 The reference is to a new parliament resulting from conflict between the king and the people, as well as to the actions of those who must be regarded as opportunists taking advantage of political and religious disputes.

8–13 These lines seem to predict the victory of the people, though at some cost.

Text 2 A prophecy of the dice that uses the numbers rather than the pictures of the dice. Though the lines are in slightly different order, the prophetic message seems similar to that of Text 1.

10. "A Prophecy by the Stars"

COMMENTARY

Always associated with "A Prophecy by the Dice," the short "A Prophecy by the Stars" also looks toward political changes. The text printed below is the most intelligible of the sixteenth-century versions, but it only sets a cosmic stage for change. The political changes to come (from a contemporary but impossibly garbled text) include the calling of a "false strong parlyament / That shall cause soo many frekes to bee shent," and "he that loketh after the apostelles place shall goo besyde." Further, "the egyll most nedes flye then ouer the mold." The piece ends with the hope that "this werr shall bee att an ende."[35]

TEXT

    The blacke shall bleed,
    The blewe shall haue his hed,
    The whyte and the blewe shall tourne all to oon,
    The sonne shall shyne [two] starres that styll stode,
    That callyd ys the fyxt shall moveable bee or none;   5
    The sonne, the moan, ouer the starres shall gone,
    That after shall neuer shyne nor keuer:
    And Iu[p]iter shall do this deed at Dover.

References to *blacke*, *blewe*, *white*, the *sonne*, *starres*, and the *moan* are all astrological.
4 *[two]* The manuscript has a sketch of a cast of a die: ⚁ .

35 The contemporary but nearly incomprehensible text is from British Library MS Lansdowne 762, fols. 96r and v. For further details, see Appendix.

CHAPTER FOUR

The Place of Political Prophecy in the 1530s

When John Dobson was investigated by Henry VIII's Council of the North in 1537, he admitted that the accusations of his parishioners were true — he had made the predictions he was accused of having made. But in admitting the charges, the vicar also offered an explanation of his actions. Dobson told his examiners that the prophecies he had repeated were not his own, that "*to his knowledge*" they were predictions that had been made by Merlin, Bede, and Thomas of Erceldoune, who had long foreseen the accomplishment of all the events "as is comphrehendid therein."[1] This is the only real defense Dobson offered the Council. If we are to come to terms with the place of prophecy in the developing crises of the 1530s, we must recognize that his somewhat curious defense of himself is crucial. Without understanding the significance of his claim, we will come no nearer to understanding how and why political prophecies were so dangerous.

As we have seen, cryptic and allusive "prophecies" like Dobson's had a long history. When our unfortunate vicar predicted that an eagle would "spread his winges ouer all this realme," he was quoting texts that had been known for centuries. Many of the images wielded as weapons in the 1530s — predictions that priests would bear arms or that babies would be cut out of their mothers' bellies, for example — had originated with Geoffrey of Monmouth.

Why were these well-worn images so potent? We might expect that a prophecy would be much more compelling if it were new or if its predictions were unique or unusual rather than reworked or recycled, but, contrary to our expectations, that simply is not the way political prophecies worked. New prophecies do appear, but revived versions of older texts are far more common, and even the "new" compositions include familiar symbols and long passages adapted from earlier pieces. Some "new" prophecies are really only *new* combinations of *old* texts. What made prophecies so appealing, in truth, was not their *originality* but their *familiarity*.

With such a long history, events "predicted" in these prophecies could not

---

[1] SP 1/127, fol. 64, italics added.

147

be dismissed as the ravings of a single disgruntled vicar, as only one example, or as the schemings of an individual aspirant to wealth or power or position. To the contrary, the political and religious crises of the present had been long foreseen. They had been predicted by men and women who had no possible personal interests in the difficulties and disaffections of the moment. Thus in the ancient character of prophecy lay their authority.

Of course it is possible to regard "prophesiers" like Dobson as cynical manipulators of the credulous, or to interpret the "defense" he offered as the desperately silly maneuver of a frightened man. To be sure, there were clever manipulators. Richard Jones, the Oxford scholar engaged in duping William Neville, clearly played his victim for a fool and just as clearly relished the game. And there were the desperate. Even at this distance, John Hale — "aged," "oblivious," "troubled by sickness" — is pitiful as he begs for forgiveness for having dabbled in prophecy. But we would be wrong to dismiss prophecies and prophesiers so summarily, for the records seem overwhelmingly to prove that most of the men and women investigated during the decade were neither cynical nor silly. They were serious about their predictions and convinced that their protests were sanctioned by a long prophetic tradition.

When John Dobson quoted prophecies he believed had originated in the visions of Merlin, Bede, and Thomas of Erceldoune, he must have been comforted by his conviction that the turmoil engulfing his country had been foretold, that, however difficult and confusing, the present was unfolding exactly as it should. But those like Dobson who resisted the political and religious revolutions of the King could not only find *comfort* for their fears but *justification* for their resistance. Henry *must* be confronted, his new order had to be challenged and overturned. Political prophecies offered authority for those like Dobson who opposed the King. They demanded this opposition, in fact.[2]

---

[2] On this, see again Chapter One, pp. 15–16, as well as Reeves and Thomas. Recall also R.W. Southern's words, ". . . prophecy was the most certain of all sources of historical information, and . . . it could provide an assured framework for the whole course of history. . . . [I]t was the only source of information about the future — information which was in itself absolutely certain, though obscure in its manner of presentation and needing careful investigation if its meaning was to be established" (pp. 159–60, quoted above, Chapter One, p. 16); see his complete essay on the significance of prophecy.

The sanction political prophecies gave to sixteenth-century resistance cannot be emphasized enough, and this is one of its unique features. It is quite distinct from the more general interest in medieval prophecy in this respect, as noted by Robert E. Lerner, for example: ". . . resort to prophecy was meant to provide edification and comfort, not inspiration for insurrection" ("The Black Death and Western European Eschatological Mentalities," p. 93).

In the explosive confrontation between royal prerogative and the individual conscience, prophecies thus were a support, even a mandate, for those who were determined to resist the power of the King and his government. But who were these opponents of royal authority? Surprising numbers of them are men who are far removed from questions of order and obedience and from the exercise of power and influence — they are prisoners in jail, travelers to and from market, tenant farmers, apprentice saddlers, innkeepers, provincial lawyers, and servants. Just as remarkable is the number of very ordinary women examined for their involvement in politically oriented comment, action, and reaction. Those who were more commonly voiceless — those outside the sphere of power, prestige, and influence of the court — found, in prophecy, a potent political voice. And only by our recognition of the significance of political prophecy will we be able to hear those voices — voices usually unheard in scholarly discussions of the exercise of Tudor royal authority.

Joining these voices in a strange new alliance are those who had formerly been an intimate part of the political and religious establishment. The state papers testify to the strong resistance of parish vicars, local parsons, priests, and chaplains, as well as of religious institutions, represented by priors, abbots, canons, monks, and friars who suddenly found themselves cut away from their traditional place in the social order. The religious no longer occupied their privileged place in the power establishment. Having lost their official voice, they joined the dissident voices of men and women who had always been outside the ruling culture.

John Dobson's use of prophecy as a challenge to Henry's authority was enough to result in his conviction and execution for treason. For those who challenged royal power in a more direct way, those like Edward Stafford, Rhys ap Griffith, or Edward Neville — in other words those whose birth and blood might be seen to offer a more familiar kind of threat to the throne — prophecy could also be a potent weapon. All three men wielded prophecy in their own interests. In addition to whatever overt or covert challenges these men might (or might not) have offered the King's power and authority, the government recognized the danger in their use of political prophecies. Prophecies were a part of each man's prosecution. At every opportunity, Henry's government thus warned those who opposed the government that their prophetic weapons would be turned against them.

These three cases are important because they remind us that prophecies were still consulted by the wealthy and powerful, just as they always had been. Very intriguing evidence of this influence is offered by a brief inscription in a sixteenth-century hand appended to a small fourteenth-century manuscript.[3] The book itself is a compilation of history and prophecy. It

[3] Lambeth Palace Library MS 527, 68 folios measuring 7⅞″ by 4½″. For a full list of the manuscript's contents, see M.R. James, *A Descriptive Catalogue of the*

begins with a lengthy chronicle occupying the first half of the book, a Latin history through Edward I containing numerous references to the prophecies of Merlin. The second item in the collection is a long Latin prophecy, the third a long extract from Geoffrey's Latin prophecies of Merlin. Several other brief prophecies are included as well. At the bottom of the manuscript's last folio is the crucial inscription: "Ex dono amicissimi mei Thomae More generosi et honestissimi viri. Daniel Gray."[4] The attribution is certainly no proof of the manuscript's provenance. Even if the book was, at one time, in More's possession, it may have come into his hands at some point in his official capacity. Still, it is interesting to speculate about when and how the collection might have come to More's attention and about why the lord chancellor might have kept it and then passed it on to Gray. We cannot answer these questions, but clearly prophecies may have had some place even inside the sphere of the court. That Henry's own lord chancellor might have had a collection of prophecies is still more evidence of how widespread was their influence, and we are left to speculate about the place of these predictions in More's own stand against royal authority. And in More's collecting and then passing along such a book of political and religious prophecy, we may see the same kind of process that the Council uncovered in Dobson's case, though on a more discrete and learned scale, of course.

The state papers show that resistance to the government's authority was thus widespread and strongly felt among all those outside the government's established order. Those at both the highest and lowest social levels actively and strongly challenged the government's new order.[5] Yet political prophecies also appealed to those still *inside*, caught within the Tudor revolution. The single most carefully compiled collection of prophecies surviving from the decade belonged to Humphrey Welles, of Hoar Cross, Staffordshire, a modestly successful, upwardly mobile government administrator who bettered himself considerably during Henry's reign, studying the law, marrying well, gaining a post in the King's government in 1538 at Cromwell's recommendation, finding powerful patrons in the Stafford family, and eventually, in 1545, becoming a member of parliament.[6] Welles kept his place as well as his

---

Manuscripts in the Library of Lambeth Palace (Cambridge, 1932), pp. 725–27. I am indebted to the Hill Monastic Library for making available to me photocopies of the manuscript.

[4] A library stamp obscures the name, suggested with a question by James, p. 727.

[5] The best account of this resistance is Elton's *Policy and Police*.

[6] For the details of Welles's biography, see Stanley T. Bindoff, *History of the Houses of Parliament: The House of Commons, 1509–1558* (London, 1982), 3, 573–74. On Welles's book (Bodl. Libr. MS Rawlinson C.813), see Appendix, pp. 57–58 and, more completely, Sharon L. Jansen and Kathleen H. Jordan, eds., *The Welles Anthology (Bodleian Library MS Rawlinson C.813): A Critical Edition* (Binghamton, New York, 1990).

head despite his evident Catholicism, at the same time collecting and transcribing five pro-Catholic, anti-government prophecies during the decade of
the 1530s. Welles's book contains "The Prophecies of Rhymer, Bede, and
Merlin," "The Marvels of Merlin," The Prophecy of the Lion, the Lily, and
the Son of Man," "A Prophecy of a New World Emperor," and "When Rome
is Removed into England."

Still, Welles managed to steer his course safely through the turmoil of the
time — despite his personal connections, his political convictions, and his
religious preference, he survived and even prospered where men like Dobson
and the duke of Buckingham did not. Welles must have kept his interest in
prophecy private while Dobson made his convictions public and while more
prominent men like Stafford used prophecies to further their own interests.
Welles's own connections to the Stafford family must have placed him under
some ongoing suspicion if not in outright danger, and his Catholicism must
have been fairly well known. Nevertheless, he was awarded a clerkship of the
summons before Henry's death, and in 1564, under Elizabeth, he was restored
to the Staffordshire bench, recommended by his bishop to the Queen's Privy
Council as "meet to continue in office; accounted of good men an adversary
of religion and no favourer thereof neither in deed nor word, but better
learned than the rest."[7]

Despite his personal yet obviously private opposition to Henry and in spite
of his spiritual convictions, he seems to have come to terms with the uneasy
religious compromise of Elizabeth's reign, since he continued in public office
and acknowledged the Queen in his will as "defender of the faythe."[8] Perhaps
Welles's career illustrates the government's tolerance of personal convictions
as long as they were kept private, and, maybe more important, a practical
Tudor acceptance of those who proved themselves useful in government
service, as Welles must obviously have done.

We cannot forget the government's own use of prophecy in our evaluation
of the place of prophecy in the conflicts of the period. Having confronted the
influence and subversive power of prophecy again and again in his investigations of dissatisfaction, protest, and rebellion, Cromwell himself finally resorted to a counter-attack in prophetic terms. Although he made no use of

[7] Quoted by Thomas Pape, *Newcastle-under-Lyme in Tudor and Early Stuart Times*
(Manchester, 1938), p. 38.
  The records of Welles's career under Edward are silent. Welles was accused of
having helped to disrupt a shire election for Mary's first parliament, trying unsuccess-
fully to have Sir Henry Stafford elected. In March 1557 he was appointed the clerk
of the mint at the Tower.
[8] A debt of gratitude is owned to my friend and colleague Kathleen H. Jordan for
having acquired a copy of Welles's will, which we transcribed together one pleasant
spring afternoon. Dr. Jordan received a copy of the will from the Lichfield Joint
Record Office, Public Library, Lichfield, to whom I extend my appreciation as well.

Thomas Gibson's reinterpreted version of "The Sayings of the Prophets," he did employ Richard Morison to author the government's prophetic efforts.[9]

Given the authority and sanction offered by prophecies originating in the predictions of Merlin and Bede, Morison's retreat in prophetic tradition makes sense. If those protesting the government's power and authority looked to Merlin or Becket or Thomas of Erceldoune for support and justification, Henry's government would go back yet farther, finding even stronger support for their own prophecies. And thus Morison's description of his prophetic text, "not lately commen out of wales, but founde in scripture, in the iiii. boke of Esdras."[10] Morison's reference to the prophecy "lately come from Wales" might be a reference to specific prophecies like the one circulated in support of Rhys ap Griffith, which the prisoners in the Ilchester jail had heard and believed, but it must also have been intended in a much more determined way to undercut Geoffrey's prophecies of Merlin. In terms of biblical time, Geoffrey's prophecies *were* "but lately" known and thus, however enduring and surprisingly credible, nowhere near as important or valid as those with scriptural authority. And so the government entered the prophetic game on prophecy's own terms.

In his recent brief overview of "Prophecies and Politics in the Reign of Henry VIII," Alistair Fox comments on the influence of political prophecy, concluding that a "profitable analogy might be drawn with those who read horoscopes in modern newspapers: few but the most credulous readers would actually believe that what they read might be literally enacted, but they derive satisfaction from discovering patterns that answer to their desires or fears. In Henrician England this happened on a vast and communal scale, which is why we cannot afford to ignore the prophecies."[11] I agree with Fox's reckoning of the "vast and communal" scale of the protest, but I think we miss the point entirely if we compare the appeal of prophecies to current newspaper horoscopes. People consult horoscopes desultorily, out of idle curiosity, perhaps for some *personal* relevance, not seriously for answers to crucial political and religious questions.[12] To reduce prophecies to the level of horoscopes is to misunderstand them entirely.

To misunderstand the real power of political prophecies is to deny their

9 See Chapter Two, pp. 57–60.
10 *An exhortation to styrre all Englyshemen*, D.iv. verso.
11 P. 91. As mentioned before, Fox's work seems based almost exclusively on secondary sources, particularly Taylor, Dodds, and Elton (*Policy and Police*), and the abstracts of the state papers in *LP*. The original documents make the seriousness of the prophecies more clear.
12 I may have to rethink these comments considering recent revelations about Nancy Reagan's manipulations of President Ronald Reagan after consulting a personal astrologer!

place in the Tudor revolution of the 1530s. At stake were not only problems of succession and of religious reformation, but the much more fundamental and ultimately more serious problem of order and obedience. At issue were questions of authority, of legitimate power and its exercise, and of the right — or duty — of resistance to power used or abused. Political prophecies challenged the government's answers to these questions. They were a serious part of this public debate, part of the popular resistance to royal power and of the negotiations to settle the confrontation. Prophecy offered a legitimacy to resistance. That the government itself, after long pursuit of the source of prophecies and tireless prosecution of "prophets," eventually resorted to a campaign of counter-prophecy is a remarkable comment on the contemporary assessment of the value and potency of such predictions. I would argue that a crucial role in the confrontations and negotiations of the decade is assumed by political prophecy — by the power and authority inherent in its poetry and tradition.

Most significant is the way political prophecy was recognized and used as a subversive tool by those determined to resist the reformations of King and parliament. In earlier times, prophecy had been used quite differently.

Geoffrey of Monmouth's prophecies had been written in Latin for an educated and influential audience, while Giraldus Cambrensis' interest in prophecies had been encouraged by Henry II.[13] During Edward I's reign, prophecy had been used to justify war with Scotland.[14] Political prophecies like "Adam Davy's Dreams" and "The Prophecy of the Eagle and the Hermit" had been addressed to Edward II to inspire him to renew wars with Scotland and even to undertake a continental crusade.[15] Under Edward III, political prophecies were inspired by the war against France and forecast his ultimate conquest of all Christendom.[16] Richard II's deposition had inspired many prophecies; John of Bridlington's prophecy had been interpreted as support for Henry IV, while the later "Six Kings" had been used against him in the Percy-Glendower rebellion.[17] Even more explicit poetry of social protest,

[13] On Geoffrey's audience and interests, see John J. Parry and Robert A. Caldwell, "Geoffrey of Monmouth" in Arthurian Literature in the Middle Ages, ed. Roger S. Loomis (Oxford, 1959), pp. 72–93; see also Taylor on both Geoffrey and Giraldus.

[14] See, for example, John Taylor, English Historical Literature, p. 149.

[15] See Taylor, pp. 92–99; John Taylor, pp. 246–47; J.R.S. Phillips, "Edward II and the Prophets," pp. 189–201; and V.J. Scattergood, "Adam Davy's 'Dreams' and Edward II," Archiv für das Studium der Neueren Sprachen, 206 (1970), 253–60, for example.

[16] See Taylor, pp. 58–62 and 82; John Taylor, pp. 241 and 247–48; and Michael J. Curley, "The Cloak of Anonymity and 'The Prophecy of John of Bridlington,'" p. 361.

[17] See Taylor, pp. 48–51, 87; Allan, pp. 185–86 and 99–100; and Curley, especially pp. 361 and 364. For a fairly detailed discussion of Henry IV's use of

while sympathetic to the "grievances and attitudes" of the common people, seems to have been written by and for a fairly restricted audience.[18]

By the mid fifteenth century, prophecy had become part of a wider campaign of propaganda.[19] It was used quite deliberately in the political rivalries of both York and Lancaster. Prophecy was employed by the "politically aware," particularly by Edward IV and his supporters, to vindicate Yorkist claims to the throne. What is interesting is that prophecies were used by the Yorkist kings, Edward IV and Richard III, to influence public opinion. Lancastrian prophecies do survive, but the overwhelming number of prophecies from the period are Yorkist — the responses of usurping governments during periods of political tension and rebellion. Prophecies support their claims of legitimacy among those whose support was crucial — "the nobility and gentry, and the increasingly educated commercial classes," as one recent scholar indicates.[20]

But the fifteenth century began to witness a new element in its divisions, instances where prophecy was not used as royal flattery or government propaganda but as protest against royal authority.[21] By the 1530s, this trickle of protest had become a flood. Prophecy was no longer a tool to make or control popular opinion. It had been appropriated as a source of power and authority for popular protest.[22] Its poetry became a persuasive popular discourse that challenged the official language of proclamation and statute.

prophecy, see Caroline D. Eckhardt, "Prophecy and Nostalgia: Arthurian Symbolism at the Close of the English Middle Ages," in The Arthurian Tradition: Essays in Convergence, ed. Mary Flowers Braswell and John Bugge (Tuscaloosa, Alabama, 1988), pp. 115–16.

[18] See John Taylor, p. 237 and J.R. Maddicott, "Poems of Social Protest in Early Fourteenth-Century England" in Ormrod, pp. 130–42, especially pp. 133–34.

[19] See Alison Allan, "Yorkist Propaganda" and Charles Ross, "Rumour, Propaganda and Popular Opinion."

On the "restricted audience" of these texts, see especially Allan, pp. 188–89. For the larger subject of political poetry in the fifteenth century, see Scattergood, Politics and Poetry, especially Chapter 10 ("English Society III: Verses of Protest and Revolt").

[20] See Allan, pp. 179 and 189; Eckhardt, pp. 116–17; and Gransden, "Propaganda in Middle English Historiography," Journal of Medieval History, 1 (1975), 363–81.

[21] See Chapter 1, pp. 18–19; for more detail, see Ross, particularly the examples he cites on pp. 16, 19–20, and 21–22.

[22] I have argued here that the ancient tradition of prophecy gave it a kind of "higher authority" than that of King and parliament. An interesting parallel appears in V.G. Kiernan's essay "The Covenanters: A Problem of Creed and Class," an analysis of Scots resistance to England during the seventeenth century:

> Most of the resisters [to King and re-established episcopacy after the Restoration] came from a downtrodden mass exploited since time out of mind by superiors against whom they had never attempted to rise. For

Only two decades after the social contest of the 1530s, Henry's daughter would find her person and her policy the subject of violent and ugly political prophecy. The texts again challenge the authority of royal power and religious reformation — but this time, their opposition is to the Queen's *Catholicism*. The texts themselves remain virtually unchanged, but the historical moment changes, and prophecies are simply reinterpreted — their *meanings*, not their words, change. This is most clearly illustrated by "The Marvels of Merlin," surviving now in eight versions, one from the fifteenth century, three from the decade of the 1530s, and four from Mary's reign.[23] "The Marvels" is marvelously adaptable, useful during the Lancastrian-Yorkist civil wars, revived under Henry to protest the government's religious reformation, then used again in Protestant protest against Mary's efforts to return to the religion it had once been used to support. Thus prophecies may provide intriguing evidence of the complicated interplay of text and context, of the way different readers find different meanings in the same complex, highly metaphoric texts.[24]

My own interest in these texts lies in the intersection of literature and history. As historical documents, they have been largely ignored, primarily because they are figurative and *literary*.[25] They're not solid "evidence," not *factual*. As literature, they have been ignored or dismissed, not only because they are cryptic and political but because they have seem to have such little literary "merit." Whatever value they had when they were created by Geoffrey of Monmouth has been de-valued by their popular re-creation and

them to rise up now and challenge authority was an immense feat in itself. They could only achieve it by having another, higher authority to look to; by virtue of firm conviction that God, through accredited representatives and the words of scripture, commanded them so to act. They were exchanging one obedience for another. As for the meaning of what they were bidden to do, God's intentions were inscrutable. For men and women haunted by fear of damnation, to defy earthly penalties by joining in prayer on a wild moor might be the most potent reassurance (p. 52).

The essay is from his collection *Poets, Politics and the People*, ed. Harvey J. Kaye (London, 1989).

[23] On these versions, see Appendix, pp. 165–66.

[24] Thus political prophecies may be an as yet unexamined part of twentieth-century theoretical debates about discourse theory, the social construction of meaning, and "semantic openendedness." My own sense is that their singular and deliberate ambiguity would contribute enormously to such theoretical and philosophical analysis.

[25] The one extensive and considered treatment of prophecy by a historian is Elton's *Policy and Police*, where cases involving prophecy, as well as rumors and magic, are examined in the context of reaction to the Tudor reformation.

transmission.[26] I would argue that we need to come to terms with the place of prophecy — its historical force and value as well as its literary appeal and merit. The literary text played a significant role in political events. Clearly poetry was regarded as a vital force in public debate.

It is also important to recognize the place of prophecy in the political and religious turmoil engulfing all of western Europe during the sixteenth century. Political prophecies, as well as dreams, apocalyptic visions, divination, magic, and astrological predictions flourished, used as ways of finding comfort and guidance in the century's confusion and oppositions. Yet they were also more than a means of finding solace. In this period of religious strife, political confrontation, international conflict, and almost overwhelming confusion and uncertainty, such prophecies and predictions became sources of real power and challenge to established authority. Increasingly, modern scholars are beginning to explore these documents, which too long have been ignored, for the new light they shed on the conflicts of the Renaissance.[27]

[26] Here, for example, is R.H. Robbins on the literary merits of political prophecy: "Of all the political poems, the prophecies are at once the most political and the least poetic. . . . many of them . . . are such doggerel that they lack interest even as *literaria curiosa* ("Political Prophecies," p. 1516), and "The majority of the prophecies are badly written and garbled, often the lines are gibberish, and numerous lines are transferred from one prophecy to another. Often the political message of the prophecy is confused in a welter of unnecessarily obscure references" (p. 1533).

[27] New works focusing on the role of prophecy in the vision in the sixteenth century have recently appeared, and their titles indicate something of the kinds of challenge these popular forms offered. See, for example, Richard L. Kagan's *Lucrecia's Dreams: Politics and Prophecy in Sixteenth-Century Spain* (Berkeley, 1990); Ottavia Niccoli, *Prophecy and People in Renaissance Italy*, trans. Lydia G. Cochrane (Princeton, 1990); and Ronald E. Surtz, *The Guitar of God: Gender, Power, and Authority in the Visionary World of Mother Juana de la Cruz (1481–1534)* (Philadelphia, 1990).

APPENDIX

Manuscript Sources and Textual Variations

Surprisingly few political prophecies have been published, perhaps because so few readers now are actually looking *for* or *at* them. Most often, unsuspecting scholars stumble across them while they are searching for something quite different. A political prophecy might be found scribbled on the flyleaf of a volume or added in the blank space left on a folio long after something else had been transcribed. The text of a prophecy might now be found in a volume otherwise full of love lyrics, or it may appear in a commonplace book among assorted memoranda, notes, and records. Under such circumstances, the prophecies have been generally disregarded.

Perhaps the best illustration of the treatment — or mistreatment — of the prophecies is the case of an anthology compiled by Humphrey Welles in the late 1530s.[1] Welles's collection has long been recognized as one of the very few manuscript sources of late Middle English lyric poetry. The fifty-one lyrics collected by Welles and copied onto the first seventy-odd folios of his anthology were published by F.M. Padelford and A.R. Benham in 1908.[2] Since then, many of these lyrics have been reprinted, anthologized, and analyzed in detail. In his introduction to the lyrics, Padelford did mention that the manuscript contained prophecies, but neither he nor anyone else took the time to transcribe them or even to examine them in any detail. Yet about one quarter of Welles's volume was devoted to political prophecy — he collected six texts, copied onto the last twenty-four folios of the volume.

These prophecies and their careful placement in the manuscript are certainly as remarkable as the lyrics preserved there. Just as he accumulated an anthology of love lyrics, Welles also gathered a representative sampling of current political prophecies. With the exception of "The Cock of the North," he had all the most significant texts, and we might quite well have proceeded in our study with only the prophecies preserved in his anthology.

---

[1] Now Bodleian Library MS Rawlinson C.813. See Chapter Four, pp. 150–51 and nn. 6–8 for details of Welles's career. On Welles's compilation of the anthology, see Sharon L. Jansen and Kathy H. Jordan, eds., *The Welles Anthology*.

[2] "Liedersammlungen des xvi. Jarhunderts, besonders aux der Zeit Heinrichs VIII," *Anglia*, 31 (1908), 303–97.

While modern readers have, until now, paid little attention to the prophecies Welles collected, earlier readers had quite a different view of their value. At some time during the seventeenth century, Welles's anthology was bound together with a second manuscript. This later collection of some sixty folios is filled completely with political prophecy, beginning with a version of "The Marvels of Merlin," a text that Welles had earlier copied into his anthology. It now seems as if some later reader or owner of the two manuscripts shared Welles's interest in political prophecy and, appreciating the similarity in the contents of the two volumes, combined them. As the composite manuscript is now bound, fully half of its 167 folios are filled with political prophecies.

A second manuscript, now held by the British Library and catalogued as Lansdowne 762, was being filled at about the same time Welles was compiling his anthology. Though transcribed during the 1530s, this volume is very different from the Welles collection.[3] Lansdowne 762 is a commonplace book, its ninety-nine folios filled with a wide variety of items.[4] The contents include practical pieces of information (such as notes of land measurement and a method of calculating the height of a church steeple), historical notes ("a certeyn letter the which King Henry the V.th sente to the King of Fraunce" and a table of the kings of England, their reigns, and their places of burial, for example), financial memoranda (for instance a bill for mason's work), medical recipes, advice for removing stains, Latin epitaphs, various other Latin pieces, including Latin prophecies, and quite a number of political prophecies. There are no lyrics, but the compiler does include a romance in the collection. Interestingly, the unknown compiler had access to John Skelton's poetry. An extract from "Collyn Clout" appears in the manuscript, titled there "The profecy of Skelton." Humphrey Welles also had access to Skelton's poetry. He included an extract from "Why come ye nat to court?" in his anthology.

Virtually nothing is known about the original collector of this volume except that, like Welles, he had London connections. The collection begins

---

[3] The Lansdowne catalogue (*Catalogus Librorum Manuscriptorum Bibliothecae Lansdownianae* [London, 1819], p. 168) says the volume was written "about the time of Henry VIII." Robbins, in his section on "Political Prophecies" in the *Manual*, gives the dates 1520–40, while Madeleine and Ruth Dodds, *The Pilgrimage of Grace*, 1, 82, narrow the date to the 1530s.

[4] The manuscript's foliation as indicated in the catalogue is flawed, indicating 106 folios. For a recent accurate collation, see the description of the manuscript in Linne R. Mooney, "Practical Didactic Works in Middle English: Edition and Analysis of the Class of Short Middle English Works Containing Useful Information," Diss. University of Toronto 1981, pp. 498–99. Professor Mooney has also generously provided me with her own handwritten notes on the structure of the manuscript for which I here express my thanks.

with a copy of the testament of "Johannes de Sharne," who is described as the rector of "Northemaston." The testament gives his date of birth as 1453. Several other names appear on flyleaves, including "Edmundus Goodwin" and "Est liber mei henrici Rowet[?]." The manuscript contains several items particularly related to London, such as the poem "An honour to london" and the item "This ys conteyned in the bulles of Pope Nicholas purchased by the Curattes of the Citie of london for offerynges of all the mensions within the said Citie of london or suburbes of the same." The contents also show an interest in ecclesiastical matters of various sorts, including a list of "the vij fridays in the yere the which be good for to faste," a note on the different sorts of friars in London, and the "vij speciall interrogacions the which a Curat ought to aske euery cristen person that lieth in the extremytie of deth," for example. Among these items is a copy of the fourteenth-century Latin prophecy of John of Bassigny and a prophecy attributed to "Johannes de Rupella," probably a corruption of John of Rupescissa, a fourteenth-century Franciscan visionary. It may well be that the collectors of this commonplace book were somehow connected with the Church, clerics of some sort in the metropolitan area.[5]

These two manuscripts, along with the prophecies in the state papers, are the most important sources of political prophecies popular during the 1530s. Robbins dated the Welles anthology between 1530 and 1540, but when the evidence of the prophecies is considered, it is possible to narrow that date. The process of compiling the lyrics probably began around 1520 or 1522, but the methods of transcription and the references in the prophecies indicate the actual copying of the collection was begun and completed about the year 1535.[6] Robbins dated Lansdowne 762 between 1500 and 1540. As a commonplace book, it was clearly filled over a number of years: the manuscript contains a table of the kings of England, for instance, with the list only

---

[5] On the manuscript's London provenance, see also R.A.B. Mynors, *Catalogue of the Manuscripts of Balliol College, Oxford* (Oxford, 1963), p. 353. I am also indebted to Professor Robert E. Lerner for his correspondence containing speculations about the compilers of the manuscript: ". . . it seems to me that the presence of the Bassigny prophecy therein (however corrupt) suggests that the compilers had access to a fairly wide range of earlier prophetic texts, plausibly from a monastic library. . . . I think that the Joh. de Rupella cited on 58r, bottom, is probably John of Rupescissa, O.F.M. — could the compilers have been monks or friars themselves?" (The manuscript also contains a note on the kinds of friars to be found in London.) Professor Lerner's comments are from a personal letter, 10 May 1990; for his original work with the texts of Bassigny and Rupescissa, see his "The Black Death," pp. 77–105.

Yet another interesting connection between the Lansdowne collection and Welles's book is the Bassigny text, a Latin version in the Lansdowne commonplace book and a heretofore unrecognized English translation in Welles's anthology.

[6] S.L. Jansen [Jaech], "English Political Prophecy and the Dating of MS Rawlinson C.813."

through Henry VII, while one of the bills included toward the end of the book is dated 1569. But once the prophecies within the collection have been read and considered, it becomes obvious they were transcribed during the 1530s, just about the time Welles's anthology was being copied.

Other manuscripts also contain prophecies from the same decade. Robbins's index in the *Manual* includes a prophecy from Bodleian Library MS Rawlinson D.1062, and he indicated the text belongs to the sixteenth century. Robbins was surely relying on the Bodleian catalogue which, in its description, dated the manuscript "saecc. xvi, xvii."[7] According to the catalogue, Rawlinson D.1062 contains "miscellaneous historical tracts in various hands," which is correct, as far as it goes. The manuscript is a composite volume, containing items transcribed on different sizes of paper, with different margins and ruling, by various hands, and of varying date, now bound together. The first item in this somewhat bewildering volume is "An Apologie of the Earle of Essex, against those which falsly and maliciously takes him to be the only hinderaunce of the peace and quiet of this countrie, 1599." This is followed by "An Admonition and Counsell or Information for the Lowe Countreys," dated 1578. The catalogue also lists several political prophecies. When we move from the catalogue to the texts themselves, we can see that at least one of the prophecies in the manuscript refers to events from the 1530s.

The same kind of examination of BL MS Cotton Vespasian E.vii reveals another item of interest. In his indexing, Robbins indicated that the manuscript should be dated between 1460 and 1480. The volume contains a chronicle from Adam to the year 2098, a table of descent for Richard, duke of York, from Brutus, assorted astronomical tables, some Latin prophecies, and, according to the British Library catalogue, "Several modern prophecies, in English and Latin verse."[8] Added to the end of this fifteenth-century volume, these "modern" prophecies include several brief texts in sixteenth-century hands, two of which seem to belong to the early 1530s.

A similar addition is found in BL MS Harley 2338, where a prophecy for the year 1536 has been copied on the last folio of a small fifteenth-century volume containing a long poem "upon our blessed Savior."[9] Although the prophecy is described in the Harley catalogue as "silly and imperfect," its date is clear, and it is indexed specifically, with incipit, in the Harley index.

Index and catalogue thus are not always specific or correct about dating political prophecies, but texts of political prophecies often are not noted in catalogue indexes at all, or, as in the case of BL MS Cotton Vespasian E.vii,

[7]   W.D. Macray, *Catalogi Codicum Manuscriptorum Bibliothecae Bodleianae, Partis Quintae, Fasciculus Quartus* (Oxford, 1898), p. 266.
[8]   *A Catalogue of Manuscripts in the Cottonian Library*, 2 (London, 1802), 480.
[9]   *A Catalogue of the Harleian Manuscripts*, 2 (London, 1808), 658.

separate items are simply listed as a group, as "several prophecies." Perhaps the best — or worst — example of this problem is BL MS Sloane 2578, a volume filled completely with political prophecies. The only printed index to the collection lists just five separate items, all appearing on the first seventeen folios.[10] Folios 18 through 111 have been lumped together and indexed simply as "Miscellaneous prophecies." The unpublished catalogue in the Student's Room of the British Library is little better, listing under the heading "Prophecies relative to events in English History, written in verse and prose," only nine items. This late sixteenth-century collection actually contains over seventy separate political prophecies.[11] Texts of political prophecies are thus most often discovered only when the covers of individual volumes are opened and the contents of each and every folio examined.

What I have collected in the present study is a representative body of the political prophecies that survive from the 1530s. More texts could have been printed, but the prophecies here seem to have been the more popular ones. I have tried to include a variety — poetry and prose, those more and less obscure, Galfridian and Sibyllic, as well as those "by the dice" and "by the stars." Most of all, I have tried to locate the texts mentioned in the trials and examinations recorded in the state papers and account for them here.

While examples of all the *texts* quoted in the state papers do survive, I have found no examples of "painted prophecies," however. Several of the cases we have examined involved prophetic pictures — of a baby with "axes and butchers knyves," for example, or of "twoo monkes paynted a-rowe, one vnder another hedlesse." William Todd described pictures like these when he was implicated for his part in Bigod's rebellion. Less gruesome references to painted prophecies were made by William Harlock, whose "calendar" contained prophetic pictures of heraldic coats of arms, and by Mistress Amadas, who simply referred to her scroll containing "painted and written" prophecies.

Prophetic manuscripts may certainly be illustrated. Bodleian Library MS 623, for example, contains diagrams. This prophetic anthology is a collection of Yorkist prophecies compiled in London about 1465. Along with prophecies attributed to Bede and the Sibyl, among others, it contains a diagram of Edward IV's descent (fol. 14v/22v), genealogical tables for the descent of Adam (fols. 29v/37v–30r/38r), a chronology of the world with prophetic diagrams and annotations (see fol. 55v/63v for example), and

[10] H.L.D. Ward, *Catalogue of Romances . . . in the British Museum*, 1 (London, 1883), 333–34.

[11] *Catalogus Librorum Manuscriptorum Bibliothecae Sloanianae* (unpublished), Vols. 2497–2719, pp. 219–221 (bound out of order, 219, 217, 222, 220, 221).

For a description of the manuscript and a list of its contents, see S.L. Jansen [Jaech], "British Library MS Sloane 2578 and Popular Unrest in England, 1554–1556," pp. 3–41.

circular diagrams of Edward IV and Henry VI in a prophetic context (fols. 63r/71r–63v/71v).

British Library MS Arundel 286 also contains an interesting illustrated text. The manuscript is described in the *Catalogus Librorum Manuscriptorum Bibliothecae Arundelianae* (London, 1840) as a fifteenth-century book, but the picture and prophecy are later additions: "An illumination representing a man in a close blue dress with a fur cap on his head, and holding a roll of paper in his hand; round this figure are some lines intended as a prophecy, with the date of 1573, about which time they seem to have been written" (p. 286). The well-dressed, bearded figure is actually pointing to the scroll he holds. The prophecy surrounding the illustration begins, in typically obscure prophetic fashion, "Wan iiij lightes begines to shine; withe viij to iiij wth xij be iuste." Since it goes on to mention "[when] maiden queene, a lande doo holde," it most likely belongs, as the date indicates, to Elizabeth's reign.

Still, neither logically plotted diagrams nor well-dressed men pointing sedately to rolls of paper is the kind of horrific prophetic picture described above. Such bloody subjects as babies with knives and headless monks seem not to have survived.[12]

Many of the depositions of the men and women questioned about political prophecies refer also to "scrolls" or "rolls." William Todd's pictures were painted on "a rolle in parchement," for example, while Mistress Amadas claimed to have a "rowyll wherein is payntyd and wryten all her profecyes." John Borobie, examined in the case of John Dobson, had explained how he had come to collect the items on his own scroll of prophecies, a scroll he had loaned to Dobson. I have found no sixteenth-century scrolls or rolls, but two of such collections survive from the fifteenth century.

Bodleian Library MS Ashmole Roll 26 is a long vellum roll that shows a genealogical line of descent for Edward IV from Adam. Along the right-hand side of this pedigree are references to Bridlington. At the end of the roll is a circle containing the names of Edward IV and his children, around which are references to Bridlington as well as to Gildas and Bede, to both of whom various political prophecies were ascribed. On the back of the Ashmole roll are extracts from Bridlington, Merlin, the Sibyl, and Becket. British Library MS Cotton Roll ii.23 is also a long scroll. The unpublished Catalogue of Cotton Charters and Rolls lists its contents, most of which are political verses or historical notes referring to events taking place between 1447 and 1452 and documenting the growth of opposition to Henry VI and support for

---

[12] A prophetic picture of a headless queen seems at one point to have come into Queen Anne's possession. The story of the incident and Anne's reaction is a late and possibly apocryphal recounting found in George Wyatt, "The Life of Queen Anne Boleigne," in *The Life of Cardinal Wolsey by George Cavendish*, ed. S.W. Singer (1827), pp. 429–30, summarized in Ives, pp. 178–79.

the Yorkist cause.[13] Among its contents are several political prophecies. Both of these scrolls have been carefully transcribed, annotated, and, though showing signs of wear on their outer rolls, preserved.

Mistress Amadas does not describe the roll she owned, but, since she claimed to have studied the prophecies on it for twenty years, it could well have been compiled in the fifteenth century and could thus have been very like the Cotton and Ashmole collections. Borobie's roll, and the other scrolls loaned and borrowed during the "commotion" of the Pilgrimage of Grace, would seem to be quite different, however. Borobie explained how such scrolls passed from hand to hand, and he described how he had extracted "clauses" from various sources and copied them onto his own roll. This piecemeal borrowing and transcribing would not lend itself to the kind of planning and diagramming that the Ashmole roll displays, nor to the fairly careful execution of the lengthy Cotton roll, 5¼" by 12' 6", the contents of which do seem to have been accumulated over a period of years, however. Borobie's scroll, and the others referred to in the examinations of the 1530s, were brief. Borobie says his was only "ij shetes of paper," while others are usually described as "little" rolls. Clearly, these rolls were ephemeral documents — easy to collect and to add to, just as easy to carry around, but not intended to be preserved forever.[14] Oddly enough, the prophetic illustration in BL MS Arundel 286, described above, *shows* just such a scroll — the man dressed in blue, encircled by prophetic lines, points to a rolled up sheet or two of what may very well be prophetic verses.

In pictures and words, in a scroll, a small quire, or a larger book, in a carefully compiled manuscript or on a disposable roll — these were the ways prophecies were collected and shared, preserved and used. What follows are bibliographic details of the ten texts included in this study.

1. *"The Prophecies of Rhymer, Bede, and Merlin"*

Supplement 3889.5, *Manual* V.291.

"The Prophecies" now exists complete in just two manuscript sources: one in Bodl. Libr. MS Rawlinson C.813 (the anthology belonging to Humphrey Welles), fols. 72v–88r and one in BL MS Lansdowne 762, fols. 75r–88r. J.A.H. Murray assigned the title to the piece, assuming that it was the prophecy that James V heard from Sir David Lyndesay, and he appended the prophecy to his edition of *The Romance and Prophecies of Thomas of*

---

[13] See O'Sullivan, ". . . BM Cotton Roll ii.23," Diss. University of London 1972.

[14] On the surviving brief folded prophetic text, Folger MS Loseley b. 546, see Chapter Three, pp. 111–12.

Erceldoune, pp. 51–61, using the Lansdowne version. He included some readings from Rawlinson, but "only the more important variations" (p. lxxxii). Unfortunately, there are also many errors in his transcription.

A considerable fragment of "The Prophecies," hitherto unrecognized and nowhere indexed, is found in Bodl. Libr. MS D.1062, fols. 111v–116r. This fragment is copied into prose lines, but corresponds approximately to lines 288–615, the third section of the poem.

In addition, lines 161–68 of "The Prophecies" existed as a separate prophecy at least as early as the fifteenth century, listed in the *Manual* as "A Prophecy by the Dominical Letters" (V.299; *Supplement* 4018.5).

Both of the complete sixteenth-century versions contain corruptions. Murray supposed Lansdowne, which he dated at 1529, to be a copy of an older northern text made by a southern scribe who turned many of the lines and rhymes into nonsense. Of Rawlinson, Murray asserted that it is a still more modernized version, but that it contains fewer mistakes (p. lxxxii). In spite of Murray's preference for Lansdowne, the Rawlinson version has been used for the poem as it has been printed here. On this version of the text as well as on the prophecy in general, see S.L. Jansen [Jaech], " 'The Prophisies of Rymour, Beid, and Marlyng': Henry VIII and a Sixteenth-Century Political Prophecy," *The Sixteenth Century Journal*, 16 (1985), 291–301.

The Bodleian catalogue is clearly in error when it indicates that the prophecy consists of seven eight-line stanzas. The prophecy as it is copied there is composed of seventy-six eight-line stanzas. In addition, lines 241–47 form a seven-line stanza, which might be regularized by adding line 251 from Lansdowne ("they shall be dreven downe into a dale") after line 241 of Rawlinson. The stanzas have varying rhyme schemes, the predominant one being cross-rhymed quatrains, but *ababbab* also appears frequently. Meter is irregular, but generally the lines are octosyllabic. Many lines have alliteration.

The *Supplement* relates this item to the romance of Thomas of Erceldoune ("As I me went þis enders day"), also printed by Murray. The "Prophecies" also shares its first seventy lines with the "Prophecies of Thomas Rymour," printed in 1603 by Robert Waldegrave in his *The Whole Prophesie of Scotland* (Murray reprinted the poem, pp. 48–51). Murray suggested that a Scottish compiler borrowed the opening lines of the original nucleus of the "Prophecies" but then appended his own account of events suited to Scottish needs (p. lxxxii).

2. "The Marvels of Merlin"

Supplement 1253.5 and 2613.5, *Manual* V.278(e and g).

As with all political prophecy, the history of "The Marvels of Merlin" as a text is very confusing. The *Supplement* (2613.5) and the *Manual* (V.278[g]) contain only one reference for the piece, a forty-eight line version found in BL MS Harley 2382, fols. 127v–128r. A second version of the prophecy can be found in both sources, indexed not under its first line but under its third. This version is found in Bodl. Libr. MS Rawlinson C.813, fols. 88v–89v (*Supplement* 1253.5 and *Manual* 278[e]). There is no apparent explanation for the poem's listing under its third, rather than its first, line. In addition to these two indexed versions, however, there are at least six other more-or-less complete versions of the same piece, ranging in date from the late fifteenth to the late sixteenth centuries.

The shape of the prophecy varies considerably from one version to the next. The versions are listed below by date:

British Library MS Harley 2382
    fols. 127v–128r
    forty-eight lines in cross-rhymed quatrains with some alliteration
    c. 1470–1500
    Supplement 2613.5; *Manual* V.278(g)

British Library MS Lansdowne 762
    fols. 50v–52r; the "Marvels" appears as the last item in a
        longer series of predictions beginning on fol. 48v
    copied into short prose paragraphs with brief titles
    c. 1530

Public Record Office, State Papers of Henry VIII
    SP 1/232, fol. 219v
    twenty lines in stanzas beginning "Flaunders and England shall fall
        at decensyon"
    mid 1530s (1534–35?)
    printed by Frederick J. Furnivall, ed., *Ballads from Manuscripts*,
        1 (London, 1868), pp. 316–17

Bodleian Library MS Rawlinson C.813 (1)
    fols. 88v–89v; the "Marvels" appears as the first 52 lines of a
        composite piece of 102 lines occupying fols. 88v–90v
    in stanzas of varying length
    mid 1530s
    Supplement 1253.5; *Manual*, V.278(e) (indexed under its third line)

Bodleian Library MS Rawlinson D.1062
  fols. 106v–107r
  copied in prose
  mid sixteenth century

British Library MS Sloane 2578 (1)
  fols. 70r–70v; the "Marvels" appears as part of a composite
    piece occupying fols. 68r–73v
  copied into short prose paragraphs with brief titles
  c. 1554–56

British Library MS Sloane 2578 (2)
  fols. 98v, 99v–100r; the "Marvels" appears as the last item
    in a longer series of predictions beginning on fol. 96v
  copied in prose
  c. 1554–56

Bodleian Library MS Rawlinson C.813 (2)
  fols. 104r–104v
  in lines of poetry but no stanzas marked
  c. 1556

Additional fragments appearing in MSS Lansdowne 762 (fol. 65r), Rawl. D.1062 (fol. 95r), and Sloane 2578 (fols. 32v and 56v–57r).

The fifteenth-century Harley version is the most regular and, seemingly, "complete" version of the text. Of the versions from the 1530s, only the copy in the State Papers stands alone and appears in quatrains. The version printed here is Bodl. Libr. MS Rawlinson C.813 (1). As indicated above, this version is the first part of a composite text, but it is closest to the earlier Harley 2382. Although it is copied into stanzas of varying length in the manuscript, it has been printed in cross-rhymed quatrains here.

The first eight lines of "The Marvels" appear as the last eight lines of another prophecy in Lansdowne 762 (fols. 63v–65r), printed by V.J. Scattergood, *Politics and Poetry in the Fifteenth Century*, pp. 386–90.

For the complete texts of the versions of this prophecy and an analysis of their relationships, see S.L. Jansen [Jaech], " 'The Marvels of Merlin' and the Authority of Tradition," 35–73. F.J. Furnivall prints the PRO version under the title "The First Prophecy" in his *Ballads from Manuscripts*, 1, 316–17.

3. "The Cock of the North"

Index 4029, *Manual* V.281.

Seventeen variants exist in manuscripts ranging in date from the mid-fifteenth century to the end of the sixteenth. These versions range from 75 to 139 lines.

Only one of the seventeen versions now known to exist dates to the 1530s, from BL MS Lansdowne 762, fols. 62r–63r, composed of eighty lines, twenty cross-rhymed quatrains, titled "brydlyngton." In the manuscript, lines 37–38 of the prophecy have been underlined.

For other printed versions, see J.R. Lumby, ed., *Bernardus de cura rei familiaris, with some Early Scottish Prophecies*, EETS, OS 42 (London, 1870), pp. 18–22, and Robbins, *Historical Poems*, pp. 115–17.

4. "France and Flanders Then Shall Rise"

Indexing in the *Supplement* and *Manual* is confused:

lines 1–4: *Supplement* 864.5, *Manual* V.304(f), described as "one cross-rhymed quatrain";
lines 5–48: *Supplement* 285.5, *Manual* V.278(c), described as "45 irregular rhyming lines";
lines 49–end: *Supplement* 3513.5, *Manual* V.304(n), described as "three quatrains."

The text is found in BL MS Lansdowne 762, fols. 53v–54v, and there is little there to indicate why it has been so strangely indexed in the *Supplement* and *Manual*. The Lansdowne catalogue clearly identifies it as one item (item #66), and the piece ends in the manuscript with "finis." There are three Latin passages inserted into the text in places where Robbins has divided the poem. He evidently regarded them as somehow dividing one prophecy into three. The Lansdowne text is here, rightfully, printed as one prophecy. Lines 49–51 are underlined in the manuscript.

Lines 1–4 are incorporated as well into a longer prophecy (134 lines), Lansdowne item #75, fols. 63v–65r (*Index* 3510, *Manual* V.276).

5. "The Sayings of the Prophets"

TEXT 1

The version printed as "Text 1" is from BL MS Lansdowne 762, fols. 48v–50v. Similar lists appear as well in Bodl. Libr. MS Rawlinson D.1062 (mid sixteenth century), Folger MS Loseley b. 546 (c. 1540), fol. 1r and v, and BL MS Sloane 2578 (c. 1554–56).

TEXT 2

Thomas Gibson's reinterpreted list of "sayings" is found in BL MS Cotton Cleopatra E.vi, fols. 401r–06r (*LP* XIII.2, 1242).

6. "The Prophecy of the Lily, the Lion, and the Son of Man"

The prose version is nowhere indexed. The verse text is listed in the *Index* as 3945 (prophecy), in the *Supplement* as 3412.3 (declaratio), and in the *Manual* as V.275.

In addition, another version in prose, not indexed, is found in Folger MS Loseley b. 546, fols. 1v–2r.

TEXT 1

The prose version is from Bodl. Libr. MS Rawlinson C.813, fols. 94v–95r.

TEXT 2

The verse version is from BL MS Lansdowne 762, fols. 52r–53v, titled there "The Prophecy of Merlyon." A second version in verse appears, in a fragmentary state, in BL MS Harley 2338, beginning

> Whanne m and ccccc togidir be knet
> And xxx and vj with hem are met
> As Merlyn sayth in þe story of Britayn
> Off Kyng Hary of Ynglond certayn
> And of the imperour, þe kyng of France
> And of othire londis many on mo. . . . (fol. 28v; *Manual* V.275).

The Lansdowne version has been printed by Scattergood, pp. 383–85.

7. "A Prophecy of a New World Emperor"

The text printed here is from Bodl. Libr. MS Rawlinson C.813, fols. 90v–94v.

After its initial attribution to the Bishop Methodius (ll. 1–7), this English text seems to be a translation of the sixteenth-century Latin version of the prophecy of John of Bassigny printed in the 1523 edition of the *Mirabilis Liber*. The English version begins about half-way into the Latin.

A contemporary Latin version, independent of the *Mirabilis Liber*, is recorded in BL MS Lansdowne 762, fols. 54v–57v.

8. "When Rome Is Removed Into England"

TEXT 1

Index 4008, *Manual* V.285.

The text printed here is a fragment of the A-text, found in PRO, SP 1/232, fol. 219v, printed by Furnivall, 1, 317.

TEXT 2

This fragment of the B-text is nowhere indexed.

The lines printed here appear as an independent prophecy in Bodl. Libry. MS Rawlinson C.813, fol. 88r–88v.

For the most complete study of "When Rome Is Removed," see Haferkorn, *When Rome Is Removed Into England*. He includes the PRO version but not Rawlinson.

9. "A Prophecy by the Dice"

Index 4018, *Supplement* 734.8, *Manual* V.297.

The *Manual* lists eleven manuscript versions.

The fifteenth-century version with glosses is Trinity College Dublin MS 516 (1450–75), fol. 118r.

TEXT 1

Printed here from PRO, SP 1/232, fols. 219v–220r, where it follows another version of the same prophecy. Furnivall prints both, 1, 318.

TEXT 2

Printed here from BL MS Lansdowne 762, fol. 96r, where it precedes a version of "A Prophecy by the Stars."

A fifteenth-century version of this prophecy is discussed by Scattergood, pp. 359–60.

10. "A Prophecy by the Stars"

Supplement 3308.5, *Manual* V.298.

The *Manual* lists four manuscript versions, but not the PRO version used here. Robbins indicates (*Manual*, p. 1530) that "A Prophecy by the Stars" is "an extrapolation (lines 28, 31, 33, 34, and 35)" of a prophecy beginning "O myghty mars that marrith many a wight," from Cambridge Univ. Libr. MS Kk.6.16, fols. 8v–10r. But since he dates *this* CUL prophecy at 1490–1510 while dating two versions of "A Prophecy by the Stars" *earlier* in the fifteenth century, it is hard to accept this conclusion. More likely the shared lines reflect typical prophetic borrowing.

The text printed here is from PRO, SP 1/232, fol. 220r, where it follows "A Prophecy by the Dice" (Text 1, see above). A somewhat more garbled version appears in BL MS Lansdowne 762, also following "A Prophecy by the Dice," see above.

BIBLIOGRAPHY

Bibliographical references for all of the sources used in this work appear in the notes. The list that follows contains only those works relevant to the study of political prophecy.

General Works on History

Anglo, Sidney. "The British History in Early Tudor Propaganda." Bulletin of the John Rylands Library, 44 (1961–62), 17–48.

———. Spectacle, Pageantry, and Early Tudor Policy. Oxford, 1969.

Bellamy, John G. The Law of Treason in England in the Later Middle Ages. Cambridge, 1970.

———. The Tudor Law of Treason: An Introduction. Toronto, 1979.

Chrimes, Stanley B. Henry VII. Berkeley, 1972.

———. Lancastrians, Yorkists, and Henry VII. London, 1964.

Davis, Norman, ed. Paston Letters and Papers of the Fifteenth Century. Vol. 1. Oxford, 1971.

Dickens, A.G. The English Reformation. New York, 1964.

———. Lollards and Protestants in the Diocese of York, 1509–1558. Oxford, 1959.

———. "Secular and Religious Motivation in the Pilgrimage of Grace." Studies in Church History, 4 (1967), 39–64.

———. "Wilfred Holme of Huntingdon: Yorkshire's First Protestant Poet." Yorkshire Archaeological Journal, 39 (1956), 119–35.

Dodds, Madeleine Hope and Ruth Dodds. The Pilgrimage of Grace, 1536–1537, and the Exeter Conspiracy, 1538. 2 vols. 1915; rpt. London, 1971.

Elton, G.R. "The Law of Treason in the Early Reformation." The Historical Journal, 11 (1968), 211–36.

———. The Parliament of England, 1559–1581. Cambridge, 1986.

———. Policy and Police: The Enforcement of the Reformation in the Age of Thomas Cromwell. Cambridge, 1972.

———. Reform and Reformation: England, 1509–1558. The New History of England. Cambridge, Mass., 1977.

———. Reform and Renewal: Thomas Cromwell and the Common Weal. Cambridge, 1973.

———. The Tudor Constitution: Documents and Commentary. Cambridge, 1960.

———. The Tudor Revolution in Government. Cambridge, 1962.

Fletcher, Anthony. Tudor Rebellions. 2nd ed. London, 1973.

Guy, John. *Tudor England*. Oxford, 1986.

Haigh, Christopher. "Anticlericalism and the English Reformation." *History*, 68 (1983), 391–407.

———. *Reform and Resistance in Tudor Lancashire*. Cambridge, 1975.

Harris, Barbara J. *Edward Stafford, Third Duke of Buckingham, 1478–1521*. Stanford, Calif., 1986.

Harrison, Scott M. *The Pilgrimage of Grace in the Lake Counties, 1536–37*. London, 1981.

Helm, P.J. *England Under the Yorkists and Tudors, 1471–1603*. New York, 1968.

Hughes, Paul L. and James F. Larkin. *Tudor Royal Proclamations: I. The Early Tudors (1485–1553)*. New Haven, 1964.

Ives, E.W. *Anne Boleyn*. Oxford, 1986.

Jacob, E.F. *The Fifteenth Century, 1399–1495*. Vol. 6 in *The Oxford History of England*. Oxford, 1961.

Jones, Ifano. "The Tudor Dynasty and the Dragon of Wales." In *Some Studies of Elizabethan Wales*, ed. E. Roland Williams. Newton, 1924, pp, 164–66.

Jones, W. Garmon. "Welsh Nationalism and Henry Tudor." *Transactions of the Honourable Society of Cymmrodorion* (Session 1917–18), pp. 1–59.

Kendrick, T.D. *British Antiquity*. London, 1950.

Levine, Mortimer. *Tudor Dynastic Problems, 1460–1571*. New York, 1973.

Levy, F.J. "The Fall of Edward, duke of Buckingham." In *Tudor Men and Institutions*, ed. A.J. Slavine. Baton Rouge, La., 1972, pp. 32–48.

———. *Tudor Historical Thought*. San Marino, California, 1967.

Loades, D.M. *Politics and the Nation, 1450–1660: Obedience, Resistance, and Public Order*. London, 1974.

Lockyer, Roger. *Tudor and Stuart Britain, 1471–1714*. New York, 1974.

Mackie, J.D. *The Earlier Tudors, 1485–1558*. Vol. 7 in *The Oxford History of England*. Oxford, 1952.

Merriman, Roger Bigelow. *Life and Letters of Thomas Cromwell*. 2 vols. Oxford, 1902.

Miller, Helen. *Henry VIII and the English Nobility*. Oxford, 1986.

Rees, J.F. *Studies in Welsh History*. Cardiff, 1947.

Scarisbrick, J.J. *Henry VIII*. Berkeley, 1968.

Simons, Eric N. *Henry VII: The First Tudor King*. London, 1968.

Skeel, Caroline A. James. "Wales Under Henry VII." In *Tudor Studies Presented . . . to Albert Frederick Pollard*, ed. R.W. Seton-Watson. London, 1924.

Smith, Lacey B. *Treason in Tudor England: Politics and Paranoia*. Princeton, 1986.

Thornley, Isobel D. "Treason by Words in the Fifteenth Century." *English Historical Review*, 32 (1917), 556–61.

Walker, Greg. *John Skelton and the Politics of the 1520s*. Cambridge, 1988.

Warnicke, Retha M. *The Rise and Fall of Anne Boleyn: Family Politics at the Court of Henry VIII*. Cambridge, 1989.

Williams, Glanmor. *Recovery, Reorientation, and Reformation: Wales c. 1415–1642*. Oxford, 1987.

——. *The Welsh Church from Conquest to Reformation*. Cardiff, 1962.

Williams, Neville. *Henry VIII and his Court*. New York, 1971.

Williams, W.L. "A Welsh Insurrection." *Y Cymmrodor*, 16 (1903), 33–41.

Wylie, James H. *History of England Under Henry IV*. 4 vols. London, 1884–98.

Zeeveld, W. Gordon. *Foundations of Tudor Policy*. Cambridge, Mass., 1948.

General Works on Political Prophecies

Allan, Alison. "Yorkist Propaganda: Pedigree, Prophecy and the 'British history' in the Reign of Edward IV." In *Patronage, Pedigree and Power in Later Medieval England*, ed. Charles Ross. Totowa, New Jersey, 1979, pp. 171–92.

Bauckman, Richard. *Tudor Apocalypse: Apocalypticism, Millenarianism and the English Reformation*. Vol. 8 of *The Courtenay Library of Reformation Classics*. Oxford, 1978.

Berdan, John M. *Early Tudor Poetry, 1485–1547*. New York, 1920.

Bloomfield, Morton W. *Piers Plowman as a Fourteenth-Century Apocalypse*. New Brunswick, New Jersey, 1961.

Brinkley, Roberta Florence. *Arthurian Legend in the Seventeenth Century*. 1932; rpt. New York, 1967.

Cohn, Norman. *The Pursuit of the Millenium: Revolutionary Millenarians and Mystical Anarchists in the Middle Ages*. 1957; rev. ed. New York, 1970.

Dodds, Madeleine Hope. "Political Prophecies in the Reign of Henry VIII." *Modern Language Review*, 11 (1916), 276–84.

Eckhardt, Caroline D. "Prophecy and Nostalgia: Arthurian Symbolism at the Close of the English Middle Ages." In *The Arthurian Tradition: Essays in Convergence*, ed. Mary Flowers Braswell and John Bugge. Tuscaloosa, Alabama, 1988, pp. 109–26 and 214–20 (notes).

Emmerson, Richard K. *Antichrist in the Middle Ages: A Study of Medieval Apocalypticism, Art, and Literature*. Seattle, 1981.

Fox, Alistair. "Prophecies and Politics in the Reign of Henry VIII." In *Reassessing the Henrician Age; Humanism, Politics and Reform, 1500–1550*, ed. Alistair Fox and John Guy. Oxford, 1986, pp. 77–94.

Frazer, N.L. *English History in Contemporary Poetry: The Tudor Monarchy (1485–1588)*. London, 1930.

Garber, Marjorie. "'What's Past is Prologue': Temporality and Prophecy in Shakespeare's History Plays." In *Renaissance Genres: Essays on Theory, History, and Interpretation*, ed. Barbara Kiefer Lewalski. Cambridge, Massachusetts, 1986, pp. 301–31.

Griffiths, Margaret Enid. *Early Vaticination in Welsh with English Parallels*. Ed. T. Gwynn Jones. Cardiff, 1937.

Herrmann, Erwin. "Spätmittelalterliche englische Pseudoprophetien." *Archiv für Kulturgeschichte*, 57 (1975), 87–116.

Jansen, Sharon L. [Jaech]. "British Library MS Sloane 2578 and Popular Unrest in England, 1554–1556." *Manuscripta*, 29 (1985), 30–41.

———. "English Political Prophecy and the Dating of MS Rawlinson C.813." *Manuscripta*, 25 (1981), 141–50.

———. "Political Prophecy and Macbeth's 'Sweet bodements.' " *Shakespeare Quarterly*, 34 (1983), 290–97.

Kinghorn, A.M. *The Chorus of History: Literary-Historical Relations in Renaissance Britain, 1485–1559.* New York, 1971.

Kingsford, Charles L. *English Historical Literature in the Fifteenth Century.* Oxford, 1913.

———. *English History in Contemporary Poetry; Lancaster and York, 1399–1483.* London, 1913.

———. *Prejudice and Promise in XVth Century England.* The Ford Lectures, 1924. Oxford, 1925.

Larkey, Sanford V. "Astrology and Politics in the First Years of Elizabeth's Reign." *Bulletin of the Institute of the History of Medicine*, 3 (1935), 171–86.

Lerner, Robert E. *The Powers of Prophecy: The Cedar of Lebanon Vision from the Mongol Onslaught to the Dawn of the Enlightenment.* Berkeley, 1983.

McGinns, Bernard. *Visions of the End: Apocalyptic Tradition in the Middle Ages.* New York, 1979.

O'Sullivan, Margaret M. "The Treatment of Political Themes in Late Medieval English Verse, with Special Reference to British Museum Cotton Roll ii.23." Diss. University of London 1972.

Pearsall, Derek. *Old and Middle English Poetry.* Vol. 1. of the Routledge History of English Poetry. Boston, 1977.

Phillips, J.R.S. "Edward II and the Prophets." In *England in the Fourteenth Century*, ed. W.M. Ormrod. Dover, New Hampshire, 1986, pp. 189–201.

Previté-Orton, C.W. "An Elizabethan Prophecy." *History*, 2 (January 1918), 207–18.

Reeves, Marjorie E. "History and Prophecy in Medieval Thought." *Medievalia et Humanistica*, NS 5 (1974), 51–75.

———. *The Influence of Prophecy in the Later Middle Ages.* Oxford, 1969.

Robbins, Rossell H. "Political Prophecies." In *A Manual of the Writings in Middle English, 1050–1500.* Vol. 5. Ed. J. Burke Severs. New Haven, Connecticut, 1975, pp. 1516–36 and 1714–25.

Ross, Charles. "Rumour, Propaganda and Popular Opinion During the Wars of the Roses." In *Patronage, the Crown, and the Provinces in Later Medieval England*, ed. Ralph A. Griffiths. Atlantic Highlands, New Jersey, 1981, pp. 15–32.

Rusche, Harry. "Prophecies and Propaganda, 1641–1651." *The English Historical Review*, 84 (1969), 752–70.

Scattergood, V.J. *Politics and Poetry in the Fifteenth Century.* New York, 1972.

Southern, R.W. "Aspects of the European Tradition of Historical Writing: 3.

History as Prophecy." *Transactions of the Royal Historical Society*, 5th ser, 22 (1972), 159–80.

Taylor, John. *English Historical Literature in the Fourteenth Century*. Oxford, 1987.

Taylor, Rupert. *The Political Prophecy in England*. New York, 1911.

Thomas, Keith. *Religion and the Decline of Magic*. London, 1971.

Webb, John. "Translation of a French Metrical History of the Deposition of King Richard the Second . . . accompanied by Prefatory Observation, Notes, and an Appendix. . . ." *Archaeologia: or Miscellaneous Tracts Relating to Antiquity*, 20 (1824), 1–423.

Williams, Glanmor. "Prophecy, Poetry, and Politics in Medieval and Tudor Wales." In *British Government and Administration: Studies Presented to S.B. Chrimes*, ed. H. Hearder and H.R. Loyn. Cardiff, 1974, pp. 104–16.

Articles on Specific English Political Prophecies

Albrecht, W.P. "A Seventeenth-Century Text of 'Thomas of Erceldoune.' " *Medium Aevum*, 23 (1954), 88–95.

Burnham, Josephine M. "A Study of 'Thomas of Erceldoune.' " *PMLA*, 23 (1908), 375–420.

Curley, Michael J. "The Cloak of Anonymity and 'The Prophecy of John of Bridlington.' " *Modern Philology*, 77 (1980), 361–69.

————. "John of Cornwall and the *Prophetia Merlini*." *Speculum*, 57 (1982), 217–49.

Eckhardt, Caroline D. "The Date of the *Prophetia Merlini* Commentary in MSS Cotton Claudius B. VII and Bibliothèque Nationale Fonds Latin 6233." *Notes and Queries*, NS 27 (1976), 146–47.

————. "The First English Translations of the *Prophetia Merlini*." *The Library*, 6th ser., 4 (1982), 25–34.

————. "The *Prophetia Merlini* of Geoffrey of Monmouth: Latin Manuscript Copies." *Manuscripta*, 26 (1982), 167–76.

Hammer, Jacob. "A Commentary on the *Prophetia Merlini* (Geoffrey of Monmouth's *Historia regum Britanniae*, Book VII)." *Speculum*, 10 (1935), 3–30.

————. "A Commentary on the *Prophetia Merlini* (Geoffrey of Monmouth's *Historia regum Britanniae*, Book VII), Continuation." *Speculum*, 15 (1940), 409–31.

————. "Another Commentary on the *Prophetia Merlini* (Geoffrey of Monmouth's *Historia regum Britanniae*, Book VII)." *Bulletin of the Polish Institute of Arts and Sciences in America*, 1 (1942–43), 589–601.

Jansen, Sharon L. [Jaech]. " 'The Marvels of Merlin' and the Authority of Tradition." *Studies in Medieval and Renaissance History*, 8 (1986), 35–73.

————. "The 'Prophisies of Rymour, Beid, and Marlyng': Henry VIII and a

175

Sixteenth-Century Political Prophecy." *The Sixteenth Century Journal*, 16 (1985), 291–301.

Lyle, E.B. "The Relationship Between 'Thomas the Rhymer' and 'Thomas of Erceldoune.' " *Leeds Studies in English*, NS 4 (1970), 23–30.

Meehan, Bernard. "Geoffrey of Monmouth, *Prophecies of Merlin*: New Manuscript Evidence." *The Bulletin of the Board of Celtic Studies*, 28 (1978–80), 37–46.

Meyvaert, Paul. "John Erghome and the *Vaticinium Roberti Bridlington*." *Speculum*, 41 (1966), 656–64.

Millican, Charles Bowie. "The First English Translation of the *Prophecies of Merlin*." *Studies in Philology*, 28 (1931), 720–29.

Rigg, A.G. "John of Bridlington's 'Prophecy': A New Look." *Speculum*, 63 (1988), 596–613.

Salter, Elizabeth. "Piers Plowman and 'The Simonie.' " *Archiv für das studium der Neueren Sprachen*, 203 (1967), 241–54.

Scattergood, V.J. "Adam Davy's 'Dreams' and Edward II." *Archiv für das studium der Neueren Sprachen*, 106 (1970), 253–60.

Smallwood, T.M. "The Prophecy of the Six Kings." *Speculum*, 60 (1985), 571–92.

Texts of English Political Prophecies

Bowers, R.H. " 'When Cuckow Time Cometh Oft so Soon,' A Middle-English Animal Prophecy." *Anglia*, 73 (1956), 292–98.

Curley, Michael J. "Fifteenth-Century Glosses on 'The Prophecy of John of Bridlington.' " *Medieval Studies*, 46 (1984), 321–39. [Of necessity, full bibliographical references for texts of the prophecies of John of Bridlington have not been supplied; for more complete listings, see Curley's notes.]

Day, Mabel. "Fragment of an Alliterative Political Prophecy." *Review of English Studies*, 15 (1939), 61–66.

D'Evelyn, Charlotte. "The Middle-English Metrical Version of the *Revelations* of Methodius; With a Study of the Influence of Methodius in Middle-English Writings." *PMLA*, 26 (1918), 135–203.

Eckhardt, Caroline D., ed. *The Prophetia Merlini of Geoffrey of Monmouth: A Fifteenth-Century English Commentary*. Cambridge, Massachusetts, 1982. [Of necessity, full bibliographical references for texts of the *Prophetia Merlini* have not been supplied; for more complete listings, see Eckhardt's bibliography.]

Furnivall, Frederick J. *Ballads from Manuscripts*, Vol. 1. London, 1868–72, pp. 316–19, 477.

———. *Political, Religious, and Love Poems*. EETS OS 15. London, 1866; rpt. 1965.

Gerould, Gordon Hall. "A Text of Merlin's Prophecies." *Speculum*, 23 (1948), 102–03.

Green, Richard Firth. "The Short Version of 'The Arrival of Edward IV.' *Speculum*, 56 (1981), 324–36.

Haferkorn, Reinhard. *When Rome Is Removed Into England: Eine Politische Prophezeiung des 14.Jahrhunderts.* Leipzig, 1932.

Laing, David. *Collection of Ancient Scottish Prophecies, in Alliterative Verse: Reprinted from [Robert] Waldegrave's Edition, 1603.* Edinburgh, 1833.

Lumby, J. Rawson. *Bernardus de cura rei famuliaris, with some Early Scottish Prophecies.* EETS OS 42. London, 1870.

Murray, J.A.H. *The Romance and Prophecies of Thomas of Erceldoune.* EETS OS 61. London, 1875.

Robbins, Rossell Hope. "Geoffrey of Monmouth: An English Fragment." *English Studies*, 38 (1957), 259–62.

———. *Historical Poems of the XIVth and XVth Centuries.* New York, 1959.

Sackur, Ernst. *Sibyllinische Texte und Forschungen.* 1898; rpt. Turin, 1963.

Sibbald, J. *Chronicle of Scottish Poetry*, Vol. 3. Edinburgh, 1802.

Wright, Thomas. *Political Poems and Songs relating to English History, Composed . . . from the Accession of Edw. III to that of Richard III.* Vol. 2. London, 1861.

———. *The Political Songs of England, from the Reign of John to that of Edward II.* London, 1839.

Wright, Thomas and J.O. Halliwell[-Phillips]. *Reliquiae Antiquae.* London, 1843; rpt. New York, 1966.

INDEX

Merlin, as prophetic authority, 2, 3, 12, 17, 37, 38, 40, 54, 58, 62, 67, 68, 105, 110, 112, 147, 148, 150, 152, 162, 168
Methodius, as prophetic authority, 43, 131, 134, 169
Monmouth, Geoffrey, see Geoffrey of Monmouth
More, Sir Thomas, lord chancellor, 21, 23; and possible ownership of prophetic manuscript, 150
Morison, Richard, propagandist, 152; *An exhortation to styrre all Englyshemen to the Defense of theyr countreye*, 59–60
Nennius, "The Omen of the Dragons," 10–11
Neville, Sir Edward, investigated for political prophecy, 52
Neville, John, lord Latimer, 30, 31
Neville, Richard, earl of Warwick, 31, 92 n9
Neville, William, investigated for political prophecy, 28; and involvement with political prophecy, 29–32; references to, 34, 66, 67, 93–94, 100, 148, 149
Northbrook, John (Exeter), accuses John Bonnefant of involvement with political prophecy, 55
Oversole, Richard (Northallerton, Yorkshire), investigated for "talk" about northern rebellion, 51
Paikok, John, priest (Rudston), investigated for political prophecy, 3
Parr, Sir William, sends prophesier to Cromwell, 47
parson of Wednesbury (Staffordshire), accused of having a book of prophecies, 40
Paul III, pope (1534–49), 23, 24, 49
Payne, John, references to, 68
Percy family, 41, 42; prophetic references to, 5, 15, 42–43, 49, 51, 98, 100, 105
Percy-Glendower revolt, and political prophecy, 98, 101, 153
Pilgrimage of Grace, 41, 52, 56, 57, 93 n14, 99, 134, 163; and causes, 23–24; and Council of the North, 1, 32; and its political significance, 5, 41; and political prophecies, 3, 41–42, 68, 94
Pole, Henry, lord Montague, 52
Pole, Reginald, cardinal (in 1536), 49, 52; prophetic references to, 5, 26
Political prophecy, confusion in, 9–10; influence of, 16–19, 147–56; laws against, 18 nn21 and 22, 19; methods, 14–16; origin and development, 10–14; stylistic features, 15 n11
types of
 Galfridian, 12, 14, 161

"painted prophecies," 13, 161
 Sibylline, 12–13, 14, 161
"Prince Edward," as prophetic hope, 31, 34, 66, 100
prior of Tortington, accused of having read a political prophecy, 40
"The Prophecies of Rhymer, Bede, and Merlin," 13, 91, 98, 100, 105, 126, 132 n29, 151; bibliographic details, 163–64; commentary, 63–68; text, 69–90
"A Prophecy by the Dice," 146; bibliographic details, 169; commentary, 144; text 1, 145; text 2, 145
"A Prophecy by the Stars," bibliographic details, 170; commentary, 146; text, 146
The Prophecy of John of Bridlington, 12, 13, 14–15
"The Prophecy of the Lily, the Lion, and the Son of Man," 132 n29, 151; bibliographic details, 168; commentary, 125–26; text 1, 127–28; text 2, 128–30
"The Prophecy of a New World Emperor," 151; bibliographic details, 169; commentary, 131–34; text, 135–40
"The Prophecy of the Six Kings to Follow King John," 12, 13, 34, 40, 45, 57, 153
The Prophecy of Thomas à Becket, 12, 13, 125 n26
The Prophecy of Thomas of Erceldoune, 12, 13
Reformation Parliament (1529–36), 21–24, 39, 133, 144, 146
the "Rhymer," see Thomas of Erceldoune
Richard II, in political prophecy, 13; interest in political prophecy, 17; and political prophecy, 153
Richard III, 63; and political prophecy, 154
Richards, John, prisoner (Ilchester jail, Somersetshire), and political prophecy, 28–29
Ryan, John, innkeeper (London), investigated for political prophecy, 54
Sandiford, site of one of the three legendary battles of political prophecy, 63, 65, 66, 98, 99
Saville, Sir Henry, reports to Cromwell about political prophecy, 47
"The Sayings of the Prophets," 59, 126, 152; bibliographic details, 168; commentary, 110–12; text 1, 113–16; text 2, 117–24
Scarisbrick, J.J., 5, 22 n3, 23 n4, 24, 25 nn6 and 7, 93 n11
between Seton and the sea, site of one of the three legendary battles of political prophecy, 98, 99
Seyman, Roger (Suffolk), accuses Richard Bishop of political prophecy, 44–46
Shakespeare, William, 16, 56 n100